Wonderfully Engrossing

I was hooked from the start… solid, [...] read that will keep you flicking through the pages and will keep you guessing… vivid writing…

Strong Woman

This book spoke to me. Lady Margaret impressed me with her ability to think her way through adverse and trying situations and turn them to her advantage.

—JUDY M. TREPANIER

Intriguing

I thoroughly enjoyed this well-written book and am anxious to follow Lady Margaret in the next book of the trilogy.

—MARLYS PEARSON

Totally Captivated

From the first word to the last, I was totally captivated by the characters, their challenges and successes as the walked the tight rope of class and court

—AMAZON CUSTOMER

Wonderful Story

… people and places put the reader back in time… into the lives of the characters…

—SHARON LACHAPELLE

Note: This story includes an infant's death, which may be a trigger for some readers.

Also By This Author

Henry's Spare Queen Trilogy

Lady Margaret's Challenge Book Two

Lady Margaret's Future Book Three

Lady Margaret's Disgrace:
Prequel to Henry's Spare Queen Trilogy
Release Date: 1 September 2021

Find Victoria online and on social media:
Author Website: *victoriasportelli.com*
Facebook: facebook.com/victoriasportelli
Instagram: vcsportelli
Pinterest: VictoriaSportelli

Dear Reader

The author will be grateful
if you leave an honest review online.
Thank you so much!

LADY MARGARET'S
ESCAPE

Henry's Spare Queen Trilogy Book One

VICTORIA SPORTELLI

Creazzo Publishing
Sioux Falls, South Dakota

Creazzo Publishing
401 E. 8th Street Suite 214-1194
Sioux Falls, South Dakota 57104
USA

Published by Creazzo Publishing in 2020
www.CreazzoPublishing.com

ISBN 978-1-952849-00-8 (paperback)
ISBN 978-1-952849-01-5 (mobi)
ISBN 978-1-952849-02-2 (ePub)

First Edition Published 2019

Credits:
Cover Design: Jennifer D. Quinlan
Interior Design: *wordzworth.com*
Map and Illustration: Lindsey A. Grassmid
Editor: Margaret K. Diehl

Names: Sportelli, Victoria, author
Title: Lady Margaret's escape / Victoria Sportelli.
Description: [Second edition]. | Sioux Falls, South Dakota : Creazzo Publishing, 2020. | Series: Henry's spare queen ; book 1 | The second edition of this work has a new cover design but no changes to the text or descriptive portions of the bibliographic record. | Interest age level: 012-018. | Summary: In 1101, King Henry engages Lady Margaret to protect his Queen Matilda. Against Norman custom, Margaret wears a sword. During his reign, Henry's Brother, Robert, Duke of Normandy invades to take Henry's crown while Robert de Belleme is also plotting to overthrow Henry.
Identifiers: ISBN 9781952849008 | ISBN 9781952849015 (mobi) | ISBN 9781952849022 (ePub)
Subjects: LCSH: Henry I, King of England, 1068-1135–Juvenile fiction. | Ladies-in-waiting–England–History–To 1500–Juvenile fiction. | Escapes--England–History–To 1500–Juvenile fiction. | Great Britain–History–1066-1687–Juvenile fiction. | CYAC: Henry I, King of England, 1068-1135–Fiction. | Ladies-in-waiting–England–History–To 1500–Fiction. | Escapes–England–History–To 1500–Fiction. | Great Britain–History–1066-1687–Fiction. | LCGFT: Historical fiction.
Classification: LCC PZ7.1.S7174 L34 2020 (print) | LCC PZ7.1.S7174 (ebook) | DDC [Fic]–dc23

For Sara
my daughter

You are the inspiration for
all my female protagonists.

Contents

England, 1101 A.D.

North Wall

SCOTLAND

Shropshire

ENGLAND

WALES

• Royal Oaks

Thames River • London

Glouchester • Margaret's Estate
Forest • Winchester
Keep

Portsmouth

NARROW SEA

• Reuen

NORMANDY

Paris •

SCALE 20   60   100
       0   40   80
          Miles

Motte and Bailey, Royal Oaks

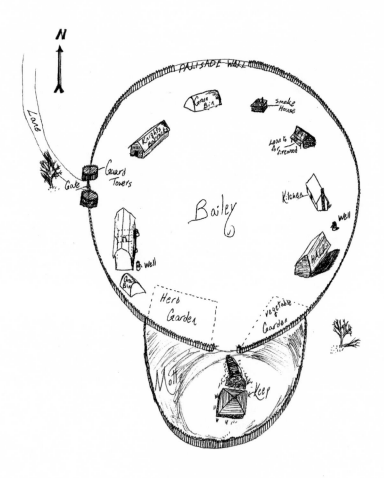

N

PALISADE WALL

Road

Gate

Grain Bin

smoke House

Knights barracks

Lean to for firewood

Guard Towers

Bailey

Kitchen

Well

Well

HALL

Grain Bin

Herb Garden

Vegetable Garden

Motte

Keep

A Royal Family

William I (the Conqueror)   m.   **Matilda of Flanders**

b. 1028 - d. 1087 A.D.   b. 1031 - d. 1083 A.D.

King of England 1066 - 1087 A.D.

Children:

Richard (Deceased)

Robert

Duke of Normandy

William II

b. 1056 A.D.

King of England 1088 - 1100 A.D.

Henry   m.   **Matilda of Scotland**

b. 1068 A.D.   b. 1080 A.D.

King of England 1100 A.D.

A Noble Family

Charles   m.   **Rosamonde**

b. 1064 A.D.   b. 1069 - 1099 A.D.

Lord, Royal Oaks Estate-1086

Children:

Margaret

Charles

(called Young Charles)

Raymond

Cecily

Characters

Normans

Henry de Beaumont, First Earl of Warwick. Holds the most lands for the Crown and is the most powerful earl. His immediate support of Henry helped make him King of England.

Lady Adela. Nine. Orphaned during King Henry's campaign to banish all traitorous men of rank.

Lady Cecily. Fourth child of Lord Charles of Royal Oaks and the late Lady Rosamonde.

Lady Claire de Clerkx. Lady in service to Queen Matilda.

Lady Margaret. First-born child of Lord Charles of Royal Oaks and the late Lady Rosamonde.

Lord Cai. Arrived in England via the invasion of 1066 A.D. with William the Conqueror, whom he served well. King William I made him an earl. He is one of the few who supports King Henry from the "old guard" of Norman lords.

Lord Charles of Royal Oaks. His estate lies three days' ride north of Gloucester in Worcestershire.

Lord William of Avondale. Widower with two young sons who strongly supports King Henry and who became Lady Margaret's undeclared champion.

Robert de Belleme, Third Earl of Shropshire and Shrewsbury. Holder of those and several other estates; the second most powerful lord in England after Henry de Beaumont, Earl of Warwick.

William I (the Conqueror), formerly Duke of Normandy. Married Matilda of Flanders. Invaded England in 1066 A.D., had himself crowned King and ruled England until he died in 1087.

Children: **Richard** died in a hunting accident.

Robert was passed over for the English crown and accepted the Dukedom of Normandy. In 1097 he joined the Grand Crusade to the Holy Land in search of wealth.

William II (Rufus) was his father's favorite son.

Henry holds land and great wealth in Normandy, which he inherited from his mother.

Normand. Squire to Lord William of Avondale.

Sir Bruis. Knight errant who serves Lord Charles of Royal Oaks.

Sir Charles (Young Charles). Son of Lord Charles of Royal Oaks and the late Lady Rosamonde and his father's heir.

Sir Cachier. Member of King Henry's corps d'elite, who serves Lady Margaret until she marries.

Sir Gailard. Member of King Henry's corps d'elite, who serves Lady Margaret until she marries.

Sir Raymond. Second son of Lord Charles of Royal Oaks and the late Lady Rosamonde.

Sir Roger. Constable of King Henry's smaller castle in Winchester. His wife is Lady Gisela.

Sir Roussel. Member of King Henry's corps d'elite, who serves Lady Margaret until she marries.

Clergy

Anselm, Archbishop of Canterbury. An important monk and theologian. In England he defended the Catholic Church's interests. He had been exiled by King William II in 1097. In 1100 Prince Henry recalled Anselm before Henry was crowned king.

Father Ambroise. Priest on Sir Charles's Royal Oak estate.

Father Gregory. One of the few Saxon priests still in England. During King William I's reign, he replaced most of England's Saxon priests with Norman ones.

Gerard, Archbishop of York. He was also King Henry's Lord Chancellor of the Realm.

William Giffard, Bishop of Winchester. Nominated to his position 3 August 1100 by Henry, probably due to Henry's efforts to win Church support for his claim to the English throne and to reward Giffard for his support.

Saxon

Cook. Head person in a kitchen who supervises a staff of bakers, undercooks, scullery maids, men, and other persons needed to feed everyone inside the bailey.

Dena. A girl on Lord Charles' estate.

Elborg. Cousin to Queen Matilda charged with protecting and serving her.

Eldene. Cousin to Queen Matilda charged with protecting and serving her.

Elric. Cousin to Queen Matilda charged with protecting and serving her.

Elstan. Cousin to Queen Matilda charged with protecting and serving her.

Garnyd. Ten, boy chosen to serve Queen Matilda at Forest Keep.

Jorgon. Hostler for Lord Charles of Royal Oaks and a friend to Lady Margaret.

Jorgon Elder. Jorgon's father and a villein on Lord Charles' estate.

Ordson. Eight, boy chosen to serve Queen Matilda at Forest Keep.

Other

Aegdyth. *(pronounced A-egg-dith)* Old Saxon name. In the late medieval period the pronunciation and spelling changed, and it became the modern Edith. (See Matilda below.)

Caitlin. Irish. As a child she was brought to London to be sold as a slave was was bought by Lord Charles as a wedding gift for his bride. She has been the nursemaid to Lady Margaret since her birth.

Cormac mac Cenedig. Scot. He served the Scots' kings Malcolm III, Duncan, and now Edgar.

Matilda, Queen of England. Half Scot and half Saxon. She was born Aegdyth and renamed Matilda (after King Henry's mother) when she married King Henry and became his queen. Henry often called her Aegdyth in private.

Preface

In 1066 A.D. England was a prosperous country that exported wool and cheeses. Citizens were free—no serfdom or feudalism—and under the rule of local earls or kings, who answered to King Harold Godwin. All lived with laws and courts we would recognize today.

William (William the Conqueror), Duke of Normandy, invaded, killed King Harold in a battle on Senlac Hill near Hastings and crowned himself king. Because William I did not want his eldest son Robert to rule England, he bought him off with his old title and all his lands in Normandy. King William had imported the custom of father-to-son rule from the continent. The Saxons, who elected their kings, hated the idea. By the time King William I died in 1087, thirty percent of England's Saxons had fled the country, died of deprivation and hunger, or had been killed outright by any Norman on a whim.

William II, called William Rufus because of his ruddy complexion, became king as his father had intended. During his twelve-year rule, William II did not marry and provide the realm with an heir. He defied the Catholic Church when he refused to fill bishops' positions and took their lands and incomes for himself. He also enraged many Norman lords and then put down their rebellion in 1097 so brutally no one dare challenge him. While boar hunting in New Forest on 2 August 1100, a lord struck him in the chest with a hunting arrow, but claimed it was an accident.

Hearing of his older brother's death, Henry raced to Winchester and seized the royal treasury. He wrote a Charter of Liberties promising the Saxons a return of some of their earlier freedoms and customs. In exchange, they supported his claim to the throne. Henry was crowned king on 5 August 1100 at Westminster Cathedral in London. Uneasy, Henry only perches on his throne. Three factions do not want Henry to be king: several barons and earls with lands in both England and Normandy, his brother Robert, and the Church.

Rumors circulate about Robert de Belleme, the second most powerful earl in England, who has the men, arms, and allies to war against Henry and win. King Henry's older brother, Robert, Duke of Normandy, is racing home from the Grand Crusade intent on invading England and taking the crown for himself. The Church is fighting King Henry in order to win back the right to name its own bishops. The Church is also maneuvering to control Henry and expects to rule England through him, but Henry is no one's puppet. The Saxons want their country back and view all this unrest as a possible opportunity to do so.

Henry believes having an heir will cement his keeping the throne, but his queen miscarried a boy babe four months after their wedding. Henry's secret is his queen is again with child. This time he wants someone who can better attend her and birth him a healthy heir. Having learned of the Lady Rosamonde's fame as a midwife to Norman women of rank, Henry is riding to Royal Oaks to bring her to Court to attend his pregnant queen.

1

Encounters

27 June 1101 A.D.

Morning

"Where is she?" asked Caitlin.

Cook replied, "Left before dawn. With a basket. Wants to be clean for May Day even if she is not allowed to celebrate."

"Too early for the stream to warm much overnight."

"Warm enough. And he's drunk again, so he won't know. Just like last month, she will have to confess getting naked, exposing herself and washing. I hope this time Father Ambroise gives her such a penance as to curtail her. Please stir that pottage for me. I must remove the loaves."

"She will die of ague," worried Caitlin.

"Will not. Too tough. Anyone who wants her dead will have to put a knife into her heart."

"Do not give him ideas! Do not even speak of such things."

"As if I'd speak to that man after what he's done to her!"

Beyond the forest and the estate's eastern border, the sun's tip peeked above the earth. As the church bell rang to announce dawn and Mass, a girl snuck through the gate of the bailey. She crept along the palisade wall toward the kitchen and dashed inside. She breathed a sigh of relief and dropped her basket inside the doorway. She sniffed appreciatively toward the hot loaves of brown bread cooling on the nearby table. She strode to the fireplace mantle to retrieve a jumble of keys and the estate scissors to tie to her girdle. As she picked her apron from a hook and donned it, she heard Cook's warning.

"Best you hurry if you want not to be caught and punished."

The girl ran out the kitchen door and dashed across the bailey, down the road, and into the church in time to hear Father Ambroise intone the first words of Mass. She slipped between the two serving girls closest to the entrance. Her first prayer was gratitude to God at not having been caught leaving the compound. After Mass, the priest dismissed parishioners according to each group's standing in the household, the master first, then his family, knights, and finally servants. With the sun now high, the girl lifted her face to the light to enjoy the coming of a warm day.

Back in the kitchen, the girl asked, "Did he ask for me?"

"No," answered Cook. She turned from ladling the pottage of boiled wheat, oats and leftover bits of squirrel into wooden bowls. "Consider yourself fortunate. Once again." The old woman wagged her finger. "Already seen to your bundle."

"Thank you. The berries already smell good."

"Welcome," came Cook's curt reply.

"Margery!" Sir Charles bellowed from the hall.

The girl, called that name by those who commanded her, returned to her role with an effort, tucking the unruly parts of herself inside. She straightened her clothes before she picked up the tray; her countenance too fell into the lines of blank propriety. As much as she disliked this, there was also a sense of accomplishment at the perfection of her charade. She crossed the space between the kitchen and the hall, reminding herself that she, Margaret, was other than, better than, what this man crudely deemed her. She whisked into the building through the servants' entrance with a platter of steaming bowls and set them on the trestle before she looked toward the head table and curtsied.

I will not react. This is only an act, not the real me. I do this every day.

"Yes, my lord?" Her voice was soft and slow.

"This butter is rancid!"

Lord Charles loved to start the day with a complaint. Today it was the chatelaine's turn to suffer his wrath.

"When was this muck churned?"

He so enjoys getting worked up, his wrath swelling like a bullfrog's pouch. He doubtless thinks himself very, very important when he is merely petty and cruel. Calm him or he will rampage all morning. "The milkmaid churned it yesterday," came her gentle reply. "I do not consume it, so I did not taste it. Shall I now?"

"No, no. Remove this trash. Bring honey instead."

Margaret curtsied and sweetly replied, "Yes, my lord. Immediately, my lord."

Inside the kitchen door, Margaret sighed, straightened her back, dipped her littlest finger into the butter and put it into her mouth. *This is fine. I will turn it into a different bowl and serve it with the midday meal; he will know no better. Of course I tasted it after I churned and*

3

salted it! Did I not pot, cover and store it as well? Rampaging again, you unwashed blob, smelling of stale ale and piss. You are no longer the man Mother once loved. Now each week you slip lower. Margaret stepped to a corner, unlocked the buttery and retrieved the honey pot.

She returned to the hall, curtsied before the head table and placed the crock and a wooden spoon before her lord. In her mind, she upended it in his lap, though that would be a waste of something more useful than the man. *If only I could give this honey to the little ones or the nursing mothers.*

"Punish the milkmaid. See to it now! And do it my way," Lord Charles ordered. "Leave the honey here; I may want more."

Keeping her eyes down, Margaret nodded and left, contempt simmering around the edges of her thoughts. *Such a strong man you are, able to order a girl hurt!* Margaret stepped carefully across the bailey so as not to kick up dust. *No rain for a fortnight. Our crops need rain now. Please, God, give use the rain we need. Your will, Oh, God, in all things.*

The barn smelled of milk and manure. The maid she sought, a ten-year-old with a round, freckled face and upturned nose, was crooning to her cows, who stared at her with their mild brown eyes.

"He is again on a rampage about butter."

The girl shrunk in horror, her body folding like wheat under a heavy rain. The last time Lord Charles had complained, he had come himself into the stable and had beaten her so badly she could not work for days. Margaret remembered tending to her, her terror that something inside the child had been broken, her hands going again and again to the girl's midsection. Keeping her countenance blank around Lord Charles had been hard.

"No, no," Margaret said. "Fear not. He expects me to do it this time. Get ready to howl."

The milkmaid was already whimpering when Sir Charles' head servant walked into the tack area and returned with an old whip handle and a saddle blanket. She looked around and placed the blanket against the outside wall.

"Ready?" Margaret smiled at the girl, silently bidding her be brave. "Come here so we can time my blows and your screams."

"Yes, mistress!" came the girl's eager reply when she saw that the wall and not herself was about to be struck.

A thump against wood. A whimper.

"Louder," Margaret instructed.

A harder blow. A wail. Another hard blow that echoed in the barn. A howl. A blow heard halfway across the bailey. A scream. The cows moved uneasily in their stalls.

If cows were not so docile, they might attack me for this, hurting their little mistress.

"Do not overdo it. Now cry."

The girl grinned, "I cannot."

Margaret reached over, grabbed the fleshy part of the girl's forearm, pinched hard and held it. *Does she not know we all must play out this farce? I cannot manage him alone.*

"Ow-u-uch!" Tears welled up in the girl's eyes. She tried to pull away and hurt herself even more. After the milkmaid's tears were flowing, Margaret let go; she felt faintly soiled and at the same time annoyed. *This is not my fault!*

"I am sorry I had to hurt you at all, but you had better show at least one bruise and evidence of having cried. You know what he is like. Now cry all you want. Just remember what you might have gotten."

Margaret returned the blanket and whip handle and walked toward the sobbing child. The girl surprised Margaret with a hug, her thin arms surprisingly strong, her mucky face pressed to the chatelaine's shoulder. Margaret hugged the girl back and kissed her on the forehead, walked through the door and slammed it shut. Margaret yelled inside her head at the lord she served. *I hate you! You horrible, vile man!*

Margaret stopped and stared at what she spotted across the bailey. A knight holding a geldings's reins and a squire with a riding gelding and a pack animal stood before the main door of the hall. The knight was a full head taller than his squire and well muscled. He looked to be in his mid to late twenties, with dark brown hair, cropped for wearing under a helmet. He was clenching a strong jaw; he lifted his chin and showed a handsome profile. His cloak was serviceable brown, his boots black. Having stopped halfway between barn and kitchen, Margaret admired the man and smiled to see him shifting his feet in annoyance in the ankle-high morning fog. *Norman. Rugged, handsome. Well appointed. Fine horse. Not accustomed to being kept waiting, I wager.*

The knight, who felt a twitch in the back of his neck, looked about and straight into the eyes of the woman wearing the trappings around her waist that informed him of her position. His eyes widened.

Margaret froze. Dark eyes stared back at her. *Why do I feel as if he is undressing me?* Unsettled, the girl ducked her head to break their eye contact and strode quickly toward the kitchen. She missed seeing the knight's smile. Kitchens were always a separate building in case of fire. This one leaned a bit and looked as though it had developed a growth on one side, a cubby Cook and Caitlin lived and slept in.

Margaret entered the run-down building and sat down to her own bowl of pottage Cook always saved for her. She sniffed appreciatively at the buttered grains before taking up her spoon.

"Someone at the door."

"I saw. Who?"

"Announced as Lord William of Avondale. 'On the king's business,' he said. He ordered the others out and sent for more food."

Margaret crossed the short distance between the kitchen shed and the hall and slipped through the side door. She peeked. Her lord's back was to her, but his body language hinted fear and displeasure at what the knight was saying. The girl ducked back into the kitchen and ladled food. She entered the hall with a heavy platter, but she looked at no one.

"This is my 'housekeeper," said Lord Charles of Royal Oaks. His tone of voice implied a hidden joke as he waved in her direction and smirked. Now on more familiar ground, Lord Charles appeared less nervous.

Lord William noted the emphasis of her title and wondered what secret the old man's meaning held. He guessed the lord's housekeeper was also his mistress. He followed Lord Charles's arm and looked directly at the woman for the second time. Dressed in drab brown from head to toe, the girl's only color was in her cheeks as she blushed at his examination and hurriedly looked at the floor. *The master's bedmate has a comely face*, thought Lord William.

Margaret's cheeks pinked as she lowered her eyes and curtsied. She deftly balanced the full tray before she rose and set the tray a distance down the table. She picked up a bowl and a pewter spoon before stepping toward the men.

As the girl leaned over to place the pottage before him, William inhaled and smelled kitchen fires, yeast, fresh bread. William inhaled again and thought, *She bears a clean woman scent and a hint of soap. Pleasant.* The knight's smile confused the girl. She looked down at her clenched hands to avoid his stare. Her cheeks pinked again.

Lord Charles began, "The king comes this afternoon with twenty men, counting these. He expects you to have a dinner ready by sundown. The king and his entourage will also need to break their fasts; they depart at dawn."

"Yes, my lord." Margaret took a deep breath and hesitantly told Lord Charles what he did not want to hear. "I'm sorry, my lord, our meat house does lack at this time. We have enough grain and other provisions, but we are short of meat, my lord."

"The king has permitted me to inform you that if you are low on stocks, Lord Charles, you may kill two of the king's deer for the evening meal."

Lord Charles stood taller and grinned at Lord William. He was now one of the few men ever given permission to kill the king's favorite hunting game. To do so unbidden was an instant death sentence.

Margaret dared not speak to the king's man. She curtsied and addressed only Lord Charles, "My lord, if you desire to send the king and his men away with provisions for a cold noon meal on horse, one more deer will provide it."

Sir William saw the housekeeper was trying to soften the blow of what other food and drink would be expended. Three kills would enable Lord Charles to be a generous host without touching his remaining meat supply. He told Lord Charles, "While I cannot increase the number of deer, both my squire Normand and I could join you and your sons in the hunt. Among the five of us, we should be able to bring down enough rabbits and other small game to provide all your housekeeper requires." Thus, Lord William told his host he was not directly accountable for his housekeeper's apparent greed.

"Good! Good!" Lord Charles responded. "If you will excuse me, I will inform my sons. Please continue to break your fast, my lord."

"May I see the stables, my lord?" Normand asked.

At the lord's nod, the squire rose to follow him. Before Lord Charles exited, he informed Lord William, "My housekeeper will do everything to see to His Royal Highness's comfort."

Margaret curtsied in silent assent and waited until Lord Charles had left the hall. She lifted the bread platter and the pot of honey from the lord's place on the dais and set it before the king's man at the table in front of the fire pit. She poured more cider into the man's mug.

"Is there anything else you require to break your fast, my lord?"

"No, no. This is enough, thank you," William answered. The steam rising from his bowl told him his meal contained a mix of boiled grains and bits of a meat. "I am Lord William of Avondale."

"I am sorry. Lord William."

"I am content," he replied smoothly. While he did not expect a formal introduction, he had hoped Lord Charles would at least tell the housekeeper his name. *Mayhap manners in the country are less formal,* he thought. "What is your name?"

"I am called Margery, my lord," she replied.

The knight looked at the stairs leading to the platform behind the dais and above the two storage rooms, both with locked doors.

"Why is the family sleeping on the guest platform instead of in their keep?"

"An accident, my lord. The keep burned in April. A servant accidentally knocked over a brazier. Terrible. She burned to death."

A lie—no, two. Let him think Fearn died that way instead of murdered.

"A wooden keep?"

"Yes. Neither King William nor his son King William Rufus granted his lordship the right to build a stone one. Think you the king is coming to grant Lord Charles permission to build a new one in stone?"

"I know not. How many beds are on the platform?"

"Three, Lord William." She said his name, bowed her head and gave a respectful curtsey to avoid angering him. "Behind that curtain is the third. The Lady Cecily sleeps there."

"Lady Cecily?"

"His daughter," Margaret mumbled.

She motioned a serving girl to stop clearing the tables and whispered what she wanted. The pair below the platform soon heard the whine and complaint of a young voice demanding to know why she had to rise so early. Lord William smiled when he heard, "THE KING!" and then feet stirring floor rushes. While they awaited the Lady Cecily, William ate and Margaret watched.

High cheekbones, sharp chin, broad shoulders. Right-handed as he ought to be… and good table manners. As another servant slipped up the stairs. Margaret pondered the king's sleeping arrangements.

"Lord William, does His Royal Highness sleep alone?"

"What?!" William blurted as he looked up from his bowl.

"Does the king sleep alone?" Margaret repeated. "Will he want the platform all to himself with his men at the bottom of the stairs? Do some sleep on the platform with him and some…" From Lord

William's expression, Margaret suddenly realized what he thought she had meant. She blushed furiously, clenched her lowered hands, and refused to meet his gaze. *How could I be so stupid to word it that way!*

While her cheeks reddened with shame, William grinned at her. When he realized she was not about to resume the conversation, William bit his lower lip to stop his voice from giving away his mirth. With brown eyes twinkling, William informed the chatelaine, "His Royal Highness will take the best bed. He will then decide who will get the others. Men will guard the bottom of the stairs and the hall doors. He will also require us to share the watch on the walls. We will do all this ourselves. Lord Charles, his sons and his men will stay with us in the hall. Please make sleeping arrangements for the Lady Cecily." He waited. "Is there anything else I may tell you?" The knight leaned back from his meal. William smiled his approval of her hazel eyes, clear skin, high cheekbones and pert nose. He cocked his head as he pondered her full lips. He noticed her delicate hands and frowned at the hard use they had seen. The length of William's stare and her own thoughts about the king's arrival had given the girl time to compose herself.

"Yes, Lord William. Does the king have aversions to any foods or herbs? What are his favorites?"

William informed her; she thanked him. William stared at her; she looked back and wondered what he was thinking. William gave her half a smile.

"Your Norman is flawless."

"Thank you, my lord."

William watched her pinch her lips with her teeth to stop her smile and wondered what amused her about his compliment. "Tell me, Margery," William intoned in such a soft voice she had to lean toward the table between them to hear the rest, "do you often beat stable walls to a chorus of false screams?" He raised his eyebrows and smirked.

Margaret frowned with worry that he might tell Lord Charles. She looked deeply into the man's eyes and saw kindness, mayhap a sense of humor. She decided to risk being discovered and beaten herself, took a step closer to the table and answered just as softly as he had spoken. "Lord Charles was displeased with the butter this morning. The last time he was 'displeased,' he beat the milkmaid so badly she could not work for days. I need her healthy. Would you have me beat a child because Lord Charles decided to demonstrate his power over a perfectly good tub of butter?"

"And careful chatelaine that you are, you will not waste it. You will simply reshape it, turn it into a new container, and serve it to your unsuspecting lord for dinner."

Margaret bit her lower lip to hide her mirth. "I would not dare!"

William winked at her. Before William could retort, she placed a finger on her lips requesting silence. She stepped back. With a flourish Lady Cecily descended the wooden stairs. At nine, Cecily should already have been betrothed. She was of moderate height with the last remains of baby fat still about her waist. With sandy hair and blue-green eyes, Cecily's features were a softer, feminine version of her father's. Lady Cecily wore a soft green bliaut over a cream-colored chemise that showed at her neck and wrists. She waited for the king's man to stand and greet her.

Margaret gave her only a cursory curtsy; her dislike of the girl was palpable. "Lady Cecily," she murmured. Just saying that was hard enough for her. "May I present Lord William of Avondale, the king's man."

He intoned the proper phrases; the girl accepted them and walked toward Lord William. As Lord Charles had reappeared from the stables, Margaret slipped away. From the servant's doorway she heard Lord Charles re-introduce his daughter and speak high praise of her. Margaret left for the kitchen before her distaste of Lady Cecily's behavior marred her face.

In the kitchen Cook pointed at the food basket and announced from across the room, "Needs a bottle of ale." Margaret unlocked the buttery door and took the three steps into the dark cellar. She reached for the reused wine bottles now filled with ale and corked, returned with two bottles and placed them in the basket. Margaret instructed a serving girl to take the basket to Lord Charles. Setting the menu for the evening meal, Margaret was busy with Cook and Caitlin, the under-cook, when the men left. They were still planning when a serving girl announced that the Lady Cecily was returning to bed.

"Oh no, she isn't!" Margaret said with force. She gave the girl instructions and left to handle the situation. "My lady!" called Margaret from the servants' entrance as she strode into the hall.

Halfway up the stairs, Cecily turned, looked down at the housekeeper and demanded, "What do you want?"

"Lord William has asked me to consult with you on matters regarding the king. It cannot wait. May I serve you while you consider his requests?"

The lady loved to have the estate's chatelaine serve her. That the housekeeper offered to do so caused the girl to smile.

"Very well. Be quick about it," Cecily ordered as she descended and sat at the end place on the dais so her servant would have to stand on the ground and look up at her.

Margaret reached for a clean mug from the side trestle and poured slowly. She faced Cecily so the stairs were out of the girl's line of vision. She stood on tiptoe to place the drink on the dais table and did not speak until Cecily had taken a sip. In the meantime, two serving girls slipped upstairs and began their work. Margaret dropped a spoon into a bowl of pottage and set it before the girl. "Well," the chatelaine began slowly. "As you are the lady of the hall and the king will credit you for the dinner, I feel it is important that you have a say in the proceedings."

"Yes, yes, go on." The girl was eager to be important.

"I will ask Lord William how close to the king you will sit." Margaret's deliberate enticement caused Cecily to look down at her.

"By Lord William if not between him and the king," the girl ordered.

"Yes," the servant intoned. She glanced up to see a pile of linens on the railing above. Margaret continued with speed so she could return to work. "With your approval, I plan to serve a barley soup to His Royal Highness and his men, should they arrive more than an hour before they dine. I'll add bread, if you like."

"You decide." The girl slurped pottage.

"If they arrive later than that, we will use the soup as the first course. I sent men to fish the river, but I am unsure of their success. If they catch nothing, the next course, or the first course, must be our smoked fish, then any small game they catch. Chickens if necessary. That will give us more time to roast the venison and boil the vegetables, which will be the main course. We still have plenty of dried apples. Would you like tarts or pies for dessert?"

"Men like tarts."

"Served with cheese or without?"

14

"Serve it and let them decide." Cecily was getting bored with the details.

"Very well. Now to the wines..."

"You know them better than I do. You take care of it." Just then a servant flung a straw mattress over the upstairs railing. "MY BED!" Cecily jumped up and looked behind and above. "You best put it together again!" she yelled to the unseen girl. Two other mattresses appeared.

"YOU did this!" Cecily spun about and accused Margaret. "You kept me down here and had them tear apart my bed out of spite. I get to eat with the king and you don't, so you wrecked my morning sleep!"

"Now, my lady," Margaret began, "I only did what Lord William ordered. The whole platform is for the king and his men. Your father will be angry if all is not as the king requires. Airing the mattresses, replacing the rushes, and putting clean linens on each bed will take hours. If His Royal Highness arrives early, your father will be furious if all is not ready. You are the lady of the household and will be held responsible."

"No, I won't. YOU will be. I'm telling Father what you did to me!"

"If you pout, if you tell him while the king and his men are here, what will go back to Court? You will be betrothed to a Norman of high standing, perhaps to the son or the brother of one of the king's men coming here. Do you want your reputation to be that of a whiner, a slug-a-bed, one who cannot manage a household?"

"If the king gets the platform, where am I to sleep?" Cecily scowled at the chatelaine's admonition. Her habit was to think of herself first.

"The king wants the hall for the men."

Still standing, Cecily reached for and slammed her spoon on the table.

"I am NOT sleeping in the stables!"

"No, no, of course not. But your father will want you safe, guarded, and close. Do you wish to sleep in the kitchen?"

"Not with the guards coming and going and getting broth before and after each watch!"

"The cook's shed?"

"It's a hovel! Cold and smelly!"

"Where then?" Margaret did not know where to put her.

"I'll sleep here. Take down my curtains and put them up in that corner. The men will have to come and go by the servants' door so I am not disturbed. I will not leave the safety of the hall. That's my decision!"

"Yes, mistress." Margaret chose not to argue. She had made Sir William's wishes known.

"What of my private things, my hair brush and such?"

"I will have the servants move your small chest. We will make you a trestle bed after dinner."

"I want my bed."

Said Margaret peremptorily, "Lord William said that is for the king's use." She turned and left the girl to her own devices. Margaret had work to do. She began it with a smile at having bested a petulant child.

Day

When Margaret reached the kitchen, she found a crowd of villeins waiting outside. Margaret, housekeeper over all, unlocked the buttery and left it open with instructions Cook be notified of every removal. Caitlin assisted in the kitchen. Margaret led a troop into the hall.

Four and a half hours later, Caitlin served wooden bowls of vegetable soup at the kitchen door to the outside workers and in the dirty end of the hall to those inside. Small groups ate standing and returned to work to make room for the next group to eat. For the king's visit, the main meal of the day had been shifted from noon to evening. The bakers and cooks worked without stopping. Mouthwatering smells of baked bread and tart shells wafted out the kitchen door and into the yard. Servants took linens and blankets from the unlocked storeroom at the back end of the hall upstairs to the platform beds. They folded the family's bedding, which had been airing outside on a rope line.

"Stack those on a trestle in a corner of the hall by the door so the family can pick up their piles later tonight," instructed Margaret. While that group worked, Margaret flew from task to task, scattering orders as she went. She headed to the stable and the yard to see how that work was progressing. In the center of the yard, she stopped and stood with her face to the sun to enjoy a breeze for a moment and then looked around. The gate was open to the hill upon which the Keep had stood. Villeins were cutting overgrown grass and piling it into small mounds. Their children were carrying the fodder to the cart outside the gate. She heard their teasing and challenges as to how fast they could work. They laughed and raced back to get more grass. She hoped the hill front would look neatly cropped even if they did not finish the back side before the king arrived. Grateful she had weeded both vegetable gardens just two days before, Margaret was pleased at how neat, prosperous and colorful they made the bailey look. She admired the many shades of green of plants gently waving in the breeze. *I miss the colors of the flowers Mother used to plant to border the gardens. Mother, your gardens are ready. Hall too. I think you would approve of our baking and cooking. I am doing my best to do as you would have done. The villeins think well of this new king. Oh, Mother. Would you could be here to meet him.*

Margaret blinked hard and ordered herself not to cry. She felt even more acutely the ache in her heart that never left her. She dabbed her eyes with the clean corner of her apron, leaned forward and wiped the sweat from her face. As she lifted her face, she sniffed and frowned. The breeze was coming toward her from right across the pig pen. First, she decided to order someone throw water over the animals covered in splattered dirt and their own waste. Then she considered clean pigs might wallow in the mud their baths might create. She decided she had better not make the smell worse. She looked down at her gunna, smudged with this and that, and reminded herself she had best wear a clean sun-bleached apron when in the hall. She wanted to look presentable for the king and his men. William's smile crossed her mind.

Margaret turned a bit right and wondered about the knights' barracks. Would they shame the family with messes the king's men might see? Just then a knight with a broom appeared at the doorway and swept dirt out the barracks door. Sir Bruis looked up, stopped, and gave her a small wave. Margaret could wave back because Sir Charles and his sons were hunting, and Cicely was inside the hall. His simple gesture cheered her as she returned to the many tasks yet to be completed. Inside the hall Margaret smiled at her workers. She always addressed people in their own language, Saxon to the villeins, Norman to the ranked, a little Latin for priests and monks. In Saxon, she said, "Perfect. You have done well."

The villeins beamed their love to her. She always took good care of their aches and pains and attended their births and deaths. This day was their opportunity to return her many kindnesses, the most important of which was she always treated them as if they mattered. To Margaret they did, and they knew it. She was like her mother that way. As she stood before them with praise in her eyes, they could see how much like her mother she had become. The women curtsied and the boys tugged at a lock of hair to show she was still a lady to them.

You wonderful people. You see me inside these clothes, behind the mask of indifference I must wear to stay safe. We play a game, you and I. You pretend I am unimportant. I pretend you have no voice. Yet we both have chosen. I to take as good a care of you as did Mother and you to watch over me and to help me when you can through all our hard days with that man. You just showed me you know I am still me. I love each of you for that.

Margaret nodded her recognition of their simple gesture and turned away to hide that her eyes were tearing in gratitude. She swallowed hard and returned to her role. Without turning back, she said, "Dena, please fetch my bag from Cook, the one I use to scent rushes."

"Yes, mistress."

"Please leave the platform so the king will step on the new rushes first," Margaret requested.

After she had scattered the dried and fresh flower petals and crushed herbs, Margaret leaned against the railing and looked at the main floor below. Just under her was the dais three steps higher than those on the floor. The table still glistened from its scrubbing. The boys had built trestle tables on either side of the rock-lined fire trough that extended down the center of the hall. They had cleaned and filled the fire pit with wood ready to be set ablaze. They had created space between the long section for warming the building and the short pile nearest the main entry door. That pile was to be for cooking meats. The girls had strewn the rushes the boys had pulled down from the stable storage area. The floor was clean and fresh. Normally all the cooking was done in the kitchen fireplace, but this day iron triangles for a spit pole had been set up at the far end of the fire trough for cooking one deer. That end danced with light and warmth as it had cooked bread and tarts all day. Wonderful smells of food, wood, and clean rushes permeated the building .

Cecily, who had done nothing all day, was ignored. She had demanded two serving girls, had gotten one, and then retreated behind her curtain. When she emerged, she was dressed in her best; she also wore a string of pearls as if she were a woman grown.

The hunters had returned with two deer carcasses, rabbits and birds. They ate standing at a table outside the kitchen door. They enjoyed soup, cold, smoked rabbit, and fresh bread dripping with melting butter given to them by Cook. Margaret served them full mugs of ale and set down full pitchers for them to enjoy.

"The game will be ready within the hour," Lord Charles stated.

Margaret replied when Cook pointedly did not. "The trough is ready; the spit poles are moved to the killing table, my lord."

"Good. You are doing well." Lord Charles' compliment was sincere.

"Thank you, my lord!" a surprised Margaret replied.

"Normand and I will help you dress the meat," Lord William offered. "Then I think I would like to sit in the hall."

"Of course! Of course!" gushed Lord Charles. "Come along, Young Charles and Raymond. If we get the hard part done quickly, we are done for the day!" The men trouped away; and, in a matter of moments, all evidence of their presence disappeared. Cooking inside and pot scrubbing outside behind the kitchen continued unabated.

"Sit before you fall," Cook advised Margaret as she grabbed the girl's hand and sat her on a stool out of the way of the kitchen workers. "Half this long day yet to go." Nodding her head in the direction of the disappearing men, she continued, "So proud of themselves, trouping about the forest, hunting and killing. Think they are doing us a favor to dress the meat. They are, but then they are 'done for the day.' Ha! Just like men!" Cook leaned against the wall. "Without us, they would eat raw meat!" Cook walked toward a work table. Margaret ordered servants to take basins and cloths to the killing table for the men to get clean there instead of inside a clean hall.

"Cook, what have I forgotten? I know I have forgotten something."

From across the room Cook answered, "Later. Eat something before he arrives. Remember, only one bowl. You have fasted since." Cook called over a servant's head.

Two bowls of soup and a half round of bread later, Margaret's head snapped as she jumped up. "Candles! I forgot candles on the head table!"

Cook strode to the girl and put her meaty hand on Margaret's slim arm. "Later, when you have the table set. Finish that mug. Until then sit, rest."

"Yes, Cook," she said as she sat on a stool, leaned against the wall and closed her eyes.

The grain wagon, again full of bags of ground wheat, oats and barley, had returned from the mill and rumbled toward the bailey.

The girl was half asleep, with Cook snoring on a stool beside her when they heard Caitlin's loud voice.

"You both best stand again. The grain wagon is back."

Margaret bounced awake and was up and going. The lady of an estate was its chatelaine, seeing to all work. Her domain included every task within the bailey and all her lord's people. Refusing any attempts Margaret had made in the last two years to train her, Cecily had become intractable and spoiled. Margaret bore the duties of the chatelaine because her mother had trained her for it, because Lord Charles had refused to remarry and because it had pleased the man to make her serve her own family. Margaret strode into the hall to check on the placement of the spit of venison to be roasted at the end of the fire pit. The boys were already slowly turning in unison each side of the spit. Margaret knew they would first warm the meat and then roast it slowly. When she saw Lord William climbing the platform steps at the back end of the hall, she threw up her hands. *Drat! Now the king will not see a perfect platform.* Frustrated, she heaved her shoulders, sighed and left for the kitchen.

William inspected the area, set his gear along the railing and changed to a clean shirt under his old, soft leather jerkin before returning to the hall. Charles and his sons had changed from a stack of clothes on a trestle meant to be the sideboard for food later and watched pages carrying their forest-colored hunting clothes toward the stable. The men enjoyed ale as they talked of the hunt and supervised the boys turning the venison. Fat hitting the logs crackled as it burned and sent up small puffs of smoke. The hunters almost drooled at the smells of cooking venison.

In the kitchen the women washed and sliced carrots, turnips, parsnips and onions; they started a fresh cauldron of water to boil the morrow's breakfast. The few squirrel bits were thrown into the barley pot to enrich the soup. The kitchen was so hot, the top half of the door was propped open. Workers walked past to get a breath of air. The fireplace, centered on the back wall, was tall enough that Margaret could have stood inside it by only dropping her chin to her chest. Each side had two brick shelves that stuck a foot into the fire box; the bottom shelves were for baking bread rounds and the shelves above were used to keep foods warm. The large cauldron on the right iron arm easily cooked soups and stews to serve forty. The two smaller cauldrons for the left iron arms held either other foods or water for cooking and cleaning. A cauldron on the floor beside the fireplace currently held scraps of food that might be used in pottage or to make a bone broth.

So practiced were the women in using the kitchen's space, large though it was, they appeared to be in a dance. From the tables and shelves to the fireplace, from the fireplace to the serving table with its platters and bowls on the shelves below. The bakers dipped their hands into bags of smashed oats, and cracked barley and rye to mix into wheat flour. The multi-grained bread was so rich with flavor and strength a poor man could live on that and ale alone. The bread and pie makers worked on separate tables on the wall opposite the fireplace. Near the outer door, which had been offset almost to a corner to avoid wind blowing out the fire, stood a table against a side wall where all meats were cut and prepared for cooking. Rain or shine, dishwashing was on an old, beat-up kitchen table outside and behind the kitchen but close enough to the kitchen well so water could easily be fetched.

Outside, hunting dogs tried to sneak into the kitchen. A servant threw bones far into the yard to keep them from under foot and watched the barking and growling animals as they fought over the little they got. Boys again raked the yard to erase the damage the hunters had done. One group, who had finished the stable, stood leaning on their rakes, refusing to help. They reeked of sweat and manure, but the stable was clean and the stalls were ready with fresh hay and water.

At the kitchen door, Margaret stood in fading sunlight as she handed half a round of warm bread to workers before she sent them home. While Margaret could see about half the bailey yard and those in it, she looked at the tree tops far beyond the palisade wall and longed to spend the evening in the quiet of the forest. As Margaret watched the sunlight fade, a brief memory flashed in her mind of her running among the trees and exploring the forest as a child. She tried and failed to remember the last sunset she had enjoyed from the palisade wall. Margaret looked away from her desired escape. *Back to work. Dream of a free afternoon another time.* She instructed select boys to wash, then come for bread before they served dinner.

Margaret sent a boy into the hall to whisper a request to Lord William. He met her at the kitchen door with the bottom half between them and in clear sight of everyone. She wanted no gossip, but she could not help but smile. *How handsome he looks, clean and hair combed. Simple green tunic, leather jerkin, grey leggings, black boots. Eyes as brown as his hair jump out of his face when he smiles. Such a smile. Food! Think food! What was I going to ask him? Oh yes.* "I can set the head table for six or seven. What does the His Royal Highness require?"

"Please set places closest to the servants' door for two retainers, then the His Royal Highness, Lord Charles and his two sons."

"Lady Cecily has her heart set at sitting at the head table. She is the lady of the estate," Margaret continued, "and I do not see her eating in the kitchen."

William remembered how Cecily hung upon her father and how he doted on her and decided. "I like Raymond, and I want him seated at the head table. We could place her on the end beside him."

"Very good, my lord," Margaret demurred, "but who will seat her?"

"I will see Raymond does it."

"Who serves His Royal Highness?"

"Two of the king's servants will wait upon all at the head table."

Margaret understood. Even with the storage rooms at his back, the king wanted no strangers serving him from the front of the dais. *Too easy to slip a knife under the table and stab a man in the guts.* "I appreciate the assistance, Lord William. I will need one of our servants to carve the venison in the hall."

The knight smiled at her diplomacy. "Of course."

"Will you please inform Lord Charles of all this?"

"I am happy to do so." William stared and smiled at her until she could stand no more and looked down. He returned to the hall.

Why does he stare at me so? What do his smiles mean? Rather than risk another close surveillance, she sent Caitlin to baste the venison in the hall. The fire sputtered and hissed from the drippings. Everyone in the hall sniffed and licked their lips in anticipation. Servants set the head table. Dena carried the pair of pewter candlesticks and beeswax candles. She promised herself to tell chatelaine how beautiful the dais table looked. Margaret and Caitlin had decided that no women but they would be in the hall so propriety would be maintained. The serving girls were not happy staying in the kitchen.

"Too bad," retorted their chatelaine. "Wine and ale will flow freely. I will not have you pawed. The king might never come here again." She concluded, "I want his memory to be one that will honor this household."

The women stared behind her and curtsied low. Margaret turned and saw Lord Charles had entered the kitchen. She too curtsied low.

"All is ready, my lord."

Lord Charles nodded in acknowledgement and pushed an empty pitcher toward her. Margaret rose and accepted it.

"None of this, no matter how well done, will change my mind or your station," Lord Charles said.

"I did not expect it would. But I do not do all this for you. I do it in memory of her." Because Margaret had turned to fetch more cool ale from the cellar, she did not see the blow her words had struck. Shocked, Lord Charles watched the villeins' eyes following the chatelaine, then return to the floor. He saw what he had not noticed since his wife's death—the love and loyalty his servants had for his housekeeper. They all were respectful. He saw the down-turned heads and shoulders of every woman curtseying; the boys were on one knee and looking at the floor. No one moved. But he could feel their hearts were with the young woman below.

In his head Lord Charles heard, *We serve you, but we love her. We do your bidding, but go away. We do not want her hurt.* Their thoughts and emotions were as real as their bodies. Lord Charles turned to Cook for affirmation. All he saw were cold blue eyes staring back. Cook, who had loved and teased the young man he had once been, was the only one brave enough to look at him. Her eyes told him she wanted nothing to do with him; she was on the girl's side. Lord Charles shuddered at the wall of strong emotions washing toward him. He felt distrust, disdain, even disgust. He told himself they were just villeins. Why should he care what they thought of him? He reminded himself the girl who had been his daughter did not deserve their support, yet they still warned him away with their very thoughts. Lord Charles was shocked at what he was feeling and dismayed they were not on his side. He was their lord. He wondered how they could be so blind to the upstart girl who thought so much of herself. Unwilling to admit defeat, Lord Charles spun on his heel and left. Only when they heard their master's retreating steps did the women and boys raise their eyes. That was as close as any ever dared to defy him. They stood in silent agreement as they waited for their leader.

When Margaret returned with the full pitcher, she saw her guardians and smiled. Then she halted. Their stances, the way they held their heads told her how close they'd come to defiance, how fierce was their loyalty. Overcome by their adoration, the girl turned away. She choked back sudden tears, then straightened her back. Turning again toward them, she first handed the pitcher to a boy and pointed toward the hall. Without realizing it, she used a motion and phrase her mother had used many times.

"Come…back to work now," Margaret intoned as she shooed them into motion as a mother hen would her chicks. After they stirred, Royal Oak's chatelaine sought the comfort of Cook's arms and ample breasts. Cook hugged the girl hard and held her head close to her own for private words. The rest of the staff pretended not to notice as they returned to their appointed tasks.

Evening

Sunlight faded first in the trees beyond the bailey and then in a half circle of cleared ground around it. Shadow crept toward the bailey wall. The guards on either side of the main gate smiled at the pleasure of seeing the bailey almost sparkle and stood a bit taller to be part of such an important event. Neither they nor almost anyone else had ever seen a royal. Shadows marched to the palisade and crept over the wall. Twilight softened edges, making everything look clean and beautiful.

"The king is coming!" a guard yelled to a boy in the yard. "Tell the hall."

The men heard from twin heralds, one boy at the hall entrance and another in the servants' doorway. Lady Cecily stepped outside her curtain and looked toward her father. In the kitchen all looked to Margaret who looked to Cook. The old woman shrugged her shoulders and returned to work. Margaret tried to show the same leadership, but she was silently out-voted. The others herded toward the kitchen door and crowded outside. They huddled together, and talked among themselves about what they might see. Margaret and Cook heard, "Wonder what he looks like? How many men do you think are with him? I want to see what they wear. Will they enter with their swords out?"

The villeins' chatelaine shrugged her shoulders at Cook and left. *Mayhap this will be the only time in my life I will see a royal. Best I make use of it.* As anxious as her help to see the king, Margaret still stood in back to give the others the best view.

The barricade gates opt wide. In rode twin heralds, one holding a colorful banner and the other blowing a trumpet, then the king alone, then his men, in pairs on their geldings and leading roundseys.

The lot looked tired, dirty, and worn out. In the center of the yard, Lord Charles greeted King Henry formally and loudly enough for all to hear.

The king looks much like the other men in his party. No, he is different. Even from that distance, King Henry radiated such power Margaret could feel it. The way he held his head, the straightness of his back and the way he looked around, as if assessing the property's value, announced his authority. The king dismounted, removed his glove as a sign of equality and shook Lord Charles's hand. That gesture demonstrated King Henry's skill of diplomacy with one of the men who ruled his land with his permission and in his name. As the retainers dismounted, the yard became a crush of boys ready to serve and men taking care of their horses and gear. The creaking of saddles as the men dismounted, the dropping of gear bags to the dusty ground, the commands of the king's knights, and the murmurs of the serving boys became the noises of the bailey.

Margaret herded her staff inside. She handed off basins of hot water and cloths so the retinue could wash hands and faces. Other boys waited for her signal to take bowls of hot soup and trays of bread into the hall.

The king and his men walked into a rush of warm air, mouth-watering smells, and boys to wait upon them. Helping carry packs, the older and stronger servants followed the knights who climbed the stairs to inspect the sleeping arrangements. Margaret peeked inside. As Lord William had all well in hand, she returned to kitchen to finish spicing various dishes.

Servants returned empty soup bowls and refilled pitchers of hard cider and ale to take back into the hall. The noises in the hall quieted as the men rested. The king and Lord William conferred on the platform. When they returned, King Henry was only slightly better dressed than Lord Charles. His shirt was a creamy white against the burgundy leather jerkin. His strong, thick leg muscles showed through the deerskin-color pants, but his brown boots were worn and a bit down at the heel, as if he had not taken time to order new ones. King Henry may have made an effort to appear no better dressed than one of his lords, but his demeanor bespoke his power. The king wore neither a crown nor a coronet; he did not need it.

In the kitchen Cook stopped a moment and asked the girl, "Well, what does he look like?"

"Who?"

"The king."

Margaret looked off for a moment.

Not as handsome at Lord William. What shall I say?

"I could feel the power in him even across the bailey. Middling tall with a thick neck. Brawny-chested. Black hair and a high forehead."

"High forehead," repeated Cook. "That bespeaks intelligence, you know."

"I like his voice, deep and resonant. Soothing, calming."

"But not as handsome as the other one?" teased the old woman.

"Which other one?"

"Your Lord William. I see how you look his way."

"I look not at him in any way!"

"Liar!"

Margaret waited in the kitchen until Cook was again busy. She slipped on a clean apron, wound the waist strings around her back and tied the ends in front. Margaret walked out while the old woman's back was turned. She inhaled the cool evening air and looked for stars. Yet the sight of these far-off heavenly lights, angels' candles, her mother used to say — did not bring the familiar sense of wonder. There was too much on her mind. Trying to anticipate whatever might happen or still be needed, she imagined the rest of the evening course by course. Lord William peeked his head out the servants' door and looked about. The firelight seeping out the doorway behind him lit his back and created a shadow with its start at his feet and its head almost touch Margaret's feet. When he caught Margaret's eye, he winked.

"Ready when you are."

The girl could not help herself; she smiled back.

"We need just a bit longer."

Lord William disappeared. Margaret wiped dry her brow with the corner of the apron; she turned back toward the kitchen to finish readying the fish course and the accompanying white wine. Hours later the feast was over, the hall tables had been cleared for men to sleep on, and the kitchen was ready for the morning. Margaret was too tired to move. Chin to chest and eyes closed, she rested on a stool with her back against a wall. When all in the hall were abed, William slipped into the kitchen. The well-oiled door hinges gave no warning.

"A boy said I was to speak with you privately after all had settled for the night," William whispered.

Margaret started awake, stood and drew him into the corner by the door. "I know why His Royal Highness came. Please tell him that none here can help him but I."

Despite William's surprise at her boldness, he nodded.

"If he would speak to me on the matter, I am sleeping in the kitchen tonight. Tell him my kitchen staff is loyal, so we can safely speak here." Margaret continued, "If any asks why we spoke, tell him

I asked if the king had been pleased tonight. Was he? Is there anything more I can do?"

"He was very well pleased. Did you not hear his toast and compliments after the meal? Nothing else need be done. I will relay your message, but I cannot say he will see you. Good night, Margery."

William's grin and soft voice were a caress to the girl's worn spirit.

"God give you good rest, my lord," she murmured as she curtsied.

William nodded and returned her parting blessing, "God give you good rest, Chatelaine." This time William called her by her title. Then he smiled, nodded, and returned to the hall. Margaret watched him until he closed the main door behind himself.

If all knights are like him, I want one of mine own. But I dare not want him.

Margaret took up her blanket and sat on the remaining sacks of ground grains. She leaned against the kitchen wall, stared at embers and was a long time praying.

Please God, let the Saxon rumors be aright. If they are not, I could die. If the king comes not, I am trapped here to the end of my days. Please God, let him seek me. Let him like my plan and need me. Please God, have him take me away from here; let me use my skills in Your service. Not knowing what else to ask for, Margaret began her evening prayers. *If it be Your will, Oh God, bless Father Ambroise, Young Charles, Raymond, and Cecily. Keep them safe and well. Bless Caitlin and Cook, Jorgon and Jorgon Elder, Aldrich and Goda, the unknown men who helped save Mother's body from beheading, and the unknown men who ride Night for me. Please keep Mother's new grave secret and Night safe. Bless Sirs Bruis and Ignace.* Margaret finished her prayer list with the knights serving the estate, every person who had worked to make the king's visit successful, and the rest of the Saxons. Too worn to wait any longer, she slid down and slept.

Midnight

A man jolted Margaret awake. He put one hand over her mouth and another on the back of her neck. He pinned her down further with a knee in the small of her back. A hard-edged whisper demanded, "Woman, what do you know of the king's business?"

She barely managed to shake her head. From the smell of the man, she knew he was not William. The stranger released her mouth. "Upon my life, I speak to the king—and only to him."

The man pulled her to a sitting position and pinned her to the wall with stiff arms. His face was but inches from hers.

"Your Royal Highness," Margery whispered in awe as she saw Henry, King of England, in dim firelight and dark shadows of kitchen gear.

Through the interior arch that led to the sleeping cubby, he saw two lumps under blankets shift. Margery saw the lumps and spotted a sentinel's back at the kitchen door.

"Back to bed. Cover your heads," Margaret hissed. She waited until Cook and Caitlin obeyed. Speaking in a hush, Margaret informed her sovereign lord, "We are now as alone as we can be, Your Royal Highness."

"What do you think you know?" Henry answered in the same hush.

"Your queen is again with child. You seek aid for her."

Suddenly furious, Henry shook the girl's shoulders so hard her head snapped against the wall.

"How?" he demanded.

"In the hall. I heard you. You asked about Lord Charles's Lady Rosamonde. When you learned she was dead, your eyes shifted away from Lord Charles; your shoulders drooped the tiniest bit. You lost interest in the rest of the evening. You thought what you had come for was no longer here." Margaret, trembling at her own temerity, rushed out her next words. "BUT help is here. All knew the Lady Rosamonde for her skills as a healer. Men wanted her because only she stitched up wounds rather than burn them or amputate. You are whole; you do not need her for that. Norman ladies asked her to help them have healthy babes. Babes lived when she delivered them. You have just lost a babe. The queen—you dare not lose this one too."

The king yanked her shoulders forward and pushed Margaret so hard her head and back slammed against the wall. Trying to refocus her eyes, Margaret blinked hard several times. The king knocked her against the wall again; this time not so hard. Chastened, Margaret looked down.

"And … " Henry asked in a hard voice.

"I … was her assistant. I accompanied her many times. I know her ways and her medicines. Since her death, I have delivered the babes on this estate. Except for a shriveled one that had been dead in the womb for weeks, every babe I have delivered since Lady Rosamonde's death is still alive."

"I know you not," King Henry rasped out his challenge.

"Lord Charles does not allow me to leave his lands," was all she would admit. "Do you want me to aid you? If so, I have questions, Your Royal Highness."

Henry released Margaret and shifted them both so they sat face to face on the sacks. They remained silent for a long moment.

Margaret took a deep breath and prayed for her own safety. *He can order my death for guessing wrong—or even for guessing aright.*

"Please tell me of your babe," Margaret began.

After the Henry answered, she asked him if any had reported the babe's appearance to him. The king was brief; he had seen his dead son himself. The babe was only four months old, almost alive, and perfect except for dark nails. The depth of the grief Henry had stifled in the telling moved Margaret, but she was afraid to show it.

"I'm so sorry, Your Royal Highness, but I must ask more. When this happened, did Her Royal Highness, the queen, have a black line under her nails where her skin ends? Did such a line develop before the babe's death?"

Even in the gloom Margaret saw a shock of recognition on her sovereign's face.

"Why, yes! I saw it when I held her hands. Several of her ladies commented on it as well."

First from Saxon gossip and now from the king's account, Margaret was cert of what had killed his first-born. As she debated whether to speak further, he took the choice from her.

"You know something. I command you to tell me."

"Sh-h-h! Your Royal Highness!" Margaret hissed. "I am afraid, my king. I am very afraid."

Henry took up the girl's hands and gripped them hard. "I am the King of England. I will protect you. Tell me."

But *no one will protect me from you if I am wrong. I will be beheaded right here.*

Margaret risked her life when she said, "My King, I fear someone may have poisoned your queen."

"Poisoned? How?"

"Her food or drink, most likely." Margaret hesitated. "There is a kind of poison that is slow acting; its main sign is an upset stomach—immediate—unless taken with food. A woman with child might think stomach trouble is part of her carrying time. Its long-term sign is black under the fingernail at the skin line. You said both she and your son had it." Margaret thought for a moment and continued, "It would take very little poison to kill an unborn. In the right doses, the mother would feel sickly, but the babe would die. Whoever poisoned the queen did so in gradual steps."

"They murdered my son!" The king finished her thought, "Through her. Is such a poison available?"

Margaret dared only nod.

"Where!" the king demanded.

"I do not know; I have only heard of it." Then to cover her lie, she quickly asked, "Who knows the queen is again with child?"

"Only I. She is afraid to tell anyone else she lose this one too. She will lose this babe if anyone learns of it. We have no time!" Henry dropped her hands and started to move, but Margaret touched his arm.

"Please, Your Royal Highness, I have a plan that may save her and your child."

Henry stared. Margaret outlined her ideas.

The king reported, "I have the location, and the men."

"We also need a priest. Mayhap one of her Saxon relatives, an old confessor who can be trusted. One who can give her hope and comfort," Margaret offered.

"A priest. What else do you request?"

"Three boons granted if I succeed." Margaret gambled the king would consent because he needed her; she hoped he did.

"What boons?" Henry asked cautiously.

36

"Small ones, Your Royal Highness. Well within your power. I think I know what I want." Margaret started with her smallest request. "Pretty clothes and some jewelry."

"Done."

"I want a dowry, so I can marry. Befitting my place, of course."

"Done. What else?"

The king was smiling at her, for surely what she wanted was far less than the proverbial 'half your kingdom' from the tales his mother had told him.

"I am not sure. I must think on it. Your Royal Highness, I have no one to sign a marriage contract. Because you are the one providing the dowry, might you be the one signing the contract?"

"Why not!" The king's tone changed. "Should you fail?"

Margaret had anticipated this and sucked in a deep breath.

"Of mine own free will, I will appear in Court and offer you my head. Then I will walk outside and set it upon the block. I do not mean to fail you, Your Royal Highness; but, if I do, all I have to give is my life."

She shuddered at the thought of failure. She had already prayed and asked God to protect her from the king's wroth, from death. *I must escape this life.*

"I accept." Anything you need?"

"One servant from this place if she is willing. If she will not come without knowing why, I will not bring her. Also, I need a purse of coins for purchases, supplies, and all else we will need before anyone knows why."

"Money! It always comes to that," the king sighed. "Very well. Soon three men will leave unseen. When they come to you, give each provisions for two days."

"Does one go to Her Royal Highness?"

Henry nodded.

"I suggest not, Your Royal Highness. Even though she remains silent, her mood, any small action may warn your enemies. She holds your future in her belly. If you bring her, sweep her away without warning, she may be safer. Please remember, no one around her must come, not her servants, her ladies, nor any of the Court, not even any of her current priests—and no food or drink comes with her."

Henry nodded.

"Two men."

Henry looked stood and looked at her hard. Fearful, Margaret clenched her hands together. The sentinel remained immobile. Henry passed. His shadow followed. Margaret sagged against the wall and expelled a long whew sound. *I still have my life! I go with the king! Now I have hope and a future. Can Lord Charles stop me?* The girl crept toward the two mummified under their blankets and shook the nearer figure.

"The king wants two days' provisions for two men anon."

Both figures uncovered their heads, but only the younger one rose. Together Margaret and Caitlin filled two empty flour sacks. Two men slipped into the kitchen, accepted the sacks and slipped out. Margaret waited to speak until Caitlin had closed the door.

"Caitlin," she whispered. "I'm wanted, but I'm not yet free."

From the cubby Cook pushed herself to her elbow. "Child, you just leaped from the cauldron into the fire. The king will be harder to serve than is Lord Charles," she warned. "And far more dangerous. Who will protect you?"

Margaret knelt beside Cook. "I have no future here. You are the one who advised me to pray for a better future. Now God has sent it. I must take it. I must. Please help me."

38

The girl pulled Caitlin next to her.

"With the king, I have a chance. He needs me. Serve him well and I can marry. What will Lord Charles do when he learns of this?"

Cook assured her, "Nothing. He's the king's vassal. The king will order him to surrender you."

"I'm going with you," Caitlin informed Margaret. "You are not going alone with anyone, not even a king. I promised your mother to take care of you and I shall." Caitlin's single nod showed her determination.

"Oh, Caitlin, you've no idea how much I need you! But I can only say we will be safe for a half year. If I fail His Royal Highness, he will have my head. Then what becomes of you?"

"I care not. We go together." Caitlin crossed her arms over her breasts.

Margaret hugged Caitlin hard. They still held each other when Cook shocked them.

"If you leave, then I leave. That old man will be even worse after you two depart. I have taken enough abuse. I am going too."

"Where? What will become of you?" Margaret knew what Lord Charles would do if he caught a villein leaving.

"My oldest brother lives alone, and needs someone to care for him. Child, with you gone, I have no reason to stay either."

"How will you get away?"

"In the rush and noise of the king's departure, I will herd everyone outside the walls to wave good-bye. While everyone is looking at the king, I will slip away."

"The danger!"

"No one will bother an old woman. Our people will not talk. I am a free woman. Your mother saw to that. He was so pleased she birthed his heir he gave her anything she wanted; she asked for Caitlin's and mine freedom."

They heard a small noise and looked toward the kitchen. Cook patted Margaret's hand.

"Just embers collapsing. We need to add wood."

"Do each of you have your paper out of the chest under the altar? Does each bear his ring seal?"

At their joint nods, Margaret un-furrowed her brow.

"Two years ago. We asked Father for them right after Lord Charles made you his slave. With his ale-addled mind, he has likely forgotten we have them," Cook informed her.

"Without the three of us, this household will come apart," Caitlin offered.

"About time," Cook countered.

Margaret imagined the estate in a week.

The baker will still bake bread, the milkmaid will still milk and churn the butter, and Reeve will still lead the Saxons in their tasks. Who will run the household, plan the meals, manage the animals, weed the garden, tend the sick, repair torn garments and all else that needs be done? Not Cecily. She refused to learn how. Not Young Charles or Raymond. They know only of hunting, fighting and swordplay. For cert not him. All he cares about is how much drink the aleman makes. Come apart it shall.

Margaret smiled to herself.

2

Departures

The women consulted about what each should take with her and how to get Cook's things outside the barricade in the morning. They were still making plans when they heard the wall guards outside. Inside the kitchen, those finishing their watch warmed themselves with a cup of hot bone broth before slipping into the barracks for a few hours' sleep. Cook, Caitlin, and Margaret started the morning's bread, ate the last of yesterday's soup and bread, and then set the morning's pottage of soaked grains over the fire. Before the household stirred, Margaret opt the door only so much as the space would fit her and slipped unseen between buildings and into the stables. She touched the young man's shoulder as she spoke his name. Jorgon shook his head to waken himself and then sat up on his straw bed amongst tack and gear.

"Yes, mistress?" he whispered.

"Jorgon, I go with the king today," she whispered back. He stared at her. "Jorgon, I want to take what's mine. Do you understand?" Margaret watched him nod. "I dare not have it seen by any here. If you bring him here, Lord Charles will kill you as soon as I leave. If you follow and bring it me, you cannot return. What shall I do?"

"Take me with you! You need me."

"True, but I am not cert for how long or what will become of you if something happens to me."

"I am a good stableman and hostler; I can find another place," Jorgon countered with false casualness.

Margaret knew he was devoted to her. The villeins had teased him about it for years. *I am wrong to play on his feelings for me. Two years. Faithful and secret and able. I need him.* Margaret outlined the women's plans and suggested Jorgon help Cook depart and accompany her until she was well away. "Surely, you can follow the king and his men. I know not where we go, but our passing should be easy to learn. No one may see you preparing the women's riding platforms for Caitlin and me. We need them."

That task done, Margaret left the horse barn and slipped back into the tiny lean-to she, Caitlin and Cook shared. She threw her few things onto an old shawl, tied the corners together, and dropped the bundle inside the cubby opening. In the kitchen Caitlin supervised the serving of the morning meal. Margaret removed the keys and scissors from her girdle and placed the symbols of her housekeeper role on the fireplace mantle. They clunked as she dropped them on the wooden beam. She turned to Cook and smiled at her as she helped the old woman ladle pottage into bowls. *Please God, may I never return. Please God, see Cook safe to her brother's hut. Your will, Oh God, in all things.*

Caitlin slipped into the lean-to with Cook as Margaret worked. The other servants were too busy to notice. The morning sky continued to lighten. In the hall only the king and Lord Charles ate their meals seated on the dais. Margaret watched them from the kitchen doorway. Lord Charles seemed pleased and then displeased. Beneath the table the man was clenching his hands together at the same time he was smiling. His head was a little bent, but his back was straight. A knight approached and asked how many horses Margaret needed. She told him Jorgon, the stable boy, knew of two women's riding platforms she and the other woman would use. She told him of their bundles. He left. Margaret again looked toward the table. Lord Charles' stiff back showed her he was upset but under control. The king had bolted his pottage and swallowed all his ale in gulps. He looked down the hall at his men leaving and appeared anxious to depart as well. When Margaret heard Cook and Caitlin behind her, she nodded to the king.

King Henry said loudly, "Well, Lord Charles, the sun is rising and we must be away."

Those men still in the hall started for the main door. Margaret slipped into the kitchen and gave Cook a quick hug and kiss. Everyone but she departed to watch the king's party. Margaret waited and paced inside the kitchen in excitement tinged with fear. *I must retrieve it before I leave else he find it and use it again.* Margaret balled up brown cloth and set it on the ground just outside the doorway. She put her back to the outside kitchen wall and slid along it to the palisade wall and along that wall. The whole time, she looked at the crowd in the bailey. *Please God, do not let anyone turn and spot me.* She reached the lean-to and slipped between the stacked wood and the wall. Carefully, she moved two logs and pulled a small box from its hiding place. Her heart raced at the thought of what she was stealing. She pocketed the item, returned the same way she had come and grabbed the brown ball just outside the kitchen door. Margaret strode into the bailey and toward her future.

While all was still covered in pre-dawn gray, the noise of the yard was of men giving servants instructions, tying gear to their saddles, boots hitting the ground as knights readied to get into their saddles, and the creaking of leather as the men settled atop their roundseys. Boys then handed up their reins of their war horses to the knights. Margaret shook out a wrinkled brown mantle and donned it. Lord William signaled for her roundsey. With a sunny smile, Lord William cupped his hands for her foot and lifted Margaret onto the platform, a seat that faced sideways. Attached to it was a leather drop to protect a woman's legs from touching the horse, and a board upon which she set her feet. Much more precarious than a man's saddle, the platform could tilt and spill a woman if she did not tie herself to the device. A sandbag hung behind the seat was the contraption's only coun-terbalance. Margaret nodded her thanks. *Good man. I like his smile.* She settled her skirt about her legs then wrapped her mantle around her. She smiled at Lord William, who looked surprised when she accepted the reins and held them correctly.

When she turned her horse's head to join the others, she first saw the king looking at her, then spotted Lord Charles on one knee to the right of the king's steed. Villeins lined the sides of the yard, spilled out the gates and stood beside the road. When they saw Margaret leaving them, they gasped. Voices rose and fell in a wave from the yard to beyond the gates. A knot of knights waited behind the king on his high-strung stallion as the animal pawed the earth and neighed.

Plainly dressed in brown servant clothes, swathed in an old, patched mantle, with her wimple wrinkled from sleeping in it, Margaret appeared rag-tag. Astride only a pony, she still held her head high, her back straight. Her face shone with a happiness no one had seen in her in two years. She smiled broadly at the sight before her. She believed her freedom was at hand as she lifted her face to the sun. Lord Charles turned, and Margaret's cheerfulness became a frown. *Can he keep me here? Then will I be dead like Mother?* Lord Charles' rising rage frightened her. His heels hit the ground hard and kicked up dust as he approached and grabbed the roundsey's reins close to the bit. His cheeks puffed ominously. The king and his men watched the pair. The villeins trembled when their lord became angry; they trembled now.

"Girl, after you leave this compound, I will never let you return!"

Margaret's temper flared. In the silence she demanded, "Have I any family in this place? Well, have I?"

"NO…you…have…not!" Lord Charles denied her through clenched teeth. "You are nothing to me."

Margaret heard leather creaking and hooves stomping. She felt suddenly warm and flushed of face. *Nothing? You will soon learn what my nothing means to this household. What Cook and Caitlin mean.* Margaret looked down at her enraged father clutching the reins so hard his knuckles were white. She decided challenging him was futile.

"Then I have no reason to stay, have I, sirrah?" she countered with false sweetness. "I have no one to object to my changing lords. I will serve the king. What becomes of me is no longer your concern." Margaret pulled on the reins to force Lord Charles to release them. He did. The pony sidestepped away from the man. She stopped her roundsey and settled him by relaxing her body and speaking softly and calmly as she stroked his neck. Two knights rode forward and positioned her between them, forcing Lord Charles to step aside. Margaret leaned forward and patted the pony's neck. When she looked up, she saw King Henry smiling at her. Beyond him, she spotted Caitlin seated uneasily upon a roundsey that was being led out of the compound. Margaret returned the king's smile and nodded she was ready to leave. *Head up. Look straight ahead. Wave to the Saxons? No, he will punish them. No looking backward. Only forward. Mother, if you are in Heaven, protect me.*

The villeins watched her departure, not the king's.

In the crush of men and horses passing through the gate, neither Lord Charles nor his children saw Jorgon and Cook standing just outside the compound. The stable boy picked up a bundle hidden beyond the gate and hustled Cook and himself down the side wall of the dry moat, around the corner, across the clearing, and into the woods.

Hours later, servants served warmed remains from the feast. When Lord Charles asked for Cook, servants admitted they had not seen her since the king's departure. When he reared out of his chair demanding to see who held the keys, the servants ran out of the hall into the yard. Lord Charles found the keys and roared his rage. No one dared enter the hall that afternoon. Children, servants, stable boys, all scattered like frightened chickens before his rampaging path through the hall, up the palisade walls, into the stable, around the compound. That night a sullen family ate cold food alone in a silent hall. Lord Charles sent for Dena, his latest bedmate. When he learned she too was missing, he smashed stools, tossed trestle stands and wrecked all evidence of the king's visit. He climbed the ladder to the sleeping platform with the estate keys in his pocket and a pitcher of ale in hand.

That night appeared the wraith that had haunted Lord Charles's lands since his wife's death two years before. All believed it to be the vengeful ghost of Lady Rosamonde astride the black that had disappeared the night of her death. The figure in scarf and mantle had first appeared in the middle of the night after Lord Charles had beaten Margaret. Other times everyone had heard it in the forest; the wall guards had seen it riding beyond the village shacks and around the edges of the moat or just inside the tree line. Each time it shrieked a wrong Sir Charles had committed. Once the wrong was done by his daughter Cecily, and it had screamed her offense. The last time the wraith appeared was after Lord Charles had ordered the milkmaid beaten.

Lord Charles had first accused first Margaret then Jorgon of faking the ghost. When he located both of them moments after the ghost had been seen, all believed the ghost was their beloved lady warning them of danger or trying to tell them something. Pondering aloud why her spirit was not at rest had netted one man a severe beating from his lord, so no one mentioned the subject again. This night the ghost rode round the compound three times while howling Margaret's name before it set off down the road the king had taken.

Too afraid of their father to seek their beds that night, Young Charles, Raymond, and Cecily huddled by the fire pit. The howling outside echoed faintly. They knew its source. Too frightened to draw attention to themselves, the boys let the fire go out rather than rise and get firewood from the corner. Cecily huddled behind her curtain and cried silent tears. In terror that the ghost's look would kill them, the guards cowered behind the barricade walls. Villeins in their huts awoke to the wailing, covered their heads, and prayed hard. Lord Charles was too drunk to hear.

The next morning the villeins reluctantly left their homes and spoke to one another about the previous night's specter. After Mass they waited in the sunshine until they were summoned before approaching the hall. They were careful to fulfill their lord's demands for fear of what Lord Charles might do if they displeased him. The household servants cleared the hall of debris without speaking to each other and as quietly as they could. When Lord Charles questioned his villeins, those who'd seen Cook leaving said nothing. A villein was a lord's chattel. Running away was considered stealing the lord's property and could be punished by death for the runaway and for any who aided, abetted, or knew of it and did not report it. Pleading ignorance was dangerous. No one remembered the Lady Rosamonde had freed Cook years before. Talk in the village was that Margaret had taken Caitlin and Cook with her. Most believed Jorgon had followed them. No one knew where Dena had gone, but none blamed her for running away. No father wanted his daughter used as she had been.

The villeins silently prayed for all them to be safe. Margaret had been so much more than just a housekeeper. Who would bind up their wounds, see to their aches and pains, listen to their complaints, protect and defend them when their lord was angry, birth their babes, comfort them as they died? They understood Margaret's desire to leave, but without her they were bereft. If they spoke of the situation, they only said "her," and everyone knew whom the whisperer meant.

3

Journey

The sun rose high and hot. Still leaves meant no breeze blew through the trees on either side of the road. Birds sang far ahead of them, stopped while the king's group passed, and resumed their calls once the party was well beyond their thickets and trees. From back of the column, Margaret spotted a bit of the king's burgundy mantle and Lord William's blue one at the front of the group. Because of no rain for a fortnight, the knight's roundseys and war horses kicked up road dust. Both Margaret and Caitlin coughed occasionally, especially when the road curved. *At least we are positioned before the baggage roundseys.*

Despite the rounder's easy ambling gate, by midmorning Margaret knew her backside would not survive the day. She had heard soft moaning behind her for the last hour, so she knew Caitlin was suffering as well. Margaret could not see her as they were both facing left. Neither dared request they be able to stop and rest. Each feared the king might return them. Margaret tried shifting in the saddle to ease her soreness, but her pony sidled and almost unseated her. After settling the beast into his previous gait, she wondered why the men rode roundseys and led their geldings. Only the king rode a stallion. When Margaret thought she could bear not another moment, she spotted a knight riding toward the group. The king and Lord William picked up their pace and soon the column stopped for a cold noon meal.

One knight assisted her descent as another helped Caitlin. Margaret was tempted to rub her backside, but she dared not among a company of men. One man agreed to be their guard as they walked into the trees. Margaret motioned Caitlin forward to accompany her. Both walked with an unsteady gait and reached for saplings to help them. *Would that I had been permitted to ride. Then I might be tougher for this journey.*

Caitlin pointed, "I see a stream through here."

Margaret waved Caitlin forward in deference to her age, but Caitlin shook her head and waved her mistress go first. *Always Norman rank first. But she is older and I love her. Why must she always insist I be first even in private?* As soon as Margaret thought she could not be seen from the road, she stopped and rubbed her backside. Margaret searched the ground. After she found a spot she liked, she asked Caitlin to stand between herself and any men who might look their way. Margaret looked back toward the road, but she saw no one through the leaves and branches. She knelt and dug a shallow hole with her fingers. She did not answer Caitlin's questions, only took out the box from her mantle pocket and set it on the ground. Caitlin gasped.

"He will poison no one else," Margaret whispered. "Jorgon made the box for me." She dropped the box into the hole and pushed it hard. After refilling the hole, Margaret tamped the ground with her foot. As a final act of defiance toward her father, Margaret crouched over the newly turned earth and pissed. Margaret reached out for a nearby dead branch and placed it over the spot. Caitlin shook her head over the girl's actions and turned away to find a place of her own over which to relieve herself. Neither saw a knight hidden by leaves and branches, watching them from the road. "Pray no one ever finds it."

Caitlin only nodded. Then she pointed toward the water. In the still part of the shallow stream, Margaret saw herself as if in a glass. She frowned. *I am older. I look old. I am old!* Margaret knelt and marred her image as she rinsed her hands, and drank small handfuls of cool water. After lightly splashing her face to cool herself, Margaret stood. "Do I look old?" She asked as she searched Caitlin's face for the truth.

"You are just worn from riding," responded Caitlin in a soothing voice. "Help me down, dear."

When Caitlin also saw Margaret's worried face in the water, she spoiled their images. Caitlin drank and stood. Margaret had dropped her wimple and undone one braid. "Stop!" demanded Margaret's former nurse as she grabbed the girl's arm. "Have you gone mad? We are among strange men, taking us who knows where, and you are exposing yourself!"

Margaret pulled herself from Caitlin's grip. When she reached for her other braid, Caitlin again grabbed her arm and began anew.

"Child, you are putting yourself in great danger. You have no one to protect your honor. They will stop me if I try. Remaining hidden is safer."

"I will not. I have been hiding long enough. Besides, I have the king's protection. He promised to take care of me."

"Lord save us! Child, he is the greatest danger of all! Before his marriage, he knew many women, Norman and Saxon alike. He took them with his winning ways and has bastard sons and daughters here and in Normandy."

Margaret shook her head in refusal.

"Right now he is saving his seed for his queen, but who knows when he will return to his old, wilder ways. He is the king and can have any woman he wants." Caitlin sucked in a deep breath and exhaled hard before she continued, "You are even more beautiful now than you were two years ago. I know you. You will let your hair go wild and then you will go wild too. This is too much freedom."

Caitlin took up the wimple that had covered her charge's head and had hidden her dark auburn hair. When she saw no agreement in her girl's face, she reasoned a compromise.

"Undo your hair if you must, but at least cover it with this. Then only the ends will show."

The girl took the wimple from Caitlin and threw it down.

"Never! I am done hiding. I will be who I am. I have risked my life for this chance. Caitlin, so much has been taken from me, Mother, a marriage, my family. I have nothing, but I am not going to BE nothing! Ever again!" When the young woman saw that Caitlin would again take up her arguments, she commanded, "I forbid you to stop me! I forbid you to speak of this again!"

Caitlin could only obey. She picked up the wimple and held it to herself. "I will not waste the fabric."

Margaret smiled at her former nurse. She always needed to have the last word. She undid her second braid and sighed as she ran her fingers through her hair. With her fingertips she rubbed her scalp, and then she pulled her hair up and out. Margaret shook her mane, grabbed a section and pulled it round her cheek. She drew the ends under her nose and sniffed. *Long enough now to touch my shoulder*

blades. Will wash you soon. And you will shine and wave in the sun.
Checking her appearance in the stream's edge, Margaret smiled. *Not so old after all.* Margaret lifted her arms to the sky to stretch out her stiffness. She faced Caitlin as her old self, confident, shoulders back, and with an air of command. "It is time the king knows who I am." With that, the young woman created a fold of her gunna under one side of her girdle and then under the other side. She smoothed down her garment, which now showed her small waist, high breasts and trim hips. *No longer need I pretend to be underfed by wearing this too big for my body.* She twirled in delight.

"Child!" Caitlin exploded in futile exasperation. "Stay hidden and safe." The older woman pleaded, "Just a little longer!"

Margaret led the way back to the road. "NO!" she threw behind her. "I am me again! I am me!" Margaret sang out as she turned away.

Caitlin knew all she could do now was watch over her. Her next thought was a prayer for protection. When Margaret reached the road, she smiled at her guardian, the knight who had seen them through the trees. His eyes widened. Simply dressed or not, the woman walked like a lady with her head high. When she curtseyed, head up and only so deeply as a Norman lady might to her equal, he perforce bowed as to an equal. The confusion showed on his face as his eyes followed her progress up the column. Men stepped back as she passed with her servant at her heels. They watched her with great interest. Several men wondered what the king had said to get her to follow him. Why was never in question. They knew their king's old habits.

Of the two seated on large rocks beside the road, Lord William was the first to spot her. Amazed at the woman's transformation, he first stared then stood in deference. With one hand holding bread and the other holding cheese, the king looked up. He saw a beautiful young woman with short, dark hair glinting golden as it stirred in the breeze. Straight backed and glowing with happiness, she beamed at him; her stride was that of a proud Norman lady. He knew her only because of her clothing. Lord William glanced back and saw the king was as surprised as he. As she approached, William puffed out his chest and stood a bit taller.

"Lord William," she curtsied, but her eyes never left his.

"Mistress?"

Her bright eyes and smile showed how pleased she was at his reaction. She gave no answer, but she did boldly wink at him. "I will introduce myself to His Royal Highness if he so wishes."

Behind her Caitlin rolled her eyes heavenward then looked toward the king.

"Come forward," said King Henry.

Margaret gave William a long smile, then she looked toward the king. The former servant stepped forward and did not stop until she was within reach of him. First lowering her lids, she curtsied and stayed down. "Your Royal Highness, I seek permission to properly introduce myself."

"Rise and do so."

Men within sound of her voice leaned forward; she had everyone's attention.

"Your Royal Highness, I am the Lady Margaret of Royal Oaks, daughter of the late Lady Rosamonde, who was the daughter of the Norman knight Raymond, made Lord Raymond of Royal Oaks by your father, King William. My grandfather fought at Hastings with your father. In her youth, my mother served your mother at Court. It is now my honor to serve you."

She stunned every man there, including the king and Lord William. Before them stood a Norman lady of high birth. Dressed in servant's clothing as she might be, she was as noble as William and more noble than many of the men present. She was also of an age to be married, perhaps past it; yet here she stood, hair unbound, unbraided, to announce to all she was still a maid. Word of who Margaret was spread quickly down the line. The king appraised her for what seemed a long time.

"You are Lord Charles of Royal Oaks' daughter?"

"Sire, I am his first-born and Lady Rosamonde's daughter." Margaret refused to relinquish her tie to her mother.

The king set down his food on the cloth at his feet, and leaned forward. "Then tell me … Margaret," his stress on her name was her first warning, "why your father would reduce your station to servant, make you his chatelaine and refuse to acknowledge you."

Margaret knew not where to begin, what to reveal, what to hide. Her eyes darted about as she thought. *Tell him only what he asks, no more. Ever.*

"Speak!"

She looked into the king's eyes and obeyed. "It saved him the cost of a dowry, Your Royal Highness. Because I am trained to be a chatelaine, reducing me to servitude also meant he need not remarry. He did this two years ago, after my mother died. You see, they fought. I sided with my mother." Margaret paused, then added, "There was no one to stop him." Margaret went no further. She preferred the short version. *If you want to know more, ask a more direct question.* Wary, Margaret watched the king take up his food.

"Continue." Henry looked up.

"Your Royal Highness, he changed my name to that of a Saxon's, ordered me to be his housekeeper, kept guard over me, and ordered me do his bidding."

"You speak perfect Norman to me and perfect Saxon to others. How so?"

"My mother trained me in both, Sire," Margaret continued in a conversational tone, trying to soften the king's mood. "She said, 'If the Saxons cannot learn Norman, then you best know Saxon.' She did."

"In the yard this morning, your father denied you had a family. Why did you ask him?" The king looked up.

"I was testing him," she admitted. "If he claimed me, then he would have to reinstate me to the position into which I was born—have to dower me to a convent or to a marriage. When he denied me before Your Royal Highness, I knew there was no hope for me there. I am not sorry to have left." Margaret shifted from foot to foot. *Stop or he will see your fear.*

"I must decide whether to send you back."

"Send me back and he will kill me," Margaret countered. "Then what help can I be to you?"

The king motioned her closer, so only she could hear him. "I want the truth, girl! Can you help me?" The king's breath was on her face; his eyes seemed to bore into her soul.

"Yes, Your Royal Highness. I told you true last night." Margaret took a short breath and continued, "But in honesty, I must now tell you my servant Caitlin knows even more than I." When Margaret saw the question in the king's eyes, she explained. "Caitlin is Celt, stolen and sold into slavery. She was a wedding gift from Lord Charles to my mother. She was present at my birth and trained by my mother before I was. They both knew a great deal. Now we are a pair, Caitlin and I." Margaret took a quick breath. "I have never known a day without her. She swore to my mother she would stay at my side. Help you I shall, but I can better help you with Caitlin's able assistance."

"I don't trust Norman gentry."

"I know, Your Royal Highness; they didn't want you to be king. But the Saxons did. And you do trust Saxons," Margaret finished for him, "which is why you were willing to take me when you thought me one. I know nothing of politics or the troubles in the land. I do know you are my only protection now, my only hope for a better life. You may trust only a few, but I am the most trustworthy person you know."

"How so?"

"Because I trust no one of the Court. You can trust me because I have no one but you upon whom to rely. I like my head on my shoulders; I intend to keep it there. You are placing your greatest hope with me. I have already placed all my hope with you. What could be more fair?"

Henry covered his mouth and chin with his hand as he thought. He looked away toward the trees. When he lifted his head and looked straight into Margaret's eyes, she froze. When he still did not speak, Margaret took such small breaths that no one looking at her would think she was alive, just a statue leaning a little toward the king.

Margaret waited and waited. "May we stay, Your Royal Highness?"

"Yes."

The Lady Margaret released an audible sigh.

"How old are you, Lady Margaret?"

The question greatly disturbed her. "I am fourteen. Too old for a really good match." Her eyes filled with unspilled tears. *I should have been married at ten or eleven, for cert after my courses had come. A year, no more than two for even a decent match. With your boons, now I have a chance.*

"Succeed in this, and I will make you a good match."

Margaret again dared to look into his eyes. "I want not some old, gray-haired, wizened thing! Half dead and with children already grown."

Henry threw back his head and roared. Everyone watched the mirthful king and the lady. Henry saw Margaret returning his smile and noted that her whole face lit up. The king reminded himself he was married to Matilda; she was the most important woman in his realm. Then he told himself to get going and to stay away from the girl. He was eighteen years her senior and old enough to be her father, not that such an age difference prevents a man from taking a mistress. *After my son is born and before she's wed,* Henry thought. "I promise. No old, gray-haired, wizened thing."

From a distance the pair looked to be in an intimate conversation, both smiling at each other. Their close stance and facial expressions gave credence to the men's willing belief King Henry had taken the lady away for his own purposes. Lord William averted his eyes then slipped away from the pair. He felt ashamed he had not seen she was a Norman and even more aghast at his thoughts about her. He knew he would have to confess to a priest his failure to protect the king from her and the desire she had raised in him.

Margaret had only minutes to eat a small chunk of bread as the rest of the column packed. She kept moving her shoulders as she ate because she wanted her clothing to soak up the sweat running down her back. *Safe for now; how soon will I again be in danger from him?* King Henry ordered the Lady Margaret placed behind him and beside Lord William in the column. Caitlin was left to ride between the last of the knights and before the baggage horses. Margaret was too afraid to anger the king by asking that Caitlin be her chaperone. The men believed their assumptions about the lady had been correct. No one had spoken to her when they believed her a Saxon and beneath them. No one dare speak to her now they knew her to be a high-born Norman lady under the king's protection.

After a time, Margaret twisted in her saddle and looked right. William only glanced her way. "My lord, I thank you for all you did yesterday to make the king's visit a success."

"You are most welcome, my lady."

She returned his half-smile and hoped he would keep talking.

"How came you to be a good rider?"

Margaret twisted his way again. "I have been riding since I was six." William only nodded. They resumed their silence as they rode along.

For the rest of that day's journey south Margaret smiled at the sun, the trees, even the road. She shook her hair. *Wonder where Night is? Did Jorgon get him away safely? When will I see him again? I am riding again and beside Lord William. Warm sun, now a light breeze. The king is leading me to a better life. This is good.*

4

--- ❧ ---

Royal Stops

The first day ended at a stone-barricaded fortress. First, Margaret marveled at the many blocks that created the great height of the palisade wall. Then she admired keep on the hill within the wall. In the bailey, the lord bowed first to the king, then to Lord William and finally to Margaret. She was now introduced by Lord William as the Lady Margaret to Lord Sebastien and Lady Ursule. They were as excited to be the king's hosts as Margaret was to be their guest. The three of them beamed at each other; Lord Sebastien helped Margaret dismount with great deference. Lady Ursule curtsied to Margaret as she landed and faced her hostess. Lord William stiffened his back, extended his left arm for her to place her hand upon; he escorted Margaret into their hall without looking at her. He left for the king's side. Caitlin joined Margaret, and they stood apart and watched for a few minutes before they joined the group. Margaret saw the need, so she helped the Lady Ursule feed her half dozen children at the end of the hall while the men ate near the lord and king on the dais.

The children, aged twelve to three, chattered questions at Margaret. Where did she come from? Why was her hair uncovered?

Was the knight her husband? Where was her party going? How soon must they leave? Margaret answered none of the questions. She asked their ages and names, and complimented them on their good table manners. In these more familiar surroundings, Margaret felt comfortable and relaxed until their mother, the lady of the manor, repeated their questions. Round from having so many babes so quickly in her youth, Lady Ursule could still scurry about attending her young ones as she tried to learn more about Margaret. The bright-eyed, curious lady received answers neither about Margaret nor regarding Margaret's relationship to the king's group. Margaret merely smiled and complimented the woman about her children and the food. That night Margaret and Caitlin slept with the women of the household on the floor of the keep. Margaret slept between the Lady Ursule and Caitlin, who had insisted on sleeping between Margaret and the door that led to the men below.

After attending Mass and breaking their fasts, the party departed. Still sore, Margaret suffered all day, but she neither complained nor slowed the party. The king ignored her. Margaret watched him whispering with a select few he called to his side. At one crossroads a pair of men rode southeast. When Margaret asked Lord William, he reported they had taken the London Road. He did not elaborate; she knew better than to ask why. Margaret looked up to see the white, fluffy clouds of the morning begin to darken. She wondered if it might rain. Sniffing the air, she decided it would not. Soon the clouds dissipated and the sky was again a bright summer blue. The sun took charge and warmed them again. Margaret took up a corner of her mantle and wiped her brow.

That evening was a repeat of the first but this time at an inn at a major crossroads. A tall wooden palisade protected by heavy, barred doors surrounded the buildings. The yard was huge, the stable very large, and the inn clean and comfortable. The king's party had the place to themselves. From the innkeeper's manner, Margaret deduced they had been expected. From the way the men moved about taking care of their horses and talked to the stable boys, Margaret realized the king had visited before. The king and his men ate in the great room on the main floor. Margaret and Caitlin rested in an upstairs room reserved for women. Caitlin insisted they also eat there. As soon as the serving girl removed the empty platters and pitchers of ale, Caitlin made Margaret help her push the bed against the door.

"I will sleep much better if the entrance is blocked."

Too tired to argue or go downstairs, Margaret obeyed. The women slept late so they did not hear the major force leave before dawn. The king had taken most of his party south, leaving Margaret and Caitlin with Lord William and an escort of six knights.

Just after dawn Margaret preceded Caitlin down the stairs. *Strange. No priest, no Mass. Will we will stop at a church before we continue?*

Margaret appeared in stages, feet, comely ankles, skirt, and then waist. At the main table William stood and pushed back the bench upon which he had been seated. Bewildered, Margaret stopped on the bottom stair. He could see her maidservant on the stair behind her looking about. Only William and six of the king's retainers remained.

"God's good morrow, my lady," he began. "His Royal Highness left before dawn. You are to break your fast. Then we depart."

Margaret stepped down and walked to the bench opposite William. Caitlin, ever vigilant, sat on the girl's side of the table down the bench yet within hearing. The knights left to prepare the horses.

The women received their pottage, bread, butter, and hot mulled wine.

"Where is the king?"

"He is for Winchester."

"Where are we for?" Margaret asked between mouthfuls.

"To a stronghold east of here." William looked at her hard before he continued. "His Royal Highness instructed me to tell you to have the household ready in three days."

Margaret nodded and continued eating rapidly. As she finished her food, the innkeeper's wife approached. The blond woman, who was much younger than her husband, was whip thin and wore her hair in a bun rather than beneath a wimple. Damp tendrils showed how hard she had been working in the kitchen.

"My lady, please take these apples for your journey."

The woman placed two small red apples on the table.

Margaret smiled. The woman was offering her best. Too early for most apples to be ripe, these might be young and a bit sour.

"Thank you, madam. That is most generous of you."

William set down his ale mug sat back, and stared at the lady before him. Before he could ask what he wanted to know, a man entered the inn.

"Lord William, a Saxon girl is at the gate asking for the lady. She's accompanied by a villein who is waiting across the clearing." The knight sounded surprised when he added, "He is holding the reins to a black war horse."

When Margaret heard the last three words, she dropped her spoon and yelped, "Night!"

In her hurry, she shoved the bench back as she stood and almost unseated Caitlin. She dashed around the end of the table toward the door, took two steps, changed her mind and stopped. When she turned back to William, she had her dagger in her hand. Startled, William pulled away. Margaret swooped past his shoulder, speared an apple and in the same stroke halved it. After wiping her knife against her hip and returning it to its sheath, Margaret grabbed both halves and headed for the door. She was too excited to hear Caitlin's, "Your mantle!"

By the time William stood, Margaret had disappeared. After William exited the inn, he swirled his mantle about him as he noted that Margaret had stopped just beyond the opened gates. She stepped forward and out of sight as he heard a loud whinny. Lord William strode through the gates, followed by his men and most of the household. What they watched held them in a trance.

Jorgon, who wore his black hair short as Norman law demanded, was a bit taller than Margaret even though he was almost two years younger. Hard work in the fields had tanned his skin and hard work in the stables had strengthened his arms and legs, which were thick with muscles that rippled when he worked. Jorgon was strong enough to hold the gelding still. The young man nodded to Lady Margaret. At her nod in return, the Saxon threw the loop of reins over the gelding's head and stepped back. The Percheron pranced in anticipation, snorted, whinnied, and pawed the ground but stayed where he was.

Noble head. He has been groomed with his mane and forelock brushed. Shiny coat. So beautiful! My Night.

Margaret placed the apple halves in her left hand and, with the right, put fingers into her mouth and gave a shrill whistle. Ignoring the chill in the air, she began their dance with a deep curtsey. The stallion tucked his right front hoof under him and returned her bow.

Margaret rose; Night followed. William watched Margaret put her hands out palms down and pump them up and down. In response the stallion lifted his front hooves and danced to the rhythm she set.

William gazed at her glowing face as she stood on her tiptoes and bounced up and down.

Margaret applauded her steed and called out words of praise and encouragement. Her horse shook his head in anticipation and his mane bobbed against his neck. Laughing, Margaret, spun to the right and stopped short as she faced her beloved horse. The black spun to his left and stopped too. Margaret spun one turn left; Night mirrored her. In her happiness, the young woman threw back her head and laughed. Sir William smiled at how happy she sounded. Her horse snorted in response. Finally Margaret leaned forward, showed her gelding her hands, now palms up. She waited; Night stiffened his front legs. In one giant motion, Margaret raised her hands high and shook them. The stallion reared high and pawed the air. Margaret clapped and yelled, "Good boy!" to her horse as his forefeet hit the ground hard. She ran toward her beloved playmate, and the horse pranced toward her.

In fear the big war horse would overrun and kill her, William bolted. He stopped when he saw both horse and woman meet. The black halted just short of knocking her over. Margaret held both hands behind her back. Night reached around her, sniffling and snorting. Margaret brought her right hand around and held it open. Night lipped the apple piece between his teeth and chomped. Margaret crooned and caressed Night's cheek with her free hand as he ate. The great horse bent his head over her shoulder, sniffing out the other half. Margaret opt her left hand behind her back and let him reach for the last of his treat. He munched; she hugged.

"I have missed you, boy," she admitted as she stroked his neck and ran her fingers through his mane. She patted his cheek and kissed his muzzle before she turned to her hostler.

"Thank you! Thank you, Jorgon. I would have been lost without him."

Margaret saw Dena sidle toward Jorgon and watched as her hostler put his arm protectively around the girl's shoulders. Margaret scowled at the petite girl with the sandy hair and bare feet. "Why is she here!"

"I told him to bring her," answered Caitlin, now standing next to the pair. "We can use her in the kitchen, and she couldn't stay behind, given what Lord Charles did to his last bedmate."

"Dena is my betrothed," added Jorgon, hoping that his friendship with Lady Margaret extended to his sweetheart too.

Another mouth to feed. Another life for which I am responsible. She did not want the responsibility, but there was no help for it now. "You had better be useful!"

"Yes, mistress! I promise!" Dena curtsied deeply.

Margaret ordered Jorgon, "You two take my roundsey. I ride Night."

Jorgon cupped his hands for his lady's foot and lifted her onto the platform he had taken from the knight, who had lent her his roundsey. She grabbed the reins as Night danced away in excitement.

"My lady!" called out Lord William.

"My lady!" Caitlin echoed, holding up the forgotten mantle.

Margaret pulled hard right and kicked Night's flank. The pair headed across the clearing as Lord William yelled, "No!" Lord William, whom the king had charged with keeping the lady safe, watched in horror as she rode straight for a wooden fence. Caitlin clasped her hands in prayer. Margaret bent low over Night's neck.

They soared over the low wooden fence. Night, who had been held in check for far too long, raced on. Lord William and his men scrambled for their horses. Margaret worked hard at pulling both on the rope around Night's nose and the reins; she finally slowed him to a trot. She turned him and returned to the inn on the road beside the field. The knight assigned to lead Caitlin set her on her steed and gave Margaret's former pony to the new couple.

Margaret's face flushed and her eyes lit with a fire William had never seen in a woman. She tossed her wind-tangled hair as Night had tossed his mane.

Now astride his own horse, Lord William leaned over, grabbed Night's reins and commanded, "Never, never do that again. You could have been killed!"

Margaret leaned back and smiled winningly. "Lord William, I have been jumping fences since I was eight. Night even longer. It is our favorite thing to do," she added sweetly.

Lord William began his argument through clenched teeth.

"Lady Margaret, a woman should not be riding a male horse. You should be on a palfrey. A woman's chair saddle is not a secure seat. Furthermore … "

Jorgon broke the deadlock by distracting them both. "Here is your cover, my lady," he said as he lifted a threadbare blue mantle and scarf toward her.

The young woman settled a faded woolen mantle around her shoulders and pinned it with an old pewter brooch. She stuffed the fur-trimmed scarf under her backside. *I will not cover my hair unless it rains.*

Margaret was now an elegant Norman lady, even if no lady would be riding a fine war horse fit for a knight of the realm. Margaret pulled wrinkled, blue leather gloves from the blue mantle's pocket, put them on with exaggerated casualness. She gave Lord William a sidelong glance. "Well, my lord, are you ready?"

Lord William snorted his disapproval and rode back to Dena and Jorgon, who was holding the reins of the roundsey Lady Margaret had been riding.

"You know the law," began Lord William. "A death sentence for a Saxon who mounts a horse. Your walking will slow us. I will protect you only while you ride with me. If either of you get on a horse after this trip, I will find you and kill you both myself."

Jorgon spoke for Dena too when he pulled his forelock and said, "Yes, my lord. We understand. We will not abuse your permission or your protection, my lord."

Night stood still while the rest of the party lined up behind the couple. Jorgon set Dena on the pony so she rode like a man; he walked to the fence. He stood on a cross rail to mount the pony and sit behind Dena. She turned and smiled at him when he put his arms about her waist; they rode behind the baggage roundseys. Lord William and Margaret turned their horses; the party followed and walked down the road that led into the forest. The sun may have risen and warmed the morning air, but not under the heavy canopy shading the riding party.

Late morning and a long walk later, William was ready to speak again.

"How came you by him?"

"He was my grandfather's then my mother's. Mother gave him to me before she died."

"Why was he not given to your father?"

"Night would not let him near and attacked each time he tried."
Was that when their feud started?

69

From the gray on his muzzle I would guess him to be…
eighteen?"

"Twenty."

"Too old to be jumping fences," William admonished.

Margaret blushed. "I know, but he was celebrating his freedom."

5

Arrival

The road had started smooth with pastures and fields on both sides. The rippling crops smelled sweet. Workers paused to watch the party pass. Dressed in common, un-dyed, wool shifts or long shirts, barefoot and bareheaded, they looked poorer than the rich fields they worked. Margaret wondered at a lord who took so ill care of his Saxons. They traveled all morning and ate chunks of bread and cheese on horse and passed a jug of ale down the line. Nothing was left by the time it reached Jorgon and Dena. Guilty at having food in her hand, Margaret hid the cheese and bread on her side opposite the workers. She waited to eat again until she was well past the villeins. Margaret smiled at the wildflowers in the ditches, the red ones tall and bold, the pale yellow small ones with petals like tiny cups. They waved in a soft breeze as if they were nodding at her as she passed. The sun warmed the party, but not so much as to be uncomfortable. The group reached a crossroads and turned east. The road got rougher, less used, as they stepped into the trees that began a deep wood of tall oaks, spruce, and pine that soon blocked out the sun and turned the air cool. Margaret guessed this wood was part of the royal forest that covered two-thirds of the country. The land rose slowly at first and then was hilly. At the hill tops, Margaret lifted her face to the sun before Night walked downhill into the dark again. They arrived at their destination by mid-afternoon.

First Margaret spotted what might be a keep top in the distance. As they climbed the road, stones appeared. Though Margaret had heard William the Conqueror had ordered such structures built, this was the second biggest she had ever seen. The top was misshapen with some parts of the square building built up and others not. She noted the stones were of even shape and size and wondered how far away the quarry was and who had hauled them to this desolate spot in the middle of the forest. Then she saw the palisade wall was also of gray stone. Margaret thought if the fortress had a well or two and enough food, a party inside could hold off an army for a year or more. She smiled at the place the king had chosen for his queen.

The men walking the stone walls around the keep stopped and stared in their direction. From the top of the east-west road she could see the hill upon which the keep stood was barren of trees and shrubs so no one could hide or set a fire in an attack. The structure watched over two great roads that intersected below it. The path that led to the mighty walls snaked back on itself three times. Margaret and the others waited while Lord William and two knights rode the switchback to the main gate. After a brief conversation with a man on the wall, they returned.

"My lady, the holder of the keep is new to me. He is called Elric and says his Saxon men are loyal to Malcolm, late King of Scotland, the queen's father. Only you know the password to gain entrance."

Margaret nodded and motioned Night forward. Lord William watched her approach the main gate. Elric disappeared from the walls and reappeared through a small gate beside the great one. After he assisted Margaret to dismount, she waved to the group below. Margaret, Elric and Night disappeared inside the walls. By the time the party reached the keep, the main gate had been thrown open.

Margaret frowned when she saw the entrance to the square stone building was up one floor and only accessible by a wooden ladder. A queen with child would be in danger of falling while using it during the winter rains. *I must find another way of getting the queen outside and strong with exercise.* The bailey yard looked much like her own at home with wooden buildings housing animals and goods. A prodigious amount of chopped wood was stacked to dry under a three-sided shed. Margaret surmised either the fortress had been unoccupied over most of the winter—unlikely—or this stone keep needed great quantities of wood to keep the place livable.

Jorgon took Night from Margaret but not before she caressed his neck and assured him she would ride him often. The old war horse seemed to understand and followed Jorgon to the stable. Caitlin and Dena hauled bundles with them. Margaret walked ahead of the others. At the foot of the ladder a Saxon held each woman's elbow in turn; another man waited at the doorway and took their bundles from them before offering a hand to pull them up. They stepped into the tower and gagged. The first level was a combination of rotting, filthy rushes, piled junk and putrid odors, especially piss and old ale.

"My apologies, my lady," Elric offered in Norman when Margaret held her nose. "The previous troop was a filthy bunch. We are still clearing their mess. We started on the upper floor and hoped to have it all gone before you arrived. This is all that we have left to remove."

"Pitch it into that old wagon outside, take it to the bottom of the hill leeward of us and burn it."

"Yes, my lady. Before sundown."

"Are there stores below? Do we have sufficient stores for all of us for a year?"

"You need to inspect them, my lady. My men are hearty eaters and drinkers; I doubt the supplies would last a year, but mayhap for seven months. Eldene knows how to make ale if you can buy enough grain."

Fearful of what might be lacking, Margaret asked to see the buttery. Elric turned over the keys and preceded her down the stairs in case she should fall. Inside the storage room, a bucket dropped through a hole in the ceiling through a brick ring and below the dirt floor. They heard the splash of water.

"Caitlin?" Margaret called up the hole.

"Yes, my lady. Just getting water to wash and cook."

Margaret was relieved a well was below the donjon. She had already seen the one in the bailey. After careful inspection, Margaret decided they might have enough dried staples and grains, but they would need more for ale plus fresh supplies and live animals.

When they returned to the first floor, she asked Elric, "Will the village provide butter and eggs? Will their lord sell us grain and whatever else we need?"

"The butter is excellent, but eggs are scarce, my lady."

"Sir Elric..."

"Just Elric, my lady. Please remember I am Saxon."

"Elric," Lady Margaret smiled up at him, "you may be, but not 'just.' I wager your family was important enough thirty-five years ago."

"That was then; this is now. Now I have to walk a very narrow path between my people and the king's."

Margaret nodded and said, "I want this keep to be totally self-sufficient: milk, butter, eggs, animals, grain, everything. Can we achieve this? Is the village safe? Will the villagers sell us what we need?"

"It is and they will if we have the coins. What their lord will charge is another matter."

Margaret smiled at his "we." She looked upward again at the noises she was hearing. *If anyone can make this place a home, Caitlin can.* Margaret walked to the stairs, lifted her skirt a modest height, and proceeded upward. Eric followed and stared as her hips swayed with each step. Her rich brown hair caught the light, glowing bronze and gold.

The second level was the hall, with a fireplace on one side and a mass of Elric's men's gear at the other end of the room. True to his word, Elric had cleared the stone floor of rushes and the fireplace of ashes. The Saxons would garrison downstairs and guard the walls, but they would dine in the hall. The women could sleep on the hall level in the alcove behind the fireplace. Arrow slits at regular intervals on all four walls lit the room but dimly.

Elric explained, "This heavy wooden door leads to a set of stairs to a third level. All that is above are the half walls of the next floor. When William the Conqueror died in 1087, work stopped, and his heir, King William Rufus, did nothing further."

Margaret watched Caitlin coax embers to life to warm the bread starter. No summer warmth reached the interior of the stone walls. Margaret shivered with the dampness of the place; she hoped a fire would warm and dry the air. Dena, wielding a broom, stood behind Caitlin. After the fire took, Dena swept the remaining debris onto the hearth to be consumed. She stopped to warm her bare feet from working and standing on the stone floor as she gazed on the red flickers. Caitlin smiled approval at the slim girl's desire to be warm, and then she swung a cauldron of water on the iron arm over the flames.

"I will fetch you a pair of thick boots," promised Margaret. *A nourishing soup will be welcome in this damp, cold place. How much firewood will we need to warm this place come winter?*

Dena smiled and curtsied her thanks.

While Elric and his men tended to the mess below, Dena received the key from Margaret and fetched salted meat and dried barley from the donjon. Lord William and his men inspected the palisade walls and walkway around the bailey. He assigned four of his men to stand watch. Margaret and Caitlin conferred about what was still needed as the women scrubbed with hot water and lye soap the dishes, spoons, cooking utensils, trestle tables, and the two wooden chairs. Caitlin stirred the pot and swung the iron arm back over the fire. The smells of a hearty soup soon filled the air.

"Thank you, Caitlin, for remembering soap, linens, salt and herbs. I am thrilled you also remembered bread starter. I was in too great a hurry to leave to remember much," Margaret admitted.

"Well, my lady, I saw that and tried to remember all we would need. I also packed your needlework. Our stay will be long, and I fear you will not have enough to do with all the waiting."

Lord William's head and shoulders appeared in the stairway. He had climbed high enough to hear Caitlin's last remark. He grimaced and gritted his teeth. William looked as if a fast escape from the fortress was his greatest desire.

"I shall leave in the morning, Lady Margaret. I must get to my own lands," he informed her through taut lips as he reached the top step.

"My lord, I cannot dismiss you; only the king can. I suggest you stay until His Royal Highness returns. He should be here in two days—three at most. On the morrow I must go into the village to obtain supplies. I need your company, Lord William. Please, will you come with me?"

'Very well, my lady." William's polite response did not match the sourness of his face, but Margaret did catch his quick change of face back to impassive. He bowed and left.

I hope I have not lost his favor. Mayhap he sees the poverty of my plain clothes and thinks me beneath him. Jumping Night angered him. Be not so bold. Be more a lady. Mayhap that will please him, and I will win back his smiles.

"He is unhappy about something, Caitlin. I know not what."

"Help me draw more water. We must finish cleaning before the bread and soup are ready," Caitlin responded.

Margaret sighed at William's coldness as she looked toward the stairwell. She turned, grabbed a bucket of water and walked to where Caitlin stood.

6

Purchases

At first the villagers just stood outside their doors and watched. Their buildings and gardens were much like those at home. Wattle and daub huts, thatched roofs, and a cloth door seemed to be universal features. These were in slightly worse repair than those she was used to. The willow withies of several needed more daub. Margaret wondered why the families did not use wet clay and debris to fill in the holes. *These Saxons might not have all the goods we need. Their gardens are weeded and look healthy. Mayhap they care more about them than the appearance of their homes. The lanes between the huts are straight and clean.*

Margaret located the carpenter, a rangy, fair-haired man with a face as freckled as a robin's egg, and ordered a bed for two built; he sold her his. She surprised the man by handing over coins without bartering. After the carpenter's neighbors saw him bite each coin and nod, they lined up to offer their wares. Before the couple started buying, Elric handed several pennies to Lord William, who used his dagger to cut them into halves and quarters against a flat black rock he had picked up. A Saxon boy shyly watched him work.

Lord William handed the cut coins to Elric and returned to standing behind the pair as they bargained and bought. Margaret created an instant market day by announcing what she sought and waiting for the villeins to appear with their goods. Each half-penny and farthing bought a great deal. Soon a full wagon lumbered away.

The villagers avoided the Norman knight, but they took to the lady and her helper because they spoke Saxon, smiled and also patted their children. The couple put their heads together and conferred over each sale. Then the lady chose, the man bargained, and the lady handed over the farthings, half-pennies and pennies. Speaking only a little Saxon, Lord William scowled through it all. He followed but a little of the morning's dealings, and he was greatly displeased at how easily Elric conversed with the lady.

"I am in need of a milch cow, laying hens, and a rooster. I will inspect any stock you are willing to sell," Margaret announced next. She visited the villagers's lean-tos so she could see how well they cared for the animals. The farmer from whom she purchased a brown and white cow was surprised by her knowledgeable questions and her careful examination of his animal. After she completed her purchases, several families volunteered to sell the pretty gray cats with white chests Margaret had seen wandering among the huts as they searched for game.

The Saxon whispered, "I do not think they can afford to sell any more until harvest."

"I know, Elric, but I want all in readiness when His Royal Highness arrives," Margaret whispered back.

She dared not ask how much Elric knew and continued to keep her secrets. Lord William was cert the lady was being kept on an accessible road for the king's pleasure. He wondered what the king would think of her cavorting with a Saxon. Unnoticed by the pair, the knight continued to mumble to himself most of the way back. After the animals had been taken to the barn, Lord William took Margaret's bag of coins, two Saxons and two knights to the bailey of the local lord. Sir Richard de Reuen bargained well and won almost every coin Margaret had remaining for all the sacks of wheat and other grains she had requested Lord William purchase.

At dinner, Margaret sat at the head table with William to her right and Elric her left. The men followed their leaders, so the two long tables perpendicular to the head table looked like Saxon versus Norman as they sat. Each spoke to their own. All enjoyed the soup of vegetables both fresh and dried, but the soup had only softened the few small pieces of dried meat. The Saxons reported game appeared scarce and spoke of the need to hunt farther away. Margaret translated for William and Elric. After the pair agreed what to do, they finished eating in silence. Margaret drank but one mug of wheat-based ale, but offered the men two, which they imbibed with enthusiasm. The villager's aleman was skilled and the spicing he used was refreshingly tart yet delicious.

As the men departed, Normans to guard duty and Saxons to unloading the wagon, Margaret asked William to stay behind. She stood as close to him as she dared and tried to win his smile with a winsome one of her own. She failed. His frown worried her, but she asked for what she needed anyway. "Sirrah, I have a boon to ask of you."

William only nodded.

"Your men will hunt on the morrow, but I have need of you on a personal matter. Will you stay with me?"

"What personal matter?"

"I cannot say."

"You mean you will not say. Woman, what is it you want from me?"

"I wish your help. Will you give it?"

"Very well." William added, "Be forewarned. I will ask the king to release me from this duty the day he arrives. I will not stay and watch what is to come." William spun about on his heel and left the floor before Margaret could inquire what he meant. She watched his body and head disappear as he walked down the stairs, but he did not look her way.

Margaret looked about the hall with satisfaction. Dena had found the mortar and pestle for grinding grain into flour, and Caitlin had scrubbed it clean. It had been drying by the fireplace and was now ready for use. Dena had scrubbed the beaten-up blue cupboard clean even though paint had peeled and cracked, exposing bare wood; sacks of wheat, oats, rye and barley leaned against either side. The men's gear was now on the floor below, so the trestle tables stayed up for meals during the day and for knights to sleep on at night. In the alcove behind the fireplace stood the double bed Margaret and Caitlin would share. They had emptied the cloth mattress, turned the fabric inside out and refilled the bag with fresh, sweet-smelling straw that had just been cut and was still bright yellow and soft.

I hope we beat all the lice out of the straw covering and the bedding.

After supper, Dena worked hard with the mortar and pestle to break open kernels of wheat and rye; then she smashed the oats she needed to add for the morning pottage. Caitlin and Margaret washed dishes before setting aside the cauldron of soaking grains Dena had prepared. At Margaret's instruction, Dena placed the only chairs on either side of the fireplace. Lord William took one; Margaret decided to join him. They sat in silence with William staring at the fire rather than looking at her. Margaret enjoyed the soft pops and crackles of the flames but could not relax.

He appears to need cheering. What can I say to lift his spirits?
"My lady?"

"Yes, Dena," Margaret replied without looking away from the knight.

"Am I to sleep in the little room too?"

"Yes."

"I trust Jorgon, my lady. I could stay with him in the stable."

Margaret heard William's faint snort and liked it not. She turned to Dena.

"That will not do, Dena."

When Margaret saw the girl's eyes and shoulders droop, she explained, "Dena, look at me. We are going to be here a long time. The men guarding us came without their women. It will not set well with them Jorgon has one to bed when they do not." Margaret raised her hand to stop Dena's objection. "It matters not how things are between you two; what matters is how it will appear." Margaret paused a moment. "You were an innocent when Lord Charles took you. If you appear the slattern now, the men will treat you as one. Behave with honor and you will be treated honorably. Do you understand?"

Dena curtsied. "Yes, my lady. I will sleep behind the fireplace."

"And I will see you better dressed."

"Thank you, my lady."

Dena left to sit beside Caitlin at a table.

Margaret turned to William, whose face mirrored both surprise and distaste. Margaret thought he disapproved of Dena's request. William thought, *You speak hypocrisy.*

"When do you think they will arrive?"

William just shook his head and stared into the fire. He watched a log break in half and send gold sparks upward from a glowing orange heart. As a boy, such a sight had reminded him of the priest's description of hell, for all that it was mesmerizing. *And maybe it still should.* Fearful of what he might say, he chose silence. They heard men below readying for the evening watch.

"I hope the priest arrives soon. It is sinful to miss Mass, and I want his protection."

William frowned again. *Why is she talking about behaving honorably or expecting the Church's protection when she is about to become King Henry's mistress?*

7

Confrontation

Saturday, 6 July

"I brought these," announced William as he climbed the last step. "Please shut the trap door so no one will join us."

"What need have you for short swords, my lady?"

"I need to know how to use one."

William moved the blades to behind his back.

"No. Women do not use men's weapons. They are not even allowed to touch them."

Margaret took a small step forward. "I need to be able to protect myself."

"From whom?"

"I do not want to know how to how to use a sword, but I must."

William shook his head in refusal. "My lady, you sleep within stone walls; the Saxons pull up the keep's ladder each night. The door below and the outer walls are well guarded. What more need you?"

"If all those fail, I will die. But if I must," Margaret emphasized each word, "I intend to kill at least one attacker."

"You are under the king's protection with good men around you. Who wants you dead?"

Margaret released a long, slow breath and tried anew.

"Lord William, His Royal Highness instructed you to assist me with whatever I might need, did he not?"

William gave a curt nod.

"What if there is a traitor among us?"

"I will give a simple order. No one may carry a blade to this floor."

"I still need to know how to use one. I ask you to do as the king requested."

William turned and departed. Discouraged, Margaret stirred the pot over the fire, tasted the stew and added a pinch of salt. William returned with wooden practice swords.

Margaret turned to Caitlin and Dena. "I order you to leave this floor, leave this building. Stay where you will until I call for you."

Both women nodded and did what they had been told.

William, who stood beside the trap door, announced, "No one learns with real weapons. I will report what you have asked me to do to His Royal Highness when he arrives."

At Margaret's nod, William lowered the trap door. Guards on the walls looked toward the occasional dull clashing sounds coming from the keep, but they saw nothing through the arrow slits. The men in the yard questioned each other to no avail.

William first showed Margaret the correct stance, how to hold the blade forward and its proper angle from her waist. Margaret quickly learned to advance and retreat, step right and left. *This*

86

footwork is like dance steps and I dance well. Next William taught her how to parry left and right to stop a blade from advancing toward her. He counted a pattern of both sword and step moves, one, two, three. Make a quarter turn and repeat. Margaret smiled to herself at how close they stood. They completed a full circle left and then right. They kept at it, first very slowly and then a bit faster each time until William was satisfied Margaret might be able to defend herself for a very short while. *She is too good at this to be a beginner,* William thought as he gave her a half smile. He glowered to hide his next thought.

"I am most reluctant to teach you how to take advantage of a fighter's momentary lapse, how to quickly thrust through a gap and injure an attacker with a cut to the arm, a thrust to his face to make him retreat, or a point into his chest."

"I insisted you do so. I also need to know how to attack."

After William showed her how to do it, without giving any warning, he attacked.

"Yell for help as you fight for your life," he commanded.

Margaret yelled, "Help! Help! I am being attacked.!"

Alarmed at hearing the muffled shouting, the guards on the parapet walkway stopped and stared at the keep. Unable to discern what Lord William and Lady Margaret might be doing, they gossiped. When the sounds stopped, they resumed their patrol. William continued the lesson for two hours more. Finally, William declared Margaret proficient enough to defend herself until a man came to her aid. Margaret's tired legs quivered; the practice blade hung from her limp, aching arm. But she was happy. *I will be respected.* She raised her left hand to wipe away sweat dripping from her brow into her eyes and from her chin. William thought how fetching Margaret looked with wet ringlets framing her flushed face and her disheveled hair. He tried not to watch the lift and fall of her breasts as her breathing slowed. He decided he had best leave and reached for her blade. Margaret did not surrender it.

"I need a real one of these, my lord. You have them. I want one."

William knocked the wooden blade out of her hand. When she reached for it as it fell to the floor, William grabbed her wrist. Margaret tried to pull away, but William yanked her and pulled her against himself. She was trapped with her hands splayed on this chest.

"No! I will not let you keep even this. Not without the king's permission."

Stunned to be in a man's arms, William's arms, Margaret froze. She looked into fierce brown eyes and felt his heart beating hard against her breasts. Her will fell into those eyes and she relaxed. She lowered her head against his chest and relaxed her knees. Her heart pounded to the beat of his. William held her even tighter to keep her upright. He lowered his head until his lips touched her hair. Reluctant to release Margaret, William held her close. Margaret closed her eyes at the delicious feeling of being held by a man, by William. *Safe. Protected. Stay. Such strength. I could lean on him forever.* Margaret pushed herself a tiny bit closer into his chest, into his arms. She felt his lips against her crown and her heart smiled. *Is this love? Is holding each other the start?* Margaret sighed in happiness. William let himself be seduced by the warmth of her, Margaret's smell, the softness of her body. He held Margaret for as long as he dared.

When King Henry's visage flashed in William's mind – those proud, keen eyes and ruddy cheeks – he stiffened first his will, then his back. *A great wrong. The king's mistress. He will kill me if he learns of it,* William reasoned to himself so he could, would release the girl. With great reluctance, William slowly loosed his arms, pulled back and stepped away. He let his hands caress Margaret's back and forearms before fully separating from her. He saw her half-op eyes, with a fringe of dark lashes, a half smile and pleasure on her rosy face. He willed himself not to bend and kiss her lips. William tamped down hard on his desire for Margaret. He reminded himself that she was the king's, repeated that thought and also that to touch her again might bring him death. Margaret felt the loss of William's warmth, felt cool and hot at the same time. She looked into his face and found a hardness and a whiteness about his mouth she did not expect. She wondered what she had done wrong.

Have I been too bold again? Is he angry with me for that?

In a harsh tone, William said, "Let the king give you a sword. I will not provide the weapon for you to be a Judith, so my liege lord can be your Holofernes."

Then William whispered "Margaret" but she did not hear him.

Margaret's heart pounded so hard in her ears she did not understand his words. Margaret had felt his hard hug and then his slow release. She gazed at William, her face filled with unspoken questions. William had gently put her from him as if trying to undo a great wrong in holding her close with desire and need in his heart. Yet his eyes seemed to drink her in even as he released her. With the lightest touch, William placed his fingertips on her shoulders and pushed so she would step back from him. Only then did he reach for the blades at their feet.

Stunned at William's embrace, Margaret wanted to say his name, call him back to her. Her face burned; her body ached. She felt frozen to the spot at the same time she burned to rush into his arms. She watched, dismayed, as he walked away from her, practice blades in hand. When William reached the trap door, he stopped as if he had decided something. He dropped the blades and strode back to her. Margaret's heart leapt to her throat at his return.

William began in a rush, "My lady, you still have time. I can sell your fine horse to dower you. I will help you escape to a convent where the king is not likely to find you. I am sure they will take you in."

"Escape? Why would I want to escape?"

William's voice turned stern. "Margaret, being the king's mistress is nothing new. Others have preceded you; others will follow you. After he has bedded and is done with you, he will marry you off to someone who wants his favor, or he will dower you to a convent. Do it now! Save your honor, your name. Save your family the shame!"

"Shame!" Margaret thundered as she awoke to his meaning. "Is that what you think? That I am to be the king's... How dare you! How dare you!" She looked about for something to throw at him. *I will hurt you! With what?* Margaret reverted to what she did when her brother Charles angered her. She stepped forward and swung her right foot. She kicked William in the shin with all her might. William grunted. "Get out!" she shrieked. Margaret kicked again, but William had jumped back. "Get out now! How dare you! How dare you!" she shouted as put her hand on her dagger hilt.

As William retreated, he countered, "Think! Think what will become of you!"

Margaret heard nothing. "I will kill you for what you said!"

With only his head above the floor, William grabbed the blades and called to Margaret, "Change your mind. I can save you, but only if you leave today."

Margaret spotted the fireplace poker. Intending to put her lesson to immediate use, she dashed to the fireplace and grabbed the poker. She spun and raced toward the man who had so insulted her. She reached the stairwell too late. In a fury Margaret grabbed the ring, yanked the door over the stairwell, and jumped on it. "Aarrgghh!" Margaret screamed as she jumped on the door again. Then she threw the poker across the room and watched it clank against the wall. "That should be your head!" she screeched.

One man on the walls peered toward a slit and glimpsed a shadow pacing with a long, black stick in its hand. He heard loud sounds but no words. At midday no one called the men to dine. Lord William warned them not to approach the keep, but they were hungry. Caitlin was in the cow shed, so they sent their youngest to ask her to intercede for them. When Margaret heard someone knocking on the trap door, she walked over and stomped on it with both feet.

"Margaret!" came the imperious call from below. "Open this door. I will provide the noonday meal."

"Bread and stew for Norman and Saxon soldiers. But not for Norman lords! Is that clear?"

"Yes, mistress," said Caitlin. She promised not to serve the man, but she did not promise to prevent him from serving himself. "Raise the door."

"Only you," Margaret ordered as she pointed to her former nurse. Margaret guarded the opening as Caitlin passed her. Wild-eyed and with hair in disarray, her color high, she peered down the hole to be sure no one else was about before plunging the poker downward and in a circle to catch anyone hiding.

Turning back to Margaret, Caitlin said in her softest, gentlest, voice, "I will need that to stir the fire, my lady." Then she held out her hand and waited.

Of long practice, Margaret calmed and handed over the poker without objection. In this manner Caitlin had been taking away what Margaret should not have since the first time she toddled to her mother's sewing basket and reached for a needle poking through a garment.

"Thank you, my lady," said Caitlin in the same gentle voice.

"You are welcome, Caitlin," Margaret answered woodenly.

At Caitlin's movement toward the fireplace, Margaret awoke as if from a trance and grabbed her mantle from its peg. She pounded down the stairs and descended the ladder unaided. In the yard, men saw her raging in a loud voice about killing "him" and saw her dashing toward the barn. They turned their backs or disappeared around corners to avoid upsetting her further.

If I see him I will gut him! As Margaret had reached the wood shed, the men entered the keep. In the stable Margaret ordered Dena to assist Caitlin and gave Jorgon an order. Soon Margaret led Night to the small gate. While Jorgon unlatched the door, a guard on the walkway above approached.

"You are leaving without an escort, my lady?" he asked. "Does Lord William know you are leaving? Have you informed the Saxon? Where are you going? Who will accompany you?" he asked in an increasingly frantic voice.

Without responding, Margaret passed through the gate with Night, got a foot up from Jorgon, and settled herself on the side saddle platform without bothering to tie herself to the seat. She pointed Night's head down the path.

Jorgon did not wait for his lady to reach the bottom of the hill. He re-latched the gate and raced for the keep. By the time he reached the hall to inform Lord William Lady Margaret had left, she was already at the bottom of the hill, deciding which road to take.

Margaret loosened her tight grip on the reins. Night raced for the first hill, kicked up dust and almost soared over the top of the road. She cared not the sun was bright and overly warm. She cared not her underarms were still wet from her morning exertions and her gunna stained dark from her sweat. She noticed not the dainty wildflowers in clusters beside the road nor the leaves rustling in the wind as she flew past the trees. She saw only open road, not the forest canopy suddenly over her. She wanted only freedom.

Free! Take us far, Night. Far away.

Hair and mantle flying, Margaret shouted her happiness. The wind cooled her first her face and then her emotions. Refusing to consider any consequences, Margaret enjoyed her mad ride into the countryside. *Almost run yourself out before I turn back. Mayhap I will turn back. I am free!*

Lord William and Elric jumped up and called names and orders after themselves as they raced for the stairs. Elric was right on Lord William's heels. When William realized Elric intended to retrieve the woman too, he ordered the Saxon to guard the keep.

"I am also charged with Lady Margaret's safety, so I am going with you. If we do not return her, I am a dead man," Elric countered in perfect Norman as he waited for Lord William to don his chain mail and grab his weapons.

"She took the north road!" yelled the sentinel as the Normans mounted and charged through the main gate.

As the knights raced up the same road, Elric, Eldene and Elborg followed on foot. Both the Normans' and the Saxons' determination to catch the lady showed in their taut expressions. She could not be that far ahead, the men reasoned. Lord William pressed his horse as did the knights who followed him. The Saxons loped on.

Far ahead of the men following the pair, Night sounded winded, so Margaret took the bit back from her horse and forced him to accept it; she pulled hard on the reins. Night tried to retake the bit, but Margaret's hands held firm. Night slowed to a canter, then a trot. Margaret let him keep his pace down a long hill, so he would cool and not fever later. She again rode in sunlight; she turned her face toward a light breeze coming from the meadow on her right. Now she noticed the clumps of blue and yellow blooms scattered among the grasses uncut by grazing animals. Now she took it all in. *Stop and rest him at the bottom.* Margaret leaned over and stroked Night's neck as his breathing slowed. She spoke soft words of praise and love. Margaret looked up to see men approaching. One rode a donkey. Those behind him walked. *Knights? No! Saxons. I am alone and without protection. Even Saxons can attack and ravage me. Turn now. Run!*

The party stopped at the crest of the hill. At that moment, Margaret heard pounding hooves behind her and turned Night. On the hill she had just descended were Lord William and knights. Margaret sat in the vale halfway between both groups, who were staring at her and each other. Not waiting to see who might move first, she spurred Night with her heels and charged up one side of the road as the knights charged down the other side. As they rode past her, the men saw her relief at seeing them. The knights became a barrier between Margaret and the unknowns.

Panting hard, Elric topped the hill. "Elstan!" he shouted, "do not move! Lord William! The king sent them! They are of us!"

"Elric! Help!" yelled the Saxon next to the donkey.

Elric ran past Margaret and the knights and halted before the man who had called his name. They hugged each other and thumped each other's backs.

Margaret watched as Elric turned and made introductions. Her relief doubled. *No fighting. A priest is on the donkey.* She watched the parties re-form into one, with Lord William at the head. Elric brought the priest's donkey forward and introduced Father Gregory to Lady Margaret. Knights and the Saxons fell behind them as they followed Lord William up the hill.

"I am very glad to see you, Father. We missed Sunday Mass getting here."

The Father turned back to answer her. "You will confess today and attend Vespers tonight and Mass in the morning, so no harm done. How came you to be ahead of your party? That is not safe behavior."

Margaret replied, "I know." *I must confess if I lie. Give no details.* She ignored the men behind her and followed the priest back to the keep.

8

Preparations

Norman and Saxons alike stood at the walls as the party walked out of the trees. After the group entered, the guards re-sealed both the main and the little gate. Margaret accompanied the priest to the ladder.

"I am Father Gregory, one of the few Saxon priests left in England."

"I am the Lady Margaret of Royal Oaks. I am keeping this keep ready for His Royal Highness's return, which should be in a few days. Would you like to rest in the keep with a mug of ale?"

"Indeed, I would," responded Father Gregory as he reached for the ladder.

As the priest climbed, Margaret said a prayer of gratitude that Father was wearing dark blue cloth pants under his black cassock. *Better for riding and more modest.* She waited until Father Gregory stood on the floor above and reached out his hand to help her when she reached the top of the ladder. *Wonder what he knows,* she thought as she climbed.

Soon all settled into their routines. As the women prepared both supper's and all of Sunday's breads, men cleaned the yard and did all the Sunday chores they could. The Saxons chatted among themselves as they worked. If any Norman understood their language, he did not reveal it. Knights tended their horses, checked on their roundseys, and ordered the Saxons to clean the stables and feed and water the animals before dark.

After Caitlin snorted her disapproval of Margaret's wild ride, the girl worked hard at the fireplace and table to regain her former nurse's good graces. She knew she would suffer a lecture as soon as they rounded the fireplace for their bed. Dena worked in silence at cleaning after the other two and stayed out of their paths. By supper the atmosphere was again calm. Father Gregory's grace was a long one; he thanked God for their safe arrival, for Lady Margret's recovery, for the knight's service and their success in the hunt. His last words were a prayer for the safety of the realm and the welfare of the king and queen.

Late. When will they arrive? I have heard Queen Matilda is very religious. I do not think she will travel on the morrow.

All sat to a nutritious stew of rabbit, squirrel, vegetables, stock thickened with flour and just the right amount of salt. Sunday's day of rest permitted only minimal cooking so they would eat leftovers from this fine meal. Everyone washed their hands and faces in anticipation of confession before Vespers.

After they had supped, the men visited at the trestle tables, Normans separate from Saxons. The women did their usual cleaning and morning preparations of pottage. They moved both chairs to one side and started two kettles of water over the fire on the other.

Father Gregory took one chair and left the other for those who wanted Confession.

The men noted a new routine. Dena carried a kettle of warmed water behind the fireplace. Washing sounds. Dena carried out a wooden bucket. Jorgon dumped the used water down the privy trough on the back wall; human debris washed down the stones behind the keep and down the hill until the outer wall stopped it. These steps were repeated several times.

A while later, the men heard, "Not me!" then "Yes, you as well!"

Sir William sat with the priest and made his confession after all the others had completed theirs. Talk between them was intense with Father asking several questions, Sir William frowning and then answering. Finally, the priest raised his hand and gave the knight absolution of his sins and then his blessing.

Margaret's taking Dena's chore was proof that the girl's denial and whining were to no avail. Jorgon was awaiting the next bucket of dirty water when, from behind the fireplace, emerged three lovely women. Each one's garments had been brushed clean and smoothed down. Each girl's hair had been groomed. Caitlin and Dena's shorn locks had curled up at the ends; Margaret's curly hair was free. Dena was wearing Margaret's daily gunna, while Margaret wore her Sunday one, which also was brown but not so thin or worn looking.

Father Gregory noticed first that the villein only had eyes for the girl, who was beaming at him. Then he noted how carefully William scrutinized Margaret. Now attired as a lady's maid, Dena reached for another kettle. Jorgon jumped forward and removed it from the fireplace hook for her. Dena led Jorgon around the corner; they returned to the hall without the kettle.

Margaret stood before the priest. "Father, if you would like to get clean from your journey, warm water and clean cloths await you." Margaret gestured to her sleeping area behind the fireplace.

"Thank you, Daughter. That is thoughtful of you to provide such luxury."

The priest was behind the wall when he heard Margaret.

"Lord William, would you care to get clean as well?"

"I thank you, but I prefer cold water. I will use the well by the stable."

Father Gregory plunged a cloth into the bucket and scrubbed his face, hands, and feet before returning to the hall. Father Gregory began the evening prayers that ended almost each day of their lives. While priests prayed at regular times during the day, the people started the day with Mass and ended it with Vespers.

The men re-formed the hall into a sleeping room with pairs of benches pushed together to make a bed next to the trestle tables, which were also beds. Knights had set their bedding on the tables and benches. Lord William stood to leave the warmth and coziness of the hall, just as Father Gregory had suggested. Sir William muttered, "God give you good rest" to the priest, who smiled his approval at the knight taking his advice. When Jorgon arrived at the stable, he found Sir William had taken his sleeping corner of piled straw, so he made a bed elsewhere. No Saxon dare ask a Norman knight why he bedded down in a stable when he could have the comfort of the hall, but Jorgon did wonder. Saxons not on guard duty slept on the rushes on the first floor.

As the others settled in for the night, Lady Margaret took the chair beside the priest.

"Father, I'm sorry I waited until after Vespers, but I want no one near to hear me. It has been far too long since my last confession," admitted Margaret. "God, I beg you to grant me absolution for the sins I have committed since my last confession." Margaret drew in a deep breath and began with, "Father, nine or ten days ago I bathed in a stream before dawn. Naked. But no one saw me," she added in a rush. *The Church may preach caring for your body is wrong, but getting clean is not really a sin. Oh, well. Confess it anyway and make him happy.*

Elric saw Father Gregory and the lady in deep, quiet conversation. He knew from the short purple stole hanging around the priest's shoulders that he was also hearing Margaret's confession. As Elric rolled into his bedding, he wondered what Normans do to require they confess so long and so often. From Lord William's stares at the lady, Eric guessed his sins, but he wondered what hers might be. He saw the lady finally stand and guessed her mouth was moving to bid the priest, "God give you good rest," the customary parting of all on their way to bed.

"Thank you, my child. The cot will keep me off this cold floor. My old bones approve," he added as he patted her hand.

Warm voice, kind smile, easy penance. Glad he came.

As Margaret rounded the fireplace corner for her bed, Elric decided Sundays were always good days to make requests of those of rank. Elric closed his eyes. On the morrow and after Sunday Mass, Elric approached Margaret and requested they withdraw to stone benches set in each side of an arrow slit on the east wall. He reminded her the morning sun was almost full up and would warm them.

"My lady, I thank you for saving my life yesterday," began Elric.

"I? How?"

"If you had not returned safely to the keep, I would have answered to an angry king." When he saw her silent assent, he pressed this small advantage. "Surely you know you are a valuable person to His

Royal Highness. He commanded me to keep you safe—as safe as the other person he has commanded me to guard."

Caitlin and Dena wiping down the tables did not bother them, but two knights approached, so both went silent until the Normans had departed. Neither trusted the men to be ignorant of the Saxon language they were using.

"She is religious and will not travel on a Sunday. I expect them on the morrow."

"I agree."

"But I could not ride for two years," Margaret added wistfully as she peered out the slit, "I have missed it so."

"I will ask the king's permission for you to ride—with a proper escort, of course. I cannot say what he will answer, but, if I have your word that you will go escorted, I will make your request known to him."

"You have my solemn oath."

"Thank you, my lady."

Margaret smiled. "It was fun, was it not?"

"Yes, my lady, it was fun."

"What know you of Lord William?"

"One of the king's barons. A great estate. Wealthy. Keeps twenty men at arms for himself and funds a dozen for the king's use. Has the king's trust. Widowed last year when his wife died birthing their second son. Why do you ask?"

"We had words."

Elric lifted his chin. "Mmmm."

He knows. I must hide my interest better.

The Saxon stood, bowed and departed. For as long as she could, Margaret stared through the slit at the sliver of a sunny sky.

9

※

Royal Arrival

Monday, 8 July

"My lady, last evening you said I could practice on your hair."

"I will sit in the archway with my back to the room so you have light and I have some privacy."

As Dena worked, Margaret discussed meals, rations, and meat supplies with Caitlin, who was working at the main table to turn a large wad of bread dough into small rounds, so they would rise and be baked in time for supper.

After Margaret rejected several suggestions, Dena announced, "Some up in a braid and some down free." Dena took up the top half of her lady's hair, braided it and fastened the braid with a leather thong. Dena smiled to herself as she tied the ends into a small bow. She held up the braid and brushed Margaret's loose hair and fluffed it high. "What think you, Caitlin?" Dena set down the braid.

"A good compromise. She appears an adult, modest, and yet has her hair down as requested. Well done."

"Thank you, Dena, for your kindness. At the estate I saw you hold hands with the little girls and playing games with them. You weeded Holen's garden when she was heavy with child and could not bend over. You are always kind to others. Do the same to the queen and she will love you too."

"You are most welcome, my lady." Dena curtsied as she blushed at Margaret's compliments.

Margaret changed places and used her brush on Dena's soft blond hair. "Now you are ready."

"Ready for what?" asked Dena.

Margaret just smiled.

"Dressed as a lady's maid, Dena can serve meals and fetch but do no scullery work. We need servants," said Caitlin.

"I can bake bread," Margaret offered.

"If Dena learns to cook, two would do."

"I will learn," promised Dena. "It is my thanks for saving me from Lord Charles." She sounded eager to be of use.

"The king wants our group to be small. I doubt he wants strangers in here," Margaret said, "but I will ask."

Not long after the main meal, Lord William returned to the hall. "Lady Margaret, a messenger from the king at the wall. His Royal Highness and his party will arrive before we sup."

"Thank you, my lord."

William turned away and then back to face her. "Can you tell me, my lady, why Elric refused the messenger entrance?"

"No, my lord, I cannot." *After what you said to me, I am not about to tell you any more than I must.* William's head was all Margaret could see. She smiled that it was where it had been two days before, but this day she had no desire to kick it. "Lord William, please send me word the moment the party is sighted."

William frowned, nodded, and disappeared.

"He still thinks the worst of you," said Caitlin. "As do all the men here. Her arrival may convince them otherwise, but what will she think? You are but a girl." Caitlin leaned in and whispered, "She will command you. She will order this place to her liking after he has departed. You had best plan how to get on her good side or you will suffer her wroth. You know you will."

Margaret chose to ignore Caitlin's warning until she had time to think more on her words. *Is there no one I can hope will treat me kindly?* "He will learn the truth soon enough. Dena, fetch Jorgon. We need the mutton carcass hanging from the rafter and the tables re-arranged."

The meal was simmering in readiness; the bread was being kept warm under a cloth. A Saxon head poked from the stairwell and announced the party was in sight. The women hurriedly left the keep and climbed the walkway ladder. They stood together as they stared at the roads below. From the south road came the caravan. Armed men rode before, behind, and beside a litter carried by pairs of roundseys front and back.

"Why do wagons accompany her?" Margaret thought aloud. "He said she would come alone."

Elric heard her. "She is alone. But she needs a bed, chairs, the fittings of a castle, does she not?"

Of course, she would want her things about her. Confinement will be difficult enough without being deprived of her comforts. Stupid of me not to think of it. Seven months is a long time. "Elric, we cannot let all those men within the walls. Too many. Might attack. One might poison the bailey well. Who will remind the king he promised to be the only one to enter now that we have the place secured?"

"I left that office to the messenger. I am not fool enough to say 'no' to the king."

Margaret noted depths of wisdom in his smile and his eyes. He seemed older than twenty.

"We Saxons will take in the wagons. Only the royals will enter. The rest will sleep beyond the walls."

"Elric, shall I meet her in the yard? Curtsey and dirty my hem. Do I lead to the ladder? Go first? Help her up? Wait? Follow her?"

"Calm yourself, my lady. Greet her in the hall. She likes well-watered wine on such a warm day. She will expect me to meet her."

Margaret lightly touched his arm. "Thank you." She instructed Caitlin and Dena to return to the keep and prepare for the king's arrival before she descended the ladder. Elric watched her sweep across the yard and climb the keep ladder. After a time, the king's head appeared in the stairwell. He was looking at and bending toward one behind him. Margaret made a deep curtsey and remained there with her eyes on the floor even as she burned to look up.

"My Queen, I present the Lady Margaret."

"Your Royal Highness, if you will but permit me to serve you, I—"

"Rise, Lady Margaret. What are those smells?"

"Mutton stew and fresh bread, Your Royal Highness."

Margaret stood and looked at the woman she was trying to save. Shaken by the queen's hard stare, Margaret looked down and then up only as far as the queen's chin. Margaret saw rich green and creme fabrics beneath a sable-trimmed mantle, which was held together at her shoulder with a many-jeweled brooch that looked like a circle of stones in a stained-glass window. The queen's necklace was three gold chains of differing lengths, each heavily braided. *She is measuring me. I am not good enough. I know it.*

"May Dena take your mantle?"

The queen undid the brooch, removed the garment and held it from her, all without looking away from Margaret. Dena sidled to the group, silently took it and disappeared.

"If you please, I have mugs of cool, watered wine."

"We will take them in the chairs," said the king.

Margaret waited for the royals to seat themselves before she turned for the tray Dena was already holding for her. At the king's wave, she approached the royals and curtseyed exactly halfway between each of them.

"Well done," the queen sneered.

Margaret's spine curved down as she shrink at the insult. She waited for the couple to pick up their drinks then lowered the tray to her side. Margaret backed well down the hall and out of the royals' lines of sight before she turned and silently stepped to the fireplace to hand Dena the tray. While the couple sipped, they held an unspoken conversation, eyes glancing, tiny shrugs, slight waves of a hand. A file of Saxons stepped out of the stairwell and set down pieces of a bed frame, ropes, chests, chairs, rolled tapestries, and five chests. Two waited by the pile as the rest disappeared. At the queen's hand wave, Margaret approached and curtsied.

The queen sighed. "Once a day will do unless it is a formal occasion or guests are present."

Margaret stood and stared at her clasped hands.

"Only this room?"

"No, Your Royal Highness. May I show you a sleeping space behind the fireplace?"

The queen rose and arched her back to release journey-stiffened muscles. Margaret motioned to the archway. The queen walked toward it. "Your Royal Highness, may I?" asked Margaret as she gestured toward the mantle and the lit candle she had left for just this purpose. At the king's nod, she stood tiptoe and reached for the holder. Before she could move away, the king touched her free hand. Margaret froze.

"Remember my command. If you must choose, save my son. For now, you had best step softly. She is not happy."

Margaret nodded at him. When she looked up, she saw the queen watching them. She ducked her head, hid her free hand behind her and stepped away from the king's chair. The queen pointed to the hole in the floor.

"The well is in the donjon below, Your Royal Highness."

At the queen's curt gesture, Margaret stepped through the archway and raised the candle high. The queen brushed past her. Even though she only looked at the floor, Margaret felt the queen's hard stare.

We may never be alone again. Say it now. Be honest.

"The king said you are not happy."

"What else did he say?"

"He told me to step softly."

"How long have you known His Royal Highness?"

Margaret thought for a moment as she counted the days. She saw the queen noticed how she counted on her fingers. "Eleven or twelve days, Your Royal Highness. He came to Sir Charles' estate, Royal Oaks, looking for my mother to aid you. When he learned she had trained me before her death, he asked me to come in her stead."

Margaret waited for a response but got none. *What does she think of me? Of this place? I have no more authority here. I am but a servant again, a servant still. He said he needed me, but she is in charge.*

In a more kindly tone than she had begun, Queen Matilda said, "Lady Margaret, please hang a tapestry between those two rings and place my chamber pot in the corner behind it. The queen stepped toward the bed. "Whose is this?"

"I bought it for you, Your Royal Highness, from the carpenter in the village. I turned the ticking and filled it with fresh straw."

"You thought of my needs." Queen Matilda sounded a bit surprised. "I have brought my own things, Lady Margaret," said the queen in a gentle voice. "Please move this bed to the back wall for you and the women. Place my bed next to the fireplace stones where I will be warmed by them. Place my rugs down where I can step on them. Fasten a tapestry to cover the archway. I will decide about the chests later."

"If it please Your Royal Highness, I will have this bed moved immediately, and you may rest in it while I set the room."

"Thank you, but I shall wait fireside with His Highness," responded the queen as she stepped past Margaret.

After the men had set up the bed, they fastened the head and foot boards with a long rope that wove through the seven holes in each. They set the sideboards between the two pieces and inserted them into the headboard and footboard notches. Each man stood at the head and the foot of the frame. After knotting one end of the rope, Elborg pulled that line tight, pulled the slack through the second hole and waited for Eldene to do the same at his end. Eldene knotted the end of the final line while Elborg picked up the second rope and started threading that rope through the sideboard holes, creating an up and down weaving through the long ropes. As Margaret watched them, she thought of the times Cook had cut strips of dough and had woven them over a pie filling when she did not have enough dough to make a full pie top. Margaret smiled at the thought and sent up a quick prayer for the old woman's safety. Finally Elborg knotted the end of cross rope. The base for the bedding was now tight five-inch squares. The Saxons lifted the bed frame, carried it where Margaret pointed and stood aside to wait for Margaret's next request.

As the queen had commanded, Margaret opened one chest and found three tickings, two straw, one down, two sets of finely woven, smooth linen sheets and four thick cream-colored woolen blankets hemmed with linen edges. Another chest held a mink throw lined with a soft woolen blanket, thick woolen rugs, goose-down pillows and pewter plate, spoons, goblets, five candlesticks and a bag of candles. She called for Dena to place three candlesticks with candles in them on the head table. Dena returned to help Margaret place the tickings and make the bed.

Margaret unrolled the tapestries that had been carried in and left in front of the bed and found they had four heavy rings across their tops. She noted both were heavy sailcloth with painted scenes, one a meadow of flowers with trees behind and the other a church with hills in the background. Margaret first thought, "The meadow will be pleasant to look at from the hall." She changed her mind when she realized the queen might enjoy waking to a church scene, but feel uncomfortable pissing behind one. She asked Elborg and Eldene to hang the meadow scene in the corner and the church tapestry facing the hall. After both items had been roped into place, the men set the empty chests against the wall and the three full ones in front of them. Margaret opt two and peered inside to find the queen's winter wardrobe, boots and shoes in one chest and her summer wardrobe in the other. Then she opt the last chest.

"Elborg, know you what this is?"

Elborg looked at a triangular stringed musical instrument with a long neck cradled in blankets on top of unknown items.

"No, but it is dear. The design on it is all inlaid woods. Very costly."

Margaret lowered the lid with care and redid the clasp. She sniffed appreciatively at the smells of mutton and carrots, leeks and turnips. Margaret returned to the hall to find the king and queen on one side of the fireplace and Caitlin stirring the stew on the other side.

"She refused to step between us," the king explained with amusement.

Dena had set the head table for five persons, Margaret on the end, Father Gregory, the queen, the king, and Lord William. The pewter candlesticks held beeswax candles, already lit. Elric and Dena served.

After a quiet meal, Father Gregory led evening prayers. The king and queen retired early, and those who had work to do tiptoed and spoke in whispers.

10

A Champion

Father Gregory's pallet flanked one side of the fireplace. Opposite him Margaret slouched in one chair with her feet in the other. She had wrapped herself in a woolen blanket the queen had given to her. At the sound of feet she came awake for the third time. Margaret saw William's startled expression at finding her hearthside, like a serving maid. At his tiptoed approach, Margaret sat upright.

"Why are you not in your own bed?"

Margaret set her feet on the floor, and William sat in the empty chair.

"I gave it to Caitlin and Dena. They work harder than I and need a good rest."

William frowned, thought of the king's reputation, and leaned forward. "What are you afraid of?"

"Nothing." Margaret's glare dared him to refute her.

"Lady Margaret, please accept my abject apologies for my offenses." When William saw her eyes soften, he continued. "I believed terrible things of you. I spoke harshly to you. I should not have. I am sorry."

"The queen is with child and I am charged with her safety."

"Elric told me."

William took up her hands. They were cold. He tried to raise her fingers to his lips. Margaret tried to pull away, but he did not release her. He felt her fingers warming in his. In the flickering firelight, Margaret was half shadow, half real. William knew she would haunt his dreams for a long time.

"Tell me what you need. Anything. I shall do it. Be it."

"I need a champion, one who comes to my defense against slander. I wear my hair down to show I am still a maid, still a good girl. If others talk, will you to speak well of me? Reputation is all I have. Will you do that for me?"

"Yes, my lady. And more." William raised her hands and kissed the tips of her fingers. He smiled at her blushing. "You have but to send the words 'Night needs you' and I will be on my steed anon."

Margaret's thanks were the tears welling in her eyes. Her hand touching his cheek was her gift. William turned his head and kissed her palm and held her hand against his face. Margaret felt warm all over.

Oh, William. Dare I hope?

Father Gregory stirred. William released Margaret and stood. He lifted Margaret's feet back onto the chair and bowed. For a moment Margaret half-feared, half-hoped he would try to kiss her. Instead, William kissed the tip of his pointing finger and with it touched the tip of her nose. He smiled at her, nodded, and tiptoed away.

Margaret pulled her cover to her chin, sunk down, and released a long, slow sigh.

The priest peered just above his cover and saw Margaret wore closed eyes and lips in a smile. Father Gregory did not return to slumber for some time. The young couple had given him much to ponder.

11

Market Day

Saturday, 20 July 1101 A.D.

Father Gregory complained, "Your Royal Highness, the Church still objects to Sunday markets. It is the Lord's day for rest."

"Be that as it may, Father, for many market day is the only day for them to barter for their needs." The king continued buttering his bread. "They do go to Mass first. For them, going to market is a day of rest. As this village holds a Saturday market, you should have no objections here."

Father Gregory said no more.

After the king left to meet with the Lord Richard de Reuen, the queen summoned Lady Margaret. Margaret smiled and nodded to the queen even though Queen Matilda was frowning at her. *What have I done wrong already so early in the day? A curtsey might help her mood, but best not. I have already given her one and only Caitlin is about.* She stayed standing and waited.

"His Highness said you may hire two boys for chores. Young ones to be safe. Today or soon." The queen surveyed Margaret's attire again. "Is that brown rag all you have?"

"Yes, Your Royal Highness," Margaret said as she dropped her head and tried not to blush. *Even my Sunday gunna is not good enough.*

The queen ordered what purchases Margaret was to make, including bolts for gowns and shifts, one pair for Dena, one for Caitlin, and two for Margaret, plus fabric for a new mantle and a strip of leather for a girdle for Margaret. The queen handed over a bag of coins. "Use what you need. I expect an accounting."

Margaret smiled her gratitude at the queen caring for all three of them and for the heavy bag she had just been handed. *Mayhap you are not so stern after all.* "Thank you, Your Royal Highness. May I also purchase shoes for Caitlin and Dena? Caitlin's are almost worn through and Dena has none. If I find only leather, the stableman can fashion sturdy shoes for them."

"Of course, of course. Take four men: two Normans, two Saxons."

Margaret looked at the stitchery on the queen's lap. "Your Royal Highness, if you will trust me with your needle, I will try to have it sharpened."

Matilda smiled at Margaret and in a kind, soft voice answered, "Thank you for thinking of it. I thought I had chosen my better needle, but I left it behind."

The queen handed over the treasured object. She smiled as Margaret wove the needle through the fabric over her heart and patted it. "Margaret, you are a good girl to have thought of it. Enjoy your outing. Remember to stop and eat something too."

Margaret beamed at her queen and curtsied her thanks anyway. She enjoyed a wonderful holiday in the small village down the west road. She noticed the lanes were mounded a bit; the sides dipped toward the stalls. *To drain off rain.* She noted the dirt-dug gutters around each hut. The villagers had pulled their tables from their homes and stood behind them or leaned against their hut walls as they waited for customers. With tables on both sides, only one person at a time could walk the narrow lane. Margaret appreciated Sir Troyes walking in front; he cleared the path and held back oncoming persons each time she stopped to look at something. Summer goods were mostly fresh vegetables or large crocks filled with fresh milk or small ones of butter. Margaret guessed a buyer would bring her own container in which to take the item home. One woman's table was cheeses of various kinds and ages. Other wares included belts, coin bags or other leather goods, all dyed or painted with colors from nature, some narrow fabrics had been woven into ribs of colorful fabrics on a hand loom, the kind Saxons used. One man had cornered piglets with a three-sided fence against his hut and was selling them at a half-penny each. The cost might be dear for Saxons, but Margaret was considering purchasing two or three to fatten on slop. She had seen all that was for sale and had stopped several times to inspect wares. With a knight before her, one after her and Saxons following, Margaret had no difficulty getting through the crowd or being accosted by strangers.

"Pots for sale? I repair pots!" a sonorous voice called above the din at the end of one lane.

The delicious smells from food stalls varied from soups and breads to wood-smoked meats. Clumps of people chatted near the food stalls. Margaret decided to feed the men before making her purchases. *With only two meals on the morrow, eating might put them in good moods. They will not be holding new goods as they eat and soiling fabric or dropping things.*

117

Margaret's escorts had noticed each of her sleeve pockets drooped with a bag of coins, but had said nothing, as was proper. Margaret paid for the sticks of broiled meat and the mugs of ale from the few coins remaining the king had given her. As they ate, the knights huddled together separate from the Saxons but in a rough circle on the side of the crowd.

Should I tell them the food is from my purse? No. Sound proud. Besides they are the king's coins and not really mine. Margaret knew the goods she wanted and the people selling them. *Eat and then return for my purchases.*

"My lady, my cloth is finer than any other in the whole of the market," the round, pleasant woman bragged. Clearly her dress was from her own weaving, so Margaret knew the quality just by looking at the woman, who had a small girl clutching her skirt.

Margaret shrugged. She was unwilling to begin bargaining at a disadvantage.

"See this length and this one and this one," offered the woman as she pulled from finer and finer rolls of linen and wool on her table.

The last one caught Margaret's attention for its warm blue color. She felt the even, solid weave.

"Did you dye this yourself?"

"No, my lady. My cousin shears the sheep and his wife spins the thread. My brother's wife dyes the wool and weaves the cloth. My brother is a fuller; he built a rollers table to flatten the wool smooth. They all live together in the country. I sell the cloth and sew garments if they are ordered. We import the linen from the continent."

"A good family business," Margaret commented.

The women bargained a long while over both the cost and how much she had to sell. Margaret finally got the price she wanted by pointing out how much she was purchasing in one sale and the advantage to the woman to sell so much at one time. Looking bored, the knights and Saxons shifted their feet as they waited. After Margaret had laid out the queen's coins, the woman's eyes lit up at all that silver and agreed to Margaret's terms. With a string, the woman measured Margaret from shoulder to heel and knotted the string at that mark. As the woman used the string to measure the blue wool roll five times that length, Margaret inspected the cloth for flaws and found none. They repeated the process for four more rolls of wool and five of linen. Margaret remembered to ask for more fabric for Caitlin's clothes as she was half a head taller than Margaret.

Margaret's next stop was to the shoe seller's table, where he had placed the shoes of the same length and width in pairs. Margaret tried on hers, but guessed the sizes needed for Caitlin's larger feet and Dena's smaller ones. Actually, there were no sizes or left or right feet. A buyer had to try on two shoes and then wear them left and right until each shoe molded to the shape of each foot. Lastly, Margaret returned to two different knitters' tables to purchase socks.

The pot seller pointed to one who might have needles for sale and informed her the man was standing outside the village because he was not allowed to be among them. "A Jew," he said. Then the man spat on the ground. Margaret strode in the direction he had pointed.

Strange clothes. Strange hair. Even smells of strange foods. So that is a Jew! Remember what Father Ambroise taught us about Jews. Keep the knights near. Stand not close.

The Jew wore not a jerkin over a shirt or tunic and Norman chausses but a shirt and cloth leg coverings that flapped in the light breeze. His surcoat went to his knees, but it had sleeves and was shut with buttons to the waist and had pockets of various sizes all down the front. She puzzled over his long side locks of dark brown hair. Everything he wore was black.

"Ah, fine lady, I regret to tell you I only sell needles," the man apologized. "Mayhap a blacksmith can sharpen yours. I do have two fine needles for sale," he added.

The peddler unbuttoned his coat halfway and pulled a square of fabric from an inside pocket. He unfolded the small square of black cloth. The needles were fine indeed, straight, sharp, and with long holes easy to thread.

The queen might like a second one. I do have the king's coins. When the Jew told her the cost, Margaret gasped. *Both bags do not hold the pay he wants.*

"I cannot pay that! Not even for Her Royal Highness."

"The queen? This needle is for the queen?" the strange man asked. At Margaret's nod, he extended his hand. "Take whichever one you like, my lady. Please tell Her Royal Highness it is a gift from a grateful Jew. I watched Her Royal Highness save my cousin from a London mob about to stone him. Tell Her Royal Highness that I, Samuel the jeweler, am always at her disposal. My family is grateful to her for saving one of us."

One person spits when he talks of a Jew and the queen saves one? Why would she do that?

"I thank you."

"No, I thank you, fine lady. You have helped me repay a debt. We Hebrew people always pay our debts."

Margaret wove the new needle above the old one. As she turned to leave, the Jew bowed and thanked her again. Margaret hovered over the blacksmith as he worked. Knowing for whom he labored made the man slow and careful. He handed over the needle, and

Margaret felt its smoothness. Touching the tip drew a drop of blood. She sucked at her fingertip and licked the spot to seal it.

"Guard that well, my lady. With that needle a man could purchase a sword, a helmet and sleeved chain mail."

Sir Troyes walked the lanes announcing her request in the Saxon Eldene had taught him in whispers. Soon families stepped forward with their sons. Margaret outlined the boys' duties and informed the families she did not want brothers. The boys would be clothed, fed, and taught manners. When she explained the queen was confining the boys to the keep for as long as she was in residence and would not allow them to visit their families, several fathers removed their boys from the group. Five boys remained. After consulting with both her Saxon and Norman escorts, Margaret chose Ordson, ten, and Garnyd, eight.

The final stop was the clothiers. Margaret bought each boy was two tunics, two pairs of leggings, two pairs of socks and a pair of boots. The boys were so excited to get footwear they forgot their shyness and chattered at each other as they tried to find shoes that fit. Ordson and Garnyd beamed at Margaret when she handed them their new garments. The party walked back from the market with each Norman and Saxon carrying a bundle.

Margaret looked up the hill to the walls around Forest Keep. *Will she permit me out again? As His Royal Highness has confined her so I may be confined too. Oh Night! Even a royal gaol is still a gaol.*

"You did well and at good cost," said the queen as she regained her purse.

Margaret blushed. Then she told of Her Royal Highness of her adventures step by step and even the bargaining and her successes. Margaret's accounting of her marketing was so lively and descriptive the queen smiled. Margaret kept talking because the queen kept smiling, nodded at her stories and looked pleased with her. Finally, she launched into her description of the Jew and her conversation. After placing the sharpened needle in the queen's hand, she added the new one. "This is your gift from the Jew, Samuel the jeweler."

"Thank you, Margaret." Then Matilda switched to the less formal mode of Norman. "I appreciate your concern for my things—and for me. You may say 'Your Majesty' while we are here."

"I only want to help, Your Majesty."

Margaret was secretly pleased the queen was allowing her to use the less formal address. *Mayhap we will get along better now. If I am careful, I can hope she may even like me.* She decided to ask about the Jew.

"Your Majesty, I do not understand why the man spat after he said, 'Jew'?"

"Ah, Jews. They crucified Jesus, you know." At Margaret's nod, Matilda continued, "They are despised for that. They are also hated because they lend money and charge usury." At seeing Margaret's frown, she added, "You borrow ten pounds, but you owe twelve or thirteen for having needed money. By a pope's decree, Christians may not charge usury and must forgive the loan and the person who cannot pay it back. Most Christians will not lend coin to another Christian for fear he will not return it. So many men borrowing go to the Saracens or to the Jews—and hate them."

Lending money for usury. Is that why Christian hate Jews? Oh, and killing the Christ, surely for that.

"The Jew said he was grateful you saved his cousin from a mob."

"I remember that. I did so to prove we Christians are good people. Christians need to be good to Jews. That way they will see us leading such good lives they will want to be one of us. Convert and leave that hated faith; their lives are made awful because of what they believe."

"Your Majesty, I know almost nothing about the world. I only lived at home and visited estates when Mother took me with her to train me for midwifery."

"I know much because I was trained to be a queen. You may leave me."

Margaret slipped away and pretended not to notice the queen turning the corner of the fireplace. When Margaret was sure the queen was abed, she tiptoed to Caitlin and Dena with her gifts.

As they supped, the king announced he would depart on the morrow. He requested an early Mass and meal. He ordered the men and horses ready an hour before dawn.

The queen described her cittern to Margaret and requested she fetch it. Margaret carefully unwrapped the instrument and wondered at what sound a triangular box might make. Picking it up still in its wrappings, Margaret carried the precious instrument like a new-born babe and gently set it on the table before the queen. *What treasures she has. Do they make her happy?* Matilda pushed back her chair, took up her cittern and began with her husband's favorite tune. Margaret was pleasantly surprised at the warm sound of the melody and how the tune soothed her mind. In Latin, Matilda sang of the glory of morning, of spring and of God's good earth, warm, fertile and ready for planting. Henry smiled at his wife and gently nodded his head in time with the measures. Afterward all in the hall applauded the queen's sweet voice and skilled playing. Henry whispered three words, and Matilda began a second tune.

After Vespers, the Normans who had escorted Queen Matilda's party were permitted to enter the hall two at a time to speak their farewells to Her Royal Highness.

Lord William bowed to the queen. "You have but to send word and I shall come." After the queen acknowledged his pledge, William turned to Margaret. "And I am at your service, Lady Margaret." The warmth in his eyes belied the formality with which he now addressed her. If the queen noticed his intense stare into Margaret's eyes and her blush in response, she said nothing.

That night Margaret again refused Father Gregory's kind offer and slept on the chairs. She wondered where William was sleeping. *He leaves with the king. Do not risk even a parting glance.*

In the middle of the night, a knight ran up the stairs, dashed to the archway, and called out, "Your Royal Highness! Your Royal Highness! Invasion!"

Everyone heard the king roar, "Who? Where?"

"Sir Robert of Normandy! Your brother. Portsmouth."

"Rouse the men! We leave anon! Summon the Saxon!"

Everyone jumped out of their beds. Father Gregory led Margaret toward the well hole. He instructed her to stay and disappeared down the stairwell. Backs against walls, the Saxons froze unless ordered by a knight to assist him. Still buckling his sword belt, the king rounded the archway. Two knights flanked him. Elric met him at the fireplace. Margaret saw only Norman backs. She stepped forward to hear their conversation.

"Did the Saxons know?"

"No, Your Royal Highness. I swear upon my life we did not. We would have warned you sooner. We stand by the Charter of Liberties our fathers signed. Kill me now if you do not believe me."

Margaret gasped.

"Seal these walls against any, all. Only I op the gate. If I lose, get her to Scotland by any means. Save my queen."

"How many? Who else?" the king demanded from the messenger.

Only after the king had left the hall did Margaret take a breath deep enough to fill her lungs. Elric spotted her and approached. "Stay out of her way," he whispered.

Elric followed the Normans. The remaining Saxons stirred. They straightened the room, packed Norman sleeping gear and carried it downstairs. A few returned and sat on benches to wait for further instructions. Margaret heard the clamor of the yard, the clang of the gates, and the thumps of the massive wooden cross beams onto iron brackets. As the sounds of men and horses faded, Caitlin and Dena slipped round the corner.

Caitlin advised, "No one will sleep. We may as well start the pottage."

The three women kept to the fireplace area and tiptoed. The Saxons not on guard sat in silence. At the usual hour queen rounded the archway and stood before the small altar table against the west wall. Margaret stood well behind her. The rest of the room followed. During Mass Father Gregory prayed for the king's safety and the success of his endeavors then added a time for silent prayer. All bowed their heads. *Oh, God, if it be Your will, let the queen keep the babe. So many lives, hers included, depend on Her Majesty bearing another son.* The queen was a long time with her head down. Father did not finish the service until she lifted it.

The men ate heartily as if to swallow their worries with the food. The queen took only two spoonfuls of pottage, sipped at her ale once, and did not touch her bread. Father's meal matched hers. Margaret cleared the table and disappeared through the archway. Margaret straightened both beds and made use of the chamber pot. She rested on her bed until summoned.

Please God, protect and defend him. We need him to keep the country whole. To keep the peace. To protect his babe, his wife. Me. I know you have a plan for each of us; please let it be good this time. I know. Your will in all things. We trust in You always, Oh Lord of Hosts. I pray for the strength to bear whatever You send my way. Your will, Oh God, in all things.

Margaret was not the only who prayed the day away. The hot, sticky day dragged in disconcerting quiet. They supped in silence. Everyone slept fitfully. The queen more than the others. Monday was as silent. Mass was even longer with silent prayer time. Father Gregory started a sermon, but he cut off his words after the queen gave him a look only he could see. Father mumbled a platitude about the will of God and finished the service. No one talked aloud, only whispered. Matilda stayed in her bed most of the day, ate nothing and only reappeared for Vespers.

Now only Saxons guarded the keep and bailey. No Normans had been left behind, not even to hunt. The women distracted themselves by cutting cloth. The queen handed her scissors to Margaret and supervised. Margaret's shifts followed the line of the queen's bliaut, which was cut in the modern fashion. Margaret cut blue fabric into fitted sleeves with a trumpet shape from just above the elbow to the wrist line. The bodice would fit to the hips then flare to a wide, flowing skirt. All that cutting required Margaret to whip stitch the cut edges to prevent raveling before she could assemble the garment.

"Your old gunna looked like a sack on your body. I expect you to cut your new garments to better fit you. You have a slim waist I want to see. Leave more length for deep hems. Ladies use more fabric in their sleeve flares and hems to show their high rank," explained the queen. "Remember to keep open a sleeve hem for carrying things. Only men have pockets inside their surcoats."

Lady Margaret's bliaut was two long strips of fabric sewn with a center seam down the front and back. A head hole was cut out with a front slit; the edges were rolled under and sewn down. The last fifth of fabric made the sleeves, which were sewn on the body of the fabric. Side seams were sewn from cuff to hem. Finally, the garment bottom and sleeve edges were hemmed. The linen shifts women wore to keep their skin from chafing from the wool were sewn the same way. Caitlin and Dena's clothes were more serviceable. Both their shifts and gunnas were left as tubes. The bodies and sleeves were loose. If a Saxon wanted more room for working and walking, she sewed a side seam to just above her knees and hemmed back the slit. Because all the seams were on the fabric edges, Caitlin and Dena only needed to whip stitch the sleeve tops before they assembled and stitched the bands of fabric into a shift or gunna. Caitlin's gunna was green, Dena's a warm brown. Dena whispered to Margaret.

"What is it?"

"Your Majesty, Dena was asking if her garments would be full enough."

Margaret hoped the queen would not ask why. The queen stared at Dena, who was looking at the floor.

"How far along is she?" The queen's voice was as hard as her expression.

"She has missed her courses twice," answered Margaret.

127

"The father?"

Margaret hesitated.

"Lord Charles of Royal Oaks." She paused. "My father." Margaret rushed the rest. "He took her against her will and kept her abed three days. Then he placed her in the hall so he could…grab her… whenever he wanted. She is an innocent." Margaret was saving what had happened to Lord Charles' previous bedmate as her final argument. She prayed she would not need it. "I brought her along to save her. The hostler Jorgon and she have been sweethearts for years. He wants to marry her."

Margaret held her breath. If the queen asked, she would have to reveal they both had run away. She was cert the queen would have them returned. Margaret shuddered to think what Lord Charles would do to them. Matilda nodded as if she understood. She looked hard at Dena and guessed the girl's fate should she and the hosteler be returned. Unless forced to do so, she decided she was not going to change servants until she knew if she was staying or fleeing.

"We need them, so they stay," said the queen before she left to nap.

With tears coursing down her cheeks, Dena looked up. Caitlin hugged her hard and spoke soft words. *Breathe,* Margaret ordered herself.

That evening the queen retired early, giving Margaret the chance for which she had been waiting. She slipped down the stairs and asked to speak with Elric. At her request they climbed a ladder to walk the parapet and look into the night. Margaret gave a hard look at the guards and they moved away. She looked up at a night sky so abundant with stars that almost no dark existed between dots too many to count. She always smiled at the swath of sky lit with so many stars it looked like a wave in an ocean of night filled with distant candle flames. *The dome over God's world with a walkway to Heaven. Be it your will, Oh God, that my soul may follow it to Your gates and spend eternity with You. Mother, are you there yet? I pray it be so.*

"My lady?"

"Whisper please," she asked as she looked far away into the forest.

A sea of stars twinkled in the black above them. The breeze had died at sunset so the leaves were only black specks against black trunks and limbs. Nothing moved and the air seemed filled with dread. Not even the coolness of the night soothed Margaret's brow, now openly furrowed with worry.

"Why is Sir Robert invading? Is he supposed to be king?" *Am I bound to a usurper? Will I be dead in a month—sooner? Can we save the queen? Ourselves? What is Scotland like?*

Elric heard the fear in her voice and understood her need to know what so directly affected her. Word among the Saxons was she was as good to them as she dared under her father's rule. He was not trusting her with any secrets; she was just uninformed, he decided. Elric stepped beside her, mimicked her stance and gazed into the night as did Margaret.

"King William, who killed our king and took our country, had three sons living. Robert is eldest, but the weakest. Norman custom is to name a son heir, but he does not have to choose the eldest. Instead, William chose his favorite, his namesake. Robert objected, saying as he was eldest, the kingship should be his. His father bought him off by giving him his old dukedom and his lands in Normandy. Robert is weak, incompetent, a spender. He would have ruined our country, sold our assets and worse. Robert's brother, King William Rufus, gave Robert ten thousand marks in exchange for his title and estates in Normandy so Robert could leave on the Grand Crusade with much coin. He returned from Acre after he learned King William Rufus had died. To get home, he had to stop and marry a foreign woman from a place called Conversano near a port named Bari in order to have enough coin to reach Normandy. Her dowry got them home and left him enough to build a small army. The man is always running out."

So that is why he must have an heir. They heard the cow lowing in the stable. The cock crowed in response. "Why did the king ask you if the Saxons knew? Knew what?"

"We Saxons have a saying: 'Know where they are and live.'"

"Because …?"

"Because in the first ten years of the Conquerer's rule, every man who had fought with our king and survived was found and executed. The Normans murdered Saxons for any offense, real or imagined, or on a whim. They burned our crops for spite; many starved to death. Some fled to other lands, even as far as Constantinople. We lost a third of our people."

Where is Constantinople? "So you keep track of all Normans."

Elric nodded.

"To stay out of their way."

"Our safety and our lives depend on knowing where the Normans are and what they are planning, doing."

"What is the Charter of …?"

"Liberties. An agreement between Saxon leaders and Henry when he was still a prince. After we regained certain rights, we agreed to support Henry's claim to the throne and not to rebel."

"Do you still support him?"

"We warned the Normans Robert had landed."

Fears somewhat allayed, Margaret left for her bed. She changed her mind and strode to a small pen next to the stable. *Coming along. I pray I am not also penned for slaughtering. He must win. He must. Oh God, Your will in all things. I pray it is for King Henry's success. If all goes well, I will live and you piglets might be big enough for the Christmastide banquet.* The piglets were bigger than they had been, but still too small to consume. Margaret counted months on her fingers. *Halfway to Christmastide already. Must get you more food. If we must flee, I will return the cow, pigs and chickens. The boys can do it.*

Elric watched his mistress scratch a pig's back before climbing back into the keep. He had almost told her the Saxons had rushed the news to the Earl of Warwick the same time they had raced to the king. Elric had not told her of the Norman lords who supported Robert's claim to the throne, nor of the army of men they had provided him. He paced the wall all night, fearing a Saxon would arrive and report the king's defeat—or worse, his death in battle.

Margaret crept into her place, now beside the queen, and lay as still as she could. Her mind rushed here and there, unable to keep a thought and unwilling to settle enough to let Margaret sleep. *What do I tell her? Nothing. Mayhap she already knows. Talking about it will do no good. Her worrying might harm the babe. Lose the babe. How to transport her? On Night? No, too dangerous. How far is Scotland? Will she keep us or abandon us once she reaches home? May I take Night with me? Cannot abandon him. Will not.*

Margaret's rush of thoughts and worries kept her awake until almost dawn. Between worries she prayed for the king's safety and for his success. She prayed hard. Finally, too exhausted to continue, she squeezed her eyes shut, thought *Your will, O Lord, in all things* and collapsed into a short, light sleep.

12

Routines

A week later the women had finished sewing the garments. They had washed and sun bleached the old clothes. Margaret's former Sunday gunna was now Caitlin's new daily one. Away from the queen, the women admired each other's new outfits and complimented each other on how well they looked.

"Your Majesty, now that you have broken your fast, we can take our morning stroll around the hall."

"If you insist."

"The ladder is dangerous for you and the yard is still muddy from the rain." Margaret tried to entice the queen. "I hope you will ask me questions as we walk."

The queen rose. "How came you to acquire that fine black? Night, is it not?"

Margaret started with her grandfather, who had bought the Percheron for his son. "Uncle Robert died young and then Mother was Grandfather's only heir. She spoiled Night, 'ruined him,' I was told Grandfather said. He gave Night to her as a wedding gift. Lord Charles and Night did not get along. I do not know why."

Margaret regaled the queen with stories of her growing up around the gelding. She tossed her head to imitate her horse, and the queen laughed. Margaret had found the queen so weak and out of good condition the royal had to work to keep even the slow pace Margaret had set. Margaret kept talking so the queen would keep walking.

"Time to turn and 'unwind' now, Your Majesty. Father—Lord Charles—promised to teach me to ride when I became six. My birthing date passed. He ignored my pleas. Young Charles was five and already learning. One day my brother teased me and said I would never be taught. I mounted Night before he could and rode him around the bailey. Father was furious. He yanked me off Night and beat me right there in the snow. Mother pulled him off me and defended me. After dinner she brought me before him and swore to him that I had not been 'ruined.' At the time I had no idea what she meant. I had the effrontery to remind him of his promise. He agreed to teach me to ride only if I promised to ride using a woman's riding platform like a proper lady the rest of my life. I promised. He taught me on an old nag, not Night, but at least I learned to ride."

"How old is Night?"

"Twenty."

"The age at which I married His Highness."

"That old!" Margaret stopped. "I am so sorry, Your Majesty." She started strolling again. "Why did your family wait so long?"

"I will not answer your question today. You have not yet told me how you came to get Night. You may finish the tale during our walk before we sup."

Margaret chuckled at the queen's pun. "Yes, Your Majesty. I promise it will be a short one."

Queen Matilda laughed as she headed for her needlework

basket. The women settled onto the stone benches on each side of an east arrow slit. On a shirt for the king, the queen was embroidering his crest on the cuffs with the thinnest wool thread Margaret had ever seen. Margaret wondered at its cost. She used heavy woolen thread to mend clothes for the men guarding them.

After dinner the queen took her nap. Before the group supped, Margaret walked with the queen and finished her story. She told the queen that her mother had bequeathed Night to her before she died. Margaret omitted using Night and her mother's mantle and scarf as revenge against her lord. She did not tell the queen of Jorgon's or his father's parts in protecting her and haunting Lord Charles after his misdeeds. She did tell the queen of scaring Lord William out of half his wits.

"I want to see Night's tricks."

"I fear climbing down the ladder may be dangerous, Your Majesty."

"I will stand in the doorway to watch."

"Night will enjoying showing you what he can do."

After the demonstration the next day, the queen and Margaret again walked the hall.

"Please tell me how you came to wait until you were twenty to marry." *Have I time still to make a good match?*

The queen related a long story of her betrothed dying, of her many suitors afterward and of her refusal of them all. When she talked of her betrothed's death, her pace slowed and her voice cracked twice. Then she stiffened her spine, picked up her pace and related why she had refused each suitor. She omitted her meeting Prince Henry, his promise to wed her, and her six-year wait in a convent before marrying a king and becoming a queen. Margaret was pleased the queen was showing more emotion than she had and was friendlier, but she would be cautious. She recalled other women carrying babes and their strong, sudden swings of emotions, happy then sad, content to irate, and worse. Margret wondered if the queen would be sorry she had shared her feelings; she decided to keep their conversations light and pleasant.

While the queen napped, Margaret strolled the walkway around the walls to breathe fresh air. Elric accompanied her. He told her the queen was half Scot from her father, the King of Scotland, and half Saxon from her mother who was a princess.

"If she ever gets sad about being here, ask her to tell the story of how her father became King of Scotland. It is quite a tale and she loves to tell it."

"Thank you, I shall remember. By my count we will be here till February, a long time." *Distracting her, keeping her interested gets more difficult every day.*

They walked until the smatterings of rain threatened to become a downpour. Elric escorted Margaret to the ladder. "Please try to stay more often after we sup. I am cert the queen enjoys your company. She likes your singing and the Saxon tales the men tell."

Elric bowed. "I thank you, Lady Margaret. I shall." He held the bottom of the ladder as Margaret climbed it.

Six days after the king's departure, his messenger sat on his horse outside the gate and reported first to Elric on the parapet walkway. Elric sent for Margaret so she too would hear the invasion had been stopped.

"His Royal Highness made a treaty with his brother at Alton. He sends his good wishes to Her Royal Highness and promises to visit as soon as he has re-secured the allegiances of his barons and earls."

Immediately, Margaret reported to the queen and repeated the message exactly as she had heard it. The queen nodded and looked away. After Margaret left her, Matilda stood and disappeared behind the fireplace for the rest of the afternoon.

Margaret took up embroidering her wedding rib. *I hope come spring that I shall be able to sew it on my bliaut for my marriage ceremony before the church door. Already we seem to have been here so long a time and yet Michaelmas is two whole months away. I pray His Royal Highness returns soon. She needs to see him to assure him she and their babe are safe.*

13

Surprise

By the end of August, despite several letters from the king and all Margaret's efforts to keep the queen entertained, Matilda's mood had soured. She complained about her daily walks, the lack of variety in her meals, her clothes starting to reveal her belly, the heat, how long the days were, and so much more. Of an afternoon, she and Margaret sat beside a west arrow slit sewing but not speaking.

"My lady, I think you should look at your horse."

Margaret's head snapped up from her sewing.

"Your Majesty?"

At the queen's nod, Margaret jumped up and dropped her work on the bench. The queen bent her head to her needlework. The girl charged across the room and down the stairwell, peppering Elric with questions about Night all the way.

At the foot of the ladder Margaret paused to search for the least muddy path to the stable.

"He is fine. Fine," repeated Elric. "I had to get you out of the keep without the queen knowing someone is at the gate."

"Who?"

Elric dared take her elbow and direct her to the parapet ladder closest to the main gate.

"This is serious, Lady Margaret. If the queen learns of him, he may gain entrance, breach our fortress."

That galvanized Margaret's attention.

"Her confessor from Court, two clerics, and six warrior priests, well armed, escorting them. The priest insists on seeing the queen."

"Did you not inform him the king himself sealed us inside?"

"I tried. But I am only a Saxon. He dismissed me and demanded to see the one authorized to keep him from Her Majesty. He threatened to excommunicate us all if we refuse them entry. Too many. Too dangerous."

They climbed the ladder. The four guards walking the parapet stopped where they could be seen from below so those trying to gain entrance would think there were more guards than they already saw. Margaret nodded approval at their strategy before she stepped forward.

Forewarned, Margaret stepped to the merlins left of the main gate and leaned between them to see the party below. She began in her most humble tone.

"Most Reverend Father, I am the Lady Margaret, who serves the queen. How may I serve you?"

"Child, you may serve me by letting us inside at once."

"Alas, dear Father, I cannot." Margaret sounded both sincere and grieved to deny him. "By the king's direct order, we are forbidden to op this gate to anyone but him. Do you precede His Royal Highness?"

"No-o," said the priest. "I think not." He began anew, "I am her confessor. I have come all the way from Winchester out of my great love for our queen."

"Ah-h-h! You too love Her Royal Highness." Margaret showed him her hands palms up as a gesture of understanding. "The king will soon arrive. Only he can hear your petition to visit the queen. She has a priest who attends her. I am cert Lord Richard, who lives down that road, will host your party while you await His Royal Highness."

"Woman, you have no power to keep me from Queen Matilda! Open this gate at once or face the wroth of the Church's authority!"

"You are right, Your Grace." Margaret raised his rank from priest to bishop. "I have no power. The king has given neither me nor anyone else here the power unbar the gate. Only the king may do that." When Margaret saw one of the clerics leaning toward the priest, she stopped him with, "Father, do you intend to excommunicate His Royal Highness, the king?"

"What? Of course not!"

Margaret sucked her lips between her teeth to hide her smile. *Ha! Startled you.* "As you have heard me say, I have no power. I can only direct you to the Lord Richard's estate until the king arrives. I am cert His Royal Highness will be very interested to know why you have come." Margaret let her implied threat hang in the air.

"You will not open this gate?"

"I cannot. The king has forbidden it. You must see him." Before the priest could make other demands, Margaret intoned a respectful, "God's good day, Your Grace, to you and all your party." Then she ducked behind the wall to descend the ladder.

Elric followed her.

"Instruct men to yell at each other, sing, something. I do not want the queen to hear him should he bellow her name."

Elric called to the men guarding the gate, "Noise."

"May I see Night now?"

141

They ignored the yelling and loud talk on their side of the gate and the noisy departure beyond the gate as they climbed down the ladder and picked their way to the stable.

"Elric, Elstan, Elborg. Why is every Saxon here an 'el' something?"

"Family tradition. In our clan all our names start with 'el.'"

"You are all related?"

"Most of us are cousins, some close, some distant."

"How strange," was all Margaret thought to say. Later, Margaret returned to her duties.

"Well?" asked the queen.

"He will be fine. I ordered Jorgon to give Night more water. Night also needs more exercise than walking in the bailey, so I adjusted his food. I will need to see to him for the next few days to supervise."

"Who was at the gate?"

Margaret maintained her composure. "Elric reported a party of knights errant were seeking Lord Richard's estate. I peeked at them for excitement."

"M-m-m." The queen poked her needle into her work. She added, "I suppose if it had been company to entertain me, His Royal Highness would not have wanted us to let them enter." She sighed. "Ah well, I must do with who I have."

"The light seems to have moved. Would you like to walk now, Your Majesty?"

A few days later, Elric reported to Margaret the king was now chasing those who had conspired with the king's brother, Lord William de Warenne, Baron Robert de Belleme, and several other landholders.

"Should we tell Her Royal Highness?" he asked.

"Definitely not! If she worries, she may lose the babe. The king must have his heir. Trust the king to defeat him. Pray for it; I shall. Keep me posted. We can be away to Scotland anon if they meet and the king falls."

"And we can hide her all the way there."

Margaret knew he meant the Saxons. "Please plan for it. Then pray we do not need it."

14

Secrets

On September 25, the king arrived and announced he had routed the traitor's army and had banished de Warenne, Earl of Surrey. He was in Normandy at Sir Robert's court. Henry informed his wife he had to be in Winchester three days hence for Michaelmas. He could only stay the night. After they had supped, the royals sat next to each other on one side of the fireplace. The arms of their chairs touched, and Henry's hand rested over hers. They smiled at each other, leaned toward each other and whispered. Henry spoke first; Matilda nodded often. When Matilda spoke, Henry pursed his lips and only nodded once; he waited until she stopped before responding. Soon the king called Margaret to them. At the king's instruction she fetched a stool and sat opposite the royals.

What is wrong? Something is wrong.

Matilda offered her unwanted posset to Margaret, who took it more out of politeness than desire. After a sip, Margaret looked up to compliment the queen on her spice mixture. When the king spoke, Margaret closed her lips.

"Lady Margaret, in my travels I had occasion to pass near your father's estate."

They know about Jorgon and Dena. They are going to send them back. Nervously fingering the pewter goblet, Margaret asked, "Did you stop there, Your Royal Highness?" She hoped using formality might assuage any anger.

"No, but I heard stories."

Margaret put her lips to her cup as she prayed they would not ask about the pair. She watched the king shift in his chair and throw a leg over the outer arm. His studied casualness fooled her not. "Please tell us why your father made your marriage contract null."

Surprised at the topic, Margaret lowered the cup and stared at the royals before beginning her tale. "In 1099, Mother and Lord Charles attended your brother's Easter Court in Gloucester. While there, Mother met a friend she had not seen in years. She had a son seventeen. I was twelve. They decided, my son, your daughter, and sent their husbands together to write the contract. The other father was a very good bargainer, for he convinced Lord Charles to agree to a greater dowry than he intended. He signed the contracts anyway. Once my parents arrived home, they argued. I heard Mother say she had made an excellent match. Young Charles and Raymond would make powerful friends. Then she said, 'With that family's connection, your precious Cecily might make an even better match than Margaret. Her sister will introduce her to the right people.'"

Margaret paused, guessed the king already knew what she was relating, and decided to be frank about the matter. "That was the problem, you see. Cecily was his pet, not me. If it had been Cecily's contract, he would not have balked at twice as much. They continued to fight over my marriage. When I asked when I would be sent to my husband's household, Mother said she wanted a little more time with me, 'after the summer.' If I had left that week, I would be a wife now." Margaret's shoulders drooped. She stared into the fire.

"Then what happened?" Matilda asked in a soft voice.

"Several days later, Mother fell ill. Not she, nor Caitlin, nor I could be cert why." Margaret looked up to the persons to whom she could make her case. They had the power to right wrongs. *Dare I tell? Will you believe me? Will the poison I buried be enough evidence? Can I even find it again? What proof have I of his poisoning his bedmate Fearn? He would say I lie for revenge. He could say I poisoned the girl. Whom would you believe? Which one of us would die? Cert not a lord.*

Margaret looked up from the cup she held. She saw they expected her to continue so she again put on her public face. "Within the week, Mother knew she was dying. She called me to her bed and bequeathed me things. Night first. Her blue mantle, scarf, and gloves, two rings, her silver-handled hair brush. I cried and begged her to stop. I promised her she would get well. She said, 'No, I will not.'" Margaret stopped. She dared not reveal her mother claimed to have been poisoned by her father over the marriage contract. Close to tears, Margaret recalled her mother's death throes, her cries while holding her stomach and begging God to take her, the flickering candles, the smell of sickness. *The worst day of my life. Always will be no matter what else may befall me.* "She died that night." Margaret stuffed a fist into her mouth to stop her tears.

The king and queen watched with great sympathy as Margaret slowly regained self control. Each had lost a much-beloved mother, but theirs had died of natural causes. They suspected Margaret's had not. They shared silent looks.

"We are so very sorry," said the queen.

"Thank you for your kindness." Margaret's chin quivered. Then she wiped away her tears. *My grief is not a public matter.* "You asked about my broken marriage contract?" At the king's nod, she finished. "Two weeks later, Lord Charles called everyone into the hall. He announced he and the other earl had nullified my marriage contract by mutual agreement. Cook demanded to know why. He had sent a message to the other family that I had lain with a villein. Given the rumors, did they still want me? He was still willing to send me to them."

Margaret closed her eyes. *How could he accuse Jorgon?* Then she opt them and finished. "Caitlin hollered, 'That is a lie and you know it! I am her nurse and would know such a thing. She never has! I can prove it!'"

'Too late!' he shouted. 'They have cancelled the contract."

"'And you got back your coins, just as you planned!'" accused Cook.

He threw the torn contracts into the fire pit. Then he grabbed my head and took out his dagger. Several men rushed forward. They told me later that they thought he was going to slit my throat."

Margaret stopped. "I wish he had. That would have been easier."

"No, no, Margaret," said Matilda. "I am grateful he did not. I would not have you here. I need you, you know."

Margaret suspected the queen had said that because she was useful to the couple. *No real kindness there, just the expectation of good service.* "Thank you, Your Majesty," Margaret responded in a tone she hoped sounded grateful. Without realizing she had done so, Margaret had slipped into the familiar mode the queen requested she use only when they were alone. The queen did not correct her. Margaret hurried through the rest. "He cut off my braid and threw it after the contracts. He renamed me and told me I deserved to be no better than a villein because I had lain with one. He ordered me to take up being a servant and his chatelaine." Margaret omitted being beaten and the rest.

"You may still have the marriage if you want it, Lady Margaret."

"I beg your pardon, Your Royal Highness?"

The king repeated the offer and explained. "The young man's wife recently died in childbirth. The babe as well. As an heir, he must marry to hold the estate. I can ask him to honor his first contract falsely broken. What say you to this?"

Margaret furrowed her brow at him.

"As king, I approve every noble marriage. If you want this match, I will order it done."

The royals watched as Margaret's stood and slipped the poker into the embers until it was red. Margaret dropped one knee, plunged the brand into the wine and set the poker against the stone to her right. After she sat, she lightly sipped the drink so as not to burn her lips. She stared at the royals over the cup.

"Your Royal Highnesses, I thank you both mightily for your generous offer, but I think not."

"Why not?" asked the king.

"Several reasons." Margaret stopped to put them in order. "They broke the contract because they thought me a slattern. Even if physicians swear I am still a maid, they will not believe it. They would agree only because you ordered the marriage. They would never forgive me for a forced marriage, and I would suffer. I do not want to live that way. Also, I do not want Lord Charles' goods or coins—or even the contents of my marriage chest." *Cecily has claimed it all for herself. If she has worn Mother's things, I want none of it back.* "When I succeed in this endeavor, I will have earned mine own dowry. I would not marry without your telling a prospective family what Lord Charles did to me. If they want me examined, so be it. They will learn I am pure, that Lord Charles' claims were false. When they agree, it will be because they want me." Margaret faced the queen next. "You married at twenty, Your Majesty, and look what a fine match you made."

The queen smiled and Margaret wondered if she agreed with her remark.

"I will be fifteen in December. I still have time."

The king looked to his lady. "That is what you said she would say and for almost the same reasons. Very well, Margaret, you will have a new match with a good family who wants you." The king handed over his cold, unfinished posset. Margaret heated and returned it.

"Thank you, Your Royal Highness."

"One more question before you go." The king sipped the drink. "Is there anything else you want to tell us?"

Margaret said the words in her head before she spoke them. "The queen may have told you Dena is also with child. Her life and food have been as safe and controlled as is Her Royal Highness's. If you seek a wet nurse for your babe, Dena might do." Margaret knew she dared only inform, not ask. Margaret wondered at the queen's strange look at her idea. The king dismissed her.

After Margaret was out of hearing, the queen whispered, "She had the opportunity and sympathetic ears. Why did she not tell you?"

"I am not sure, my love, but she is still hiding something else. Of that I am cert. I believe the Saxons' stories; they are never wrong. The hostler and Dena are runaways. As long as no one comes to claim them, do nothing. As Lord Charles' bedmate, the girl was probably brought along to save her life. We know she is carrying his brat."

"What of the ghost and hauntings? I thought you were going to accost her."

"No need, my dear. She used her wits to create her mother's ghost, which only appeared when her father beat someone or did something terrible. I was told the hostler and his father helped. That last sighting has the Saxons believing the ghost followed and is protecting Margaret. The girl, the horse, and the hostler are here, so there will be no more trouble."

"I wonder what else she is hiding."

The king looked after Margaret's departure and then at his wife. "No matter at this time, my dear. She takes excellent care of you." He paused to stroke his wife's hand. "I will give you the short sword she wants."

Matilda snorted, "It is unnatural, a woman touching a sword, much less using it. Even if it is to protect me."

"I know, my dear, but you dare not touch a man's weapon and risk our heir. As she is the only Norman here, she is the only one who can even pick it up without incurring a death sentence. Besides, it amuses me to think of a woman acting the man. No harm done if only Saxons see her. She is a fierce little thing, and she will protect you fiercely. Her life depends upon it."

"As you wish, my husband."

"You may give her the short sword after I leave, but touch only the sheath."

Matilda reminded Henry she needed coins to pay everyone on Michaelmas. He told her his money bag was with his things at their bedside and asked her to remind him to give her the coins she needed before they went abed. Henry patted Matilda's hand.

"You know, I have not seen you this content … and pink and healthy… since that day I spotted you running barefoot in the meadow. How long ago?"

She frowned as if she had to figure it then smiled back at him.

"Ages ago. Eight years… I think."

They both knew how long ago they had met—to the day.

Matilda laughed.

Henry lifted his wife's hand and kissed the back of her fingers. "My Aegdyth, you are even more beautiful now than you were then."

Henry stood. Matilda pushed herself out of her chair. Hand in hand they disappeared around the fireplace.

15

Dull Days

On Michaelmas, after the queen had paid each person his or her wage, she and Margaret walked.

"His Majesty and I are creating a new race," began Matilda. "We will join the Norman race with the Saxon race and create a new one. We call it 'English.' Soon only the English race will live in England."

Margaret tried to hide her shock with a question. "Your Majesty, how can this happen? We are totally separate peoples, different languages, lands, and customs."

"Through marriage between Norman and Saxon. Their children will be the new race. We have already begun. Elric has asked me to intercede to the king because he wants to wed Aurore, daughter of a Norman lord. As she is only a third daughter, the king has agreed to send a letter to the lord giving royal permission for the match."

"A letter of permission from His Royal Highness is as much an order as permission?" guessed Margaret.

"Margaret, I like that you are both quick and clever."

"May I ask another question?" At the queen's nod, Margaret chose her words carefully. "I lack understanding, Your Majesty. A man's seed is a tiny babe. He plants it into his wife. She grows it big enough to be birthed. She is just the carrier."

"Not so, Margaret. We Saxons know a babe seed can gain something from the mother. We know not how, but either a boy or girl babe can have its mother's eye color or hand shape and such." The queen added, "Of course, whether you birth a boy or girl stays the same. The babe starts as a boy unless the mother is too overbearing and her strength cuts off his male parts and turns the babe into a girl."

I wonder if that is true. Is that a man's excuse for having given her a girl seed at the first? Birthing a girl can deprive a man of an heir; now he can blame his wife for birthing a girl instead of taking responsibility for having given her that girl seed. If so, then the king would be responsible for her birthing a girl. Do not ask questions. Say nothing. Margaret nodded a silent agreement, and the queen switched to a new topic as they walked.

The weeks dragged. Leaves had changed to brilliant reds, oranges and golds before they fell. Tempers flared more often; feelings were more easily hurt. One morning the ladies were asked to sit on a bench in the middle of the hall. Elric requested they keep their eyes closed no matter what noises the men made. When the queen demanded to know what was going to happen, Elric promised her a pleasant surprise. Elric and his men made scraping and other noises as they were obviously moving the trestles, boards and benches about the room.

When Margaret opt her eyes, she squealed. They were surrounded by a maze of benches, trestles upright or on their sides and table boards leaning this way and that. The men challenged the queen to walk her way out of the maze without moving or going over or under any of the barricades. The queen sat a long time looking at the jumble of wood; Margaret waited for her. After repeatedly being blocked and doubling back, the queen stomped her foot and glared at the men.

"Show me the exit!"

"Your Royal Highness," Elric bowed low, "one man walked the maze and gained exit before you opt your eyes. Surely, two ladies could match his wit."

Elric picked up two mugs of cider from the head table and walked to the end of the course. With that hint, the queen and Margaret soon joined him and received their prizes. Elric won a kiss on the cheek from a cheerful queen.

"You are a dear one, Elric, to find a new way to entertain me. You have my thanks."

Margaret was so grateful for Elric lifting the queen's mood she was tempted to kiss him as well. Despite the men's teasing, Margaret shook her head. "It would not be proper."

"Come now, Margaret, one kiss but only on the cheek. I shall supervise," warned the queen.

Margaret's face colored several shades as she lightly pecked Elric.

"You can tell she is a maid. She lacks skill to kiss!" said one man.

The queen replied, "And none of you will teach her. That is only her husband's office."

The queen dismissed the men, who fetched the women's wraps from their starting point. Matilda and Margaret enfolded themselves into their warm, woolen shawls and walked around the edges of the maze as the Saxons returned the jumble of wood to upright trestles with board tops and benches beside each table. The remainder of the queen's day was a happy one despite the chill emanating from the stone walls.

"Caitlin, in the three months we have been here, I have heard more singing, more music played and more stories told than ever I heard before. I remember none of this at home. Why is that?"

Caitlin stopped swirling water and starter into the flour and grains and thought for a moment. "You were four, Young Charles, three, and Raymond two. Late August. A severe wind storm broke off many ripe heads of grain. It was followed by days of rain. Ruined most of the harvest. Then an icy winter. Your…Lord Charles and your mother knew we would all starve before the next harvest."

"Was that when mother started midwifery—to gain coin for grain?"

Caitlin nodded.

"She and Lord Charles went to Christmas Court in Winchester. They took our minstrel to help him find work elsewhere and her lyre, cittern, and one other instrument, the name I remember not, to sell for grain. While there, my lady helped a local woman give birth, a breech delivery. When both lived, her reputation was made. Norman ladies of rank hired her; she was gone from estate to estate until after Easter.

"Lord Charles came home with grain from the sale of the instruments. When Lady Rosamonde returned with even more coin from her services than he had made selling the instruments, they argued about her getting at least a lyre. They started fighting then.

"He had promised to buy her new instruments and get a new minstrel when they were again prosperous. He never did. He punished her for leaving often and earning coins by refusing her a household minstrel. He forbade song and story and the hall went silent. She left as often as she was asked for and took you along. Your family started splitting apart then. A pity."

"And they never stopped arguing?"

"Never act proud at doing better than your husband—at anything. Men like it not."

Milch pail in hand, Dena walked up the stairs, and the conversation turned to how much the cow had given. As the rainy, gray days continued, keeping the queen's spirits high was more difficult. She was bored. She tired easily and slept. The king did not visit. She refused another offer of a maze. Margaret consulted Elric; they made plans. After the men had supped, they stayed in the hall, but none sang or offered to tell a tale.

"Please tell us how your father came to be King of Scotland, Your Majesty," asked Margaret with pride that now all used that title. *She has softened despite her dark moods.*

"Yes. Do," chimed Elric as he waved the other seven men not on guard duty to reseat themselves.

The men looked eager and mouthed agreements.

"You see, Your Majesty. You have a willing audience."

The queen made a dismissing motion to the men. "Everyone knows that story."

"We do not," spoke the women together.

"I have not heard it," said Eldene.

"Nor I," said another.

"Please do so," coaxed Father Gregory. "A new tale will entertain us all."

"Very well, Father, because you asked."

Caitlin and Dena cleared the head table and set a pewter goblet of watered wine before the queen. The queen straightened her shoulders and adjusted her leg robe.

"Malcolm the Second, King of Scotland, died without living sons. My grandfather, Duncan the First, was his grandson. Grandfather had been elected king because of his prowess in battle and his negotiating skills. The highlanders, who chose to live their old ways deep in the high hills of the north country, treated those living near the English border with disgust and called them 'lowlanders.' Grandfather preferred to live among the lowlanders because he admired their modern ways." Queen Matilda dripped hatred with her next words. "In 1040 Anno Domini the evil Macbeth killed my grandfather so he could be king. My father and his brother fled the country to save their lives and lived in northern England until they could attack the usurper."

In detail Matilda told of her father's seventeen years of adventures, courage, suffering and struggles and of her uncle's support of his older brother. "Finally in 1057, Siwald, Earl of Northumbria, gave my father the men and arms he needed. Father marched over the North Wall into his homeland. He killed Macbeth in a battle near Lumphanan and became the next Scots king, the right one." She spoke with great vigor in defense of her family and her father's rule. Then the queen's face fell, "Father and his eldest son, my brother Edward, died in 1093 in a battle at Alnwick. Mother was too grief stricken to live. She died a week later."

When they saw the queen again fading, Father Gregory asked, "How did you come to live with us, Your Royal Highness?"

The queen looked up to see a still-eager audience.

"A civil war. I went to my mother's family for safety" was all Matilda said before she looked down and lapsed into silence and memory.

"We heard you met His Majesty when you were in a meadow and he was not yet the king. You were running barefoot and chasing novitiates," teased Elborg.

The queen blushed. "True." Then she added, "I ran all the way into the convent to escape him. He followed me and asked who I was."

The queen turned to Margaret. "I was fourteen when I met him. My brother, Donald the Third, King of Scotland, tried to marry me off, but I refused. I would have waited a lifetime for my lord. Six years was long enough!"

The men applauded and cheered their queen. They respected her deeply held religious habits, stern though they sometimes were. They watched over her and tried to lift her spirits. They loved her for her kind and gentle ways. Now they praised her for diverting them past bedtime.

"Well done, my queen, for the best storytelling we have had. Do promise us more."

"Not tonight, Elric. I am done. Now off to bed, all of you."

Behind Matilda's back, Elric winked at Margaret. Everyone readied for bed. Margaret sent Caitlin and Dena to their bed and supervised the banking of the fire. At the queen's bedside, Margaret undid the queen's braids, shook out her hair and brushed it until it looked like shining spun gold. She helped Matilda undress and watched her climb under the coverings. As she said her own evening prayers, she doffed her bliaut and shoes and slipped under the covers wearing her chemise and socks. Since the king's first departure, the queen had requested her company. The queen rolled to Margaret and gave her a sisterly kiss on the cheek. "Thank you, Margaret. You have tonight reminded me His Majesty and I are not the only royals who struggle to keep our crowns, steady a nation, and plan its future. I know you arranged their request. You are a dear one!" The queen rolled back toward the fireplace stones and curled up under the heavy pile of blankets and the mink bed throw.

Margaret smiled in the dark and did not move until she heard the queen's steady breathing. Then she rolled outward and touched the short sword on the floor. *I doubt we fool you regarding anything, my queen.* Margaret closed her eyes.

16

Dangerous Misstep

On her return from scavenging for roots, Margaret dismissed her guards, petted Night and rewarded him with a dried apple. She left the stable and climbed the keep ladder. With one hand she pulled up the front of her mantle and skirts. She held a full basket in the other. King Henry saw her head in the stairwell and stood. Both royals noted her hair was in disarray from the wind and her cheeks flushed from the cold.

"Your Royal Highness, how good … "

"Put that down. Come hence!" ordered King Henry with eyes flashing.

Margaret looked to the queen and found no pity. She prayed she would be able to use the explanations she had prepared. Margaret stopped out of the king's reach and froze in a curtsey.

"No false obedience, girl. You have treated my queen like a villein. Why? Rise and answer!" roared Henry.

Margaret did so. Her eyes betrayed her confusion. "Your Royal Highness, I am at a loss. I am giving Her Royal Highness my total attention. She is my greatest concern. I am giving her the best of care."

"Best of care!" thundered the king.

Caitlin and Dena had already disappeared behind the fireplace; Garnyd and Ordson had followed them. The men below stayed there.

"You force her to make bread as if she were a servant. When she refused, you told her she will not eat unless she makes bread. You will not treat my queen in this manner!"

"No, Your Royal Highness." Margaret's voice shook.

The king sat beside his wife and patted her hand. "There, there, my dear. All is well again."

Margaret stayed frozen in place until she saw Matilda's smug look abate. Margaret spoke just above a hush. "Please Your Royal Highness, would you be so kind as to place your hand over your babe?"

"Why?" he demanded.

"To show you why I asked Her Royal Highness to make bread." Henry looked at his wife before he did so. Margaret addressed the queen. "If it please Your Royal Highness, would you please tighten your stomach muscles as hard as you can?"

The queen reluctantly did so and looked surprised. She repeated her action. Then she gave her husband a small smile.

"Why is this special?" he asked.

"Your Royal Highness, last month she could not do that. When I examined her four weeks ago, her stomach was already sagging from the weight of the babe. When the babe gets heavier, I feared she may miscarry it."

Margaret had their full attention now. *Regain their trust or die. I must succeed. What words will convince them and save me? Oh Lord, be my strength and tell me what to say. Breathe. Breathe. Dear God, let my every breath be a prayer. Your will in all things.*

"Your Royal Highness, I have seen this before. Women who do not wait between children often have muscles that sag. Sometimes they lose the next one. I understand the need to hurry, but doing so does put this babe in danger."

Margaret looked toward the queen but only so far as her hands in her lap. "Your Royal Highness, when I met you, you lacked the strength to walk for any length of time. At first, I thought having you walk briskly twice each day would be enough. After you started showing, I saw you sitting on the bed. Your stomach already touched the covers instead of your babe riding high under your heart. I needed a new way to strengthen you. Now you pull your muscles around the babe, and it is riding high where should be."

The queen pouted. "You might have told me what I was doing."

"I did, Your Royal Highness. I was also pointing at the babe when I said it."

"I do not remember that part." The queen frowned petulantly.

"Well, Your Royal Highness, you are modest. I may not say 'with child' or even 'babe' when men are about. Perhaps I spoke too softly." Margaret took a deep breath and risked her life again. She looked toward the king. "Your Royal Highness, may I relate how I did it?"

He sighed. "In all fairness, I suppose I should hear your side." Henry leaned back into his chair.

"I started by asking for her help. I gave her a quarter batch of dough, took a quarter myself, and gave Dena the other half. We stood on either side of Her Royal Highness and showed her how to knead the dough. She pushed her fingers into her loaf to mark it. We called it 'the queen's round.' The men begged for hers because her rounds are so light. She is a good baker. Truly. Soon I increased the ball to half, then three quarters, then a full ball. The men are eating prodigious amounts of bread, so we appreciated the queen's help. Sometimes the queen was in a good mood. When she was not, she worked the dough so well the bread was even lighter. Those times, Your Royal Highness, I believe you pretended the dough was my head."

"Sometimes it was."

"Just as the babe started lifting, Her Royal Highness decided to stop. I could not let her do that. When I tried to reason with her and failed, I made my threats. I would not have carried them out, Your Royal Highness. I swear I would not have."

"So you forced her to make bread. You used her foul moods against her for her own good."

Margaret nodded. To the queen she curtsied and gave an honest apology. "I am deeply sorry to have offended you, Your Royal Highness. I regret causing you any pain or sorrow. But I must tell you honestly, Your Royal Highness, if I had to do it over again, I would. You know how strong you must be—all over—to carry this babe to its full size. You know what it is to give birth. I was trying to get you ready the best way I know how."

The king cocked his head toward Margaret. "So you march her like a soldier and work her like a villein."

"There. You have me, Your Royal Highness. I have revealed my secret."

"How so?"

"A Saxon with child works hard. She cooks, cleans, grinds grain for bread, carries water and small children, bends, stoops, rests a bit, rises and starts again. She is more likely to birth a strong, healthy babe than a lady of rank who sits all day and is coddled. No fine, white bread for her. A villein eats good brown bread. Lots of it."

Margaret's last comment was for the queen, who had complained of the lack of that luxury food. She took a deep breath and tried again to save herself. *He had come looking Mother. Mayhap mentioning Mother will help my cause.*

"Mother, the Lady Rosamonde, taught me that every woman with child thinks she is the only one in the world to suffer as she does. We tell each one she is unique and have designed a special treatment for her. Then we treat her like all the others. For strength of lungs, legs, and stomach, we walked them twice a day. For healthy bodies and babes, we fed them like villeins. Now that you know what to do, you need us no longer."

Please God. Let him dismiss me, not execute me. Dismiss us all so I may save them from his wroth.

Without speaking, the king and queen looked at each other and decided. King Henry addressed his subject. "Yes, we do. You care for my queen and divert her. In the night if a noise startles you, you reach for the short sword. One night a guard dropped something. You jumped out of bed and came round the fireplace ready to behead him. During the day you wear the sword. Her Majesty has seen you put your hand to its hilt and stand between her and the stairs until you see the head of the person coming up them. You make her do what she must at the risk of her wroth." The king said the last part slowly and with feeling. "You take as good care of her as I would were I here. For that, I am grateful."

I am still alive. *I am still wanted. Thank you, God. Now I must re-win her favor. Please God, help me do so.*

The king took his wife's hand and looked into her eyes. Still lovingly gazing at his wife, the king issued his ruling. "Margaret, we trust you."

Margaret choked back sudden tears and muttered her thanks. While she dared not touch the king, Margaret burned to show her gratitude. She knelt before the queen, put her head on the queen's lap and hugged her legs.

"Your Royal Highness, I beg you. Please forgive me."

"Margaret, what am I to do with you?" She mussed Margaret's hair even more and lifted her head with both hands and smiled at the girl. "I forgive you."

Margaret beamed at her.

"Now what?"

Margaret's eyes twinkled. "You could let me have my way."

The king threw back his head and roared. The queen playfully tweaked her nose. Margaret again lay her head in the queen's lap and felt a royal hand upon it.

"Well enough, my dearest. In matters regarding your health, I am on her side."

Margaret rose and gave the queen a loving look. "If I may be so bold, Your Royal Highness, may I remind you that it is time for your afternoon walk?"

"But Henry, I am bored beyond my patience! I have nothing to do and no one new. I can bear this no more!"

Margaret waited for King Henry to look her way.

"I agree with Her Royal Highness, but getting her up and down the ladder for outside walking is treacherous. Please tell me what else I may do."

Margaret stepped back to give the royals the room. She walked away facing the royals before giving them her back. Basket in hand, Caitlin joined her at the fireplace.

"Girl, you are good! Your mother always said, 'Nobles are difficult, but royals are impossible.' She would have been proud of you."

Margaret whooshed a great breath as if she had been holding it a long while.

"I still have my head and we still have places." Suddenly hungry, Margaret said, "The stew smells delicious; is that venison?"

Caitlin nodded and replied, "He brought it already dressed. And the vegetables too. I dare not refuse him. For all our sakes, I pray it is safe. Let us add the wild onions you found and hope they kill any possible poison."

"Caitlin, my life was almost forfeit. Mayhap yours. The others too. I forgot to step lightly. That I am not in charge. Do not let me forget again."

"Next time, child, he will not forgive you."

"I know."

They worked to prepare an excellent meal.

17

Changes

The royals supped on delicious venison stew from the deer the king had brought and on the queen's own loaves. They appeared relaxed and amiable. The king called for Elric, Margaret, and Father Gregory to stay and ordered the rest to tarry below. As commanded, Elric closed the trap door. He joined the priest and Margaret at the first trestle table.

Still seated at the head table, the king stretched his legs, clasped his hands behind his head, and leaned back as if he were at ease.

"Which rumor shall I relate first?" The king paused dramatically and glanced at his wife seated beside him. "The queen is dead. I am leaving her body in this keep. You are guarding it with one, two, no six, captive women, each carrying a child. At the right time, they will give birth, and the queen will die in childbirth. I will have everyone here murdered and buried in the forest. I will choose a boy, claim he is mine, and take him to Winchester to be my prince."

Three sets of eyes popped wide in shock. When no one spoke, the king continued.

"Second rumor. The queen is not with child. Several women with her are. At the proper time the queen will pretend to have given birth and will take one of their sons as hers. I will have everyone here murdered to keep her secret."

"Rumor three. Need I continue?" the king demanded more than asked as he pulled in his legs and sat forward over the table. "With almost as many rumors flying about the countryside as we have roads, something new must be done."

No one dare ask the king what. Clearly, he had already set his course. He spoke to them so they could give their approval. With quick silent looks, the three cautioned each other to wait until the king revealed his plan.

"The queen must be seen alive, healthy, and with child. She will again give birth with witnesses present." The king glared at Margaret. "This matter is not about the queen's boredom, girl. I will not have the birth of my son in doubt."

Margaret nodded hard. Twice.

"The question is where? Two principal cities. Which? I am for London. The White Tower is a mighty keep and has high walls to defend us. Many vendors will keep her food supply safer. Her Highness wants Winchester, ancient seat of power, to remind the people of our son's direct line to the Saxon kings. What say you?"

London. Less chance of poisoning. Some protection. Might use poison again. Dead next time. Winchester. Smaller. Easier to spot strangers but fewer vendors. Which set of knights or guards is more loyal?

When Elric realized Margaret would not speak, he did. "Your Royal Highnesses, both cities have their advantages. We have maintained defense of this place well. Now rumors drive us out. Whose plan is that? Whichever city you choose, the queen will be vulnerable. I like this not. May we stay? Will you bring trusted men to see she is with child and have them watch her birth the babe? On roads we could be attacked."

"Men I trust enough to be in her presence are close enough to me to be accused of lying," King Henry countered. "We cannot stay."

Margaret decided to address the queen first. "Your Royal Highness, surely all know your heir's direct line to the throne through yourself to the old Saxon kings and Winchester. Whichever you choose, we must assure your safety." Margaret looked to the king. "Your Royal Highness. We need your queen separate from others. A floor with a door guarded day and night. You have trusted these twelve Saxons. Can they not secure your queen? Caitlin, Dena, and I can continue to cook for the ones behind the door. I trust Elric, Elstan or Eldene or the Saxons you choose to secure safe food. The water supply must be secure too. I am for whichever place keeps Her Royal Highness safest. A fortress within a fortress. Can that be done?"

"Yes."

The king faced Elric. "As to her transport, we will wait for the roads to dry. Every road and stopping place will be secure. On the morrow I am for Warwick for more than enough men." The king took his wife's hand and challenged Elric. "Think you I will risk her?"

"Of course not, Your Royal Highness," Elric backtracked. "But the thought of her leaving here will give me nightmares."

"No worse than mine, boy. No worse than mine."

Margaret pressed the king while he was still in a haunted mood. "Your Royal Highness, on the way will these men and we women remain the queen's inner circle, a circle of protectors within a circle of knights to ensure that no one can reach your lady?"

She watched the king nod without his taking his eyes from his wife.

"I will pray many times a day for your success, Your Royal Highnesses," offered Father Gregory.

Elric raised the trap door and left for guard duty. The others prepared for bed.

As long as the king stays where he belongs, I will sleep. I will keep what good reputation I may still possess. Margaret stepped to settle into the chairs before the fireplace.

"Lady Margaret, I insist you take my cot. I will bed on a trestle table." When Margaret tried to object, Father raised his hand to stop her and added, "I have been living soft for too long. A night on hard boards will remind me."

Accustomed to the guards coming and going, Margaret slept, but she faced the trap door with her sword on the floor below her right hand. At each turn of the guards, she awoke and lifted one eye to be sure of who approached. After Mass the next morning, the royals ate alone. Margaret was serving them when she heard a terrible sound. She dropped the milk pitcher to the table.

"God in Heaven! Someone is torturing a cat!"

The king and queen burst into laughter. Margaret covered her ears. The king laughed even harder. Eldene soon appeared.

"Your Royal Highnesses," the man yelled to be heard. "A party of Scots at the gate. They insist upon seeing the Her Royal Highness."

The screeching sounds died away for a moment, making Eldene appear to be yelling the last bit. The howling resumed, so he yelled again.

"They say they are from King Edgar. They have come to confirm the queen is alive and well. One …Corman, I think, swears he will keep up that caterwauling…

While Eldene took a breath, the royals smiled at each other.

"...until we let him in. In bad Saxon he said, 'Nay go home ,..something...I see me...something.' Then he took out that weapon."

Clearly, Eldene had never heard a bagpipe. but then neither had many of the other southern Saxons.

"Describe him please," ordered the queen as she swayed to music from home.

"Short. Long hair pulled back. Bearded. Bowlegged. Older. Wrapped in a blanket with one end over his shoulder."

"Cormac, my lord. He was my father's seneschal and rocked me to sleep my first night on earth. I have trusted him with my life more than once. Please let him in! It is Cormac!"

"Just Cormac," ordered the king.

Matilda bolted the last of her meal and downed the milk Margaret had poured for her. The noise outside stopped. With a hasty "my lord," Matilda rose and paced in front of the table.

Henry smiled at Margaret. "A diversion. Just as you requested."

"Perfect timing, Your Royal Highness."

Margaret strolled hearthside. *They were outraged yesterday. Now they are happy this morn.* Margaret started to shake her head in disbelief and then stopped herself. *I am safer if I keep away from them.*

The queen rose on tiptoe and called out Cormac's name as his head appeared in the stair pit. She dashed to the old Scot and let him enfold her. Matilda tried to place her head on his shoulder, but she was too tall to do so. The man uttered a stream of strange, harsh-sounding words but in a happy, loving tone.

Matilda pulled Cormac toward her husband. In her happiness she forgot formality.

"Henry, this is Cormac." Then she remembered. "King Henry of England, may I present Cormac, the King of Scotland's emissary."

"Cormac mac Cennedig, Your Royal Highness," said the Scot as he bowed from the waist.

Matilda looked surprised at his words, but she said nothing.

"Welcome, Cormac mac Cennedig. What messages bring you from His Royal Highness, King Edgar?"

"None, Your Royal Highness." Cormac's thick accent made his Norman difficult to understand. "Me king requested I speak with his sister, your queen, because of rumors we have heard." Cormac squeezed Matilda's hand as he looked at her. "Me bairn is alive and well. I am to take word to King Edgar." Cormac released the queen's hand and bowed low. "With your permission, Your Royal Highness."

"Do so. First break your fast. These women will see your men are fed. By my command, no one may enter; they must eat beyond the walls."

Cormac had the good sense not to ask why the king had sealed the keep. "Your Royal Highness, with your permission I will tell me men we have found the queen and she is well and with child." Cormac turned and asked, "How many months, dearie?"

"Six and a bit more."

"You look wonderful, me sweet bairn," said Cormac as he patted the hand he still held.

"Thank you, Cormac."

At the king's nod, Cormac backed away, turned and left the hall.

"I want him to stay."

"As you wish, my dear. But I will not have the whole party stay. Let them return to your brother with whatever information will set his mind at ease." The king paused then added, "I suppose we must

let in one or two men—weaponless and under guard by my men—
to see you and speak with you. I will not risk you on the ladder or
the parapet."

After the Scots ate, men entered the hall, one weaponless pair at
a time, to see the queen. She informed them she was well, in good
health, in good spirits, and protected. The queen greeted each man
warmly and asked after their families. She told each of them how
grateful she was for their coming such a long way on her behalf. The
last Scot reported they would depart at once for home. She asked
him to thank her brother, the king, for his concern. The Scot thanked
King Henry profusely for the supplies he gave them and said farewell
to Cormac. The queen handed over a message Father Gregory had
written for her.

After the last pair of Scots had left the royal presence, Matilda sat
beside her husband for a quiet visit. Always cautious, Henry stayed
the day while several of his men followed the party north. The next
morning Henry left for Lord Warwick's main estate and more men.

18

Scottish Tales

"Give me the news from home, Cormac."

"I have many stories to tell, Your Royal Highness. You walk this time of morning. May I will join you and begin?"

An hour later Caitlin was still kneading bread dough with Dena and Margaret. Caitlin nudged Margaret with her elbow and pointed her head toward the middle of the room. Margaret looked up to see the queen stomping toward them and gesturing while the short-legged Scot was trying to keep up, trying to placate the woman in Scots' words. The queen was spewing Scottish behind as she came toward the work table. With arms akimbo, she halted.

"Duck. Stay down," advised Caitlin.

I will play deaf.

A moment later, the queen appeared at Margaret's side. "Give me some."

Matilda slammed the ball on the table and punched it with such vigor she was likely to kill the yeast and make the dough ball unfit. Margaret signaled Caitlin. In concert, Caitlin slipped a bowl of flour with a well of warm water in the center as Margaret deftly drew the queen's dough ball left and away. The queen did not notice the change until she sloshed water onto her gown. That caused her to stop ranting in Scottish and switch to Norman.

"What am I doing with this?"

"You are stirring the flour into the water and starter, Your Royal Highness." Caitlin dared take the queen's hand and swish it around in the bowl. With each pass the queen's fingers dragged a little more flour into the middle. "Good," said Caitlin as she released Matilda's wrist.

Matilda played until the mixture became a sticky mess. Then she concentrated on turning the flour and water into a usable ball. After dropping the dough on the floured table, Matilda rolled rather than kneaded it. She wiped her hands with a rag and returned to Cormac, who had leaned his shoulder against a wall with his head sagged to his chin. As Matilda approached he righted himself and tried to smile as if all was well with him. The pair resumed their walk, this time at a more measured pace. However, the queen's conversation remained intense. Later Matilda dismissed Cormac, who headed for a distant arrow slit from which to gain fresh air as she returned to the bread table alone. The queen grabbed a ball of dough and kneaded it firmly and steadily for several minutes before she was ready to speak.

"My brother, the king, intends to yield to Magnus' demands!" Margaret frowned.

Matilda explained, "Magnus is a Norse chief, a thief! He took some of the Hebrides—islands to the west of Scotland. Our islands! He planted some of his people on them, claiming the islands are 'their ancient sites.' Hah! Now he wants more of them. I fear Edgar will give into his demands again!" Matilda snorted in disgust as she cut that ball into quarters and covered them to raise. "He is weak! Father would never have yielded even one uninhabitable rock, much less a half dozen choice, occupied islands. When my brother Duncan was king, he would have laughed at the emissary's demands and sent him back to Magnus in pieces. Edgar is going to surrender our islands without a fight! Our people dug wells in solid rock, built houses, started crops, and made the land productive. Father always said, 'A king who will yield even a rock will eventually yield a realm.' He was right! Edgar will lose all of Scotland to those invaders if he is not careful."

While Matilda had been venting, Cormac had snuck to the lower floor, and Margaret had been making bread rounds. She covered them to rise. She gestured toward the open room, a silent invitation for the queen to walk with her.

"Dear God, I wish I were a man!" said Matilda as Margaret walked beside her, guiding her with her body as close as she dared be to the queen's body. "He is a fool! A fool!"

After each time around the hall's perimeter, Margaret slowed their pace. Doing so slowed the queen's fevered enumeration of her brother's faults. The smell of baking bread soothed Margaret but did nothing to ease Matilda. Margaret inhaled deeply each time they passed the fireplace, but she gave up when Matilda did not take the hint. Finally, Matilda stopped halfway down one wall and stared across the room.

"I thank God I married a strong man. Henry will never surrender even an inch of soil. During his reign, every Norman and Saxon will yield to his will—or be dead. He secures the country. I provide the heir." Matilda rubbed her belly and spoke to it. "I will teach you never to surrender what is yours," the queen promised her unborn child. The queen looked up to see Margaret staring at her.

All your explanations of the politics, Court, people, situations were your own thoughts and opinions. I thought you were just mouthing the king's words. You are a pair. You advise him. I never realized you care about all of this as if you will rule. You may rule as a regent if the king dies before your son is a man.

The queen interrupted Margaret's thoughts. "You will not repeat any of this."

"No, no. Never." Margaret curtsied. "Your Royal Highness, what we say on our walks is private. It always has been." *Have I reassured you? Am I safe?*

"Good!" The queen turned on her heel and called down the stair well in Scottish, "Cormac, come here. I want the rest of the bad news now!"

She mumbled "Idiot!" in Norman before she returned to her native tongue. Margaret was glad to escape.

19

Caravan

Both All Souls Day and All Saints Day passed without a word from the king. The first days of November were bright and so cold anyone who ventured outside saw his breath. On their walks Margaret explained her practices of childbirth. The queen described Winchester until Margaret envisioned a clear picture of their destination. Desperate to leave, all awaited word to move. Everyone plunged into depression during two days of hard rain; their spirits began to lift after it stopped.

Three afternoons later a messenger arrived accompanied by men, wagons, two litters, and roundseys. He handed up a sealed document from the king. The Saxons readied their gear. The women prepared to move the contents of the keep. Only the queen slept. Before dawn, the Saxons removed everything from the hall. They packed the foodstuffs last and set their own guard around the wagon. The queen paced with Cormac keeping her company. Before Ordson and Garnig left for the village, they said farewell to the queen. When she gave each two pennies, the boys bowed and swore their eternal love to her.

Queen Matilda looked around the hall now empty but for trestle tables, the old blue cupboard, and the empty cauldrons and pots on either side of the fireplace. "I shall not miss this place," she told Margaret, "but I shall miss our talks as we walked the walls of this prison." Margaret curtsied her thanks. "You have been very good to me, Margaret. I thank you for that."

"It is my honor to serve you, Your Royal Highness, whenever and wherever you desire. I too shall miss our quiet times together." Margaret walked to the stair pit and waited for the queen to depart.

Just as the underside of the sun lifted from the land, the king rode into sight at the head of three hundred knights on their horses, as if they were expecting an attack. They were followed by squires on roundseys and pack animals. Fifty men were to remain to hold the keep.

Saxons led the sets of roundseys carrying two litters into the keep grounds. The king assisted the first veiled woman down the ladder and into the first litter. Elric and Eldene escorted the second veiled woman. Margaret and Caitlin followed.

Margaret approached the ornate queen's litter. She said, "Your Royal Highness" and then poked her head through the curtains to speak to the person within. Any spy or murderer would assume the queen occupied the first litter. Caitlin crawled into the unadorned second litter as Jorgon held Night for Margaret. She rode behind the litters and before the foodstuffs wagon. The twelve Saxons walked before, beside, and behind their formation. They were followed by the queen's goods again traveling with her in wagons that had been left outside the keep walls. More knights followed those wagons. The end of the caravan was a foodstuffs wagon and unknown items roundseys carried. Only after the group had left Forest Keep did the men staying to guard the roads below enter the bailey.

The sky was a sunless gray. No rays poked through. The fields looked wounded with rows of cuts and piles. Dark earth with the stubble from stalks whose heads had been harvested appeared abandoned. No birds sang from the leafless branches. Riders could see far into the trees on each side of the road. The sounds of the group were the creaking of leather saddles, the strike of hooves against the earthen road, and the groaning of the leather harnesses on the roundseys as they gently swung the litters side to side as the ponies proceeded. Margaret heard all that and a few whispers from the knights before and after their section of the train.

At noon Margaret carried cold food from the foods wagon to the litter occupants, who did not leave their covered couches. The party stopped only for food to be passed up the line from the pack animals. She noted the king did not eat. That night only the king, the Saxons, Margaret and the food wagon accompanied the litters into the inn yard. Inside the walls, the Saxons dropped the huge logs that sealed the heavy wooden gate. Knights surrounded the outside walls, ate their suppers over camp fires, and slept upon the ground. Inside the walls, Caitlin and Dena cooked from the wagon contents. Margaret served the royals. The royals ascended the stairs to sleep in rooms Caitlin had prepared. Margaret slept on the inn floor by the fireplace between Caitlin and Dena.

In the morning Dena, dressed in royal garb and veil, again she reclined in the queen's litter. The innkeeper and his family re-entered their business only after the last of the column had disappeared down the road. Each day's routine was the same. The length of each trip was determined by the slow-moving litters and the distances between inns.

Margaret looked down and saw Eldene walking beside her.

"Eldene, who rides beside the king?"

"Sir Henry de Beaumont, Earl of Warwick. He supported King Henry's claim to the throne and is the king's greatest ally."

"And the two men behind the king and the two men directly behind us?"

"The only other Norman barons in all England besides Warwick whom the king trusts." Eldene pointed as he named them. "Lord Robert of Muelan, Warwick's brother. Lord Richard of Redvers. Lord Robert fitz Hamon. Lord Roger Bigot. These five were the only men to follow the king when he faced his brother Robert's invasion. All the other knights with us are these barons' men."

We really are safe. Margaret relaxed on her riding platform; Night felt it and slowed his gait a bit.

"Winchester is only two days more, my lady."

"Any other lords with us?" Margaret had been looking for Lord William.

"No. See the twelve knights just behind us?" Eldene added with a smile. "They are the ones he gave for King Henry's use."

Thank you, William, for your men.

20

Private Audience

That night, after a simple meal of bread and soup, Margaret brushed Matilda's hair.

"Is there anything more I may do for you, Your Majesty?"

"No. I never realized sitting or lying down all day could be so exhausting."

"How fares the child, Your Majesty?"

"He is well. Would you like to feel for him?"

The queen lay on the bed. Gently, Margaret felt the babe, who was resting sideways with his head to the queen's left hip. The babe kicked.

"I fear I have awakened him. I am sorry. He feels small. Are you sure he is due the first week in February?"

The queen harrumphed. "I am cert we counted aright."

Margaret colored. "Please report any spotting or leaking at once, Your Majesty. We will stop immediately to rest you."

"Margaret, I will do nothing to endanger our heir."

Margaret apologized for her words and helped the queen to bed.

"God give you good rest, Your Majesty."

Margaret carefully stirred the wood in the two braziers so they would continue to warm the room as the night progressed. She tip-toed out of the room and down the stairs. She stopped halfway and watched the king conversing with a knight. For the first time she did more than look his way; she really saw him. Henry's traveling clothes might have been a drab gray, but his appearance was still imposing. *His black hair is still untouched by gray. How straight he sits as if still in a saddle. Does he relax ever? Even at seeming rest he radiates power. Is that what made him king or is it the result of becoming the king?* She knew how hard he could be. She had witnessed his winning ways, and now she watched him only appearing to be somewhat at his ease. Just then Henry looked up. At a word from the king, the knight stood and left. Henry gestured to Margaret. Dismayed to be ordered into his presence, Margaret walked to the bottom of the steps and paused. She looked to Caitlin seated by the fireplace, who nodded, stood and moved closer. Careful of her reputation and of her virtue, Margaret curtsied a respectable distance from the king.

"She guards you well," remarked Henry as he scowled at Caitlin, but he did not order her away. "Oh sit, Margaret. I will not eat you."

Margaret chose the chair opposite him. *With a table between us, I am safe.*

"How fares my queen?"

"Tired." At the king's gesture she began a full report. She ended with, "The babe seems a bit small. They grow most the last two months, so you will know more by Epiphany. I have no concerns."

"Good. She will reside in the old palace beside the Cathedral. My most trusted people will guard the entry door. We will build an inner gate for the top floors of the keep; our Saxons will guard that. She will be safe."

Margaret appraised Henry. *Actually a bit taller than average, handsome mustache, broad-chested, burly. Calm. Needs no crown or royal clothing. Was he heartless or practical when he told me to save his son over the queen? Does he truly love her or only pretend to?*

"What thought have you given to your rewards?"

"Your Royal Highness, my wishes have changed little."

"You are a shrewd one. You want clothes and dowry 'befitting your place,' you said. I figured it to be little enough when I thought you were Saxon."

She frowned. "Will you honor my boons now that you know my rank?"

"I always keep my bargains." The king sat forward. "When others keep theirs."

Margaret refused to give in to her desire to lean back; she kept her hands on the table.

"Then I shall ask for enough lands and property and dowry to make a good match; I want to marry a lord."

"Is that all you want?"

"Yes, Your Royal Highness. I want a normal life. Be a wife. Manage my husband's household. I will bear his children and help him raise them up to be good people loyal to you."

"You need a man who cares for you."

"I need to be accepted by polite society, by a family and a man from polite society." That was as much as she dared say to inform the king she had no designs on him. She wanted him to have none on her. *I am going to my marriage bed a virgin. I will be faithful all my life—no matter what.*

"That sounds like a dull life, Margaret."

"I pray so, my liege," she countered.

"And your third boon?"

"I am saving it until I know what more I may need." *I am not giving that one away until I must. You have the power to grant me control over mine own life, but will you give it?*

"Remember what I told you in secret. As the King of England, I need an heir for the stability of my realm and to continue my line. Having an heir matters more than anything else, more than any one person. I want her to live, but I need my heir more."

You told me to keep your queen healthy. Get your heir born healthy. But if I must choose between them, save your son. Do you truly love her but are being practical or are you heartless and she is disposable? Give voice to those questions and I will die.

"Smart girl. You think of details others miss. You hope for the best but plan for the worst. You should be one of my advisors." Henry paused as his eyes brightened. "Margaret?" Henry smiled winningly. "What advice would you give me now?"

The way Henry looked at Margaret and said her name unsettled her.

Is he courting me to be one of his… ? It had better not be for that. Snake about to strike? No, you don't.

She attacked. "Your Royal Highness, I would choose my regent with care."

The king looked about to spot any who might be listening to them. "What need have I for a regent?" Henry hissed.

"What need have you of an army of over three hundred fighting men when half would have been more than enough to escort your very popular queen? Each day on our journey more knights join us. What need have you of them once the queen is safe within the castle?"

Henry eyes widened in surprise she had noticed the increase of soldiers.

"You are besieged with 'Roberts,' Your Royal Highness. You have an uneasy peace with your brother, who is only the Narrow Sea away. Another foe is the Earl Robert de Belleme from the Severn River. Men talk. He supported your brother. He has an army of his own within your realm."

When the king's pupils widened further, Margaret was sure of his intentions.

"The size of your company tells me de Belleme is dangerous."

Henry grabbed Margaret's folded hands and pulled hard. Her ribs slammed against the table, knocking the breath out of her. She tried to pull back and gasped for a breath.

"How?"

Margaret inhaled. "I listen." She chose to lean forward to ease the pressure on her shoulders only to press her ribs harder into the table edge; they hurt. She whispered, "Were I you, I would ride hard and fast. Strike before anyone realizes this is an army with two purposes."

"Dear God, am I that transparent to a girl!"

"I am grown, Your Royal Highness. I attend to what I overhear." Margaret turned to her real purpose. "Your Royal Highness, I plead with you not to tell the Her Royal Highness. If she worries, she may lose your babe. Please—whatever you do—remain cheerful and circumspect. Just this once, do not tell her your plans."

Henry released Margaret and stared at her.

"You said I take as good care of her as would you, as do you. I will keep my silence. Please do not let her fear for your safety."

"Thank God you are not a man!" was all Henry could think to say.

21

Winchester

Monday, 25 November

The column was a long time crossing the River Itchen and riding through the east gate of Winchester town. High Street was empty. Someone had ordered the shuttering of every window. Margaret glimpsed the top of a castle keep and guard towers behind the cathedral and its close. The group was riding past the cathedral on their left when Margaret spotted in the distance a large castle with a stone palisade and tall keep.

Why are we staying in the smaller, older castle and not the one ahead? It has a taller, larger keep. It looks newly built with its shiny stones and regular features. Why are we not staying in the big castle?

The party turned left, marched south down a narrow lane past the west end of the cathedral, turned left and back eastward. Those in front stopped at the main gate of the smaller castle. Over the years, soot from many fires in the bailey had darkened the bottom half of

191

the four-storied keep behind the old stone walls with broken flint rocks cemented to it. Only the king, the litters, Lady Margaret, the foodstuffs wagon, the Saxons and thirty knights entered through a barbican. Margaret counted the buildings.

Chapel. Keep. Hall. Kitchen. Outbuildings. They are all small in a tightly packed bailey yard. I see a space between the buildings that may lead to a back yard area behind the keep.

From outside castle walls Sir Robert of Moulan supervised the dropping of the portcullis, the closing of the main gate and the lifting of the drawbridge.

Inside the closed compound, Elric helped Margaret dismount. "Where will Night stay?"

"I will see him well cared for. You must go to the queen."

Margaret put a hand through the litter curtains. After the queen stood, she pulled away from Margaret's hand with neither thanks nor recognition. Caitlin bounced out the opposite side and called for Dena, who exited her litter, bareheaded and ready to serve even though she wore one of the queen's garments.

The queen placed her right hand on the king's left forearm.

A tall, imposing, well-dressed man with gray hair above his ears stepped forward. "Your Royal Highnesses, welcome home. All is ready."

The royals and he spoke of matters in voices too low to be heard by others. King Henry and Queen Matilda walked to the hall and climbed wooden stairs wide enough to hold only them. Sir Roger, the castle's constable, followed the royals, and Lady Margaret followed him.

I like the double doors. They are tall, heavy, nail studded and impressive.

Margaret walked through a second set of doors. Her eyes popped. The hall teemed with people. *There are too many them to be safe! What is the king thinking to have invited them all!* Margaret stepped into the hall. Down the room and behind a four-steps dais, she saw a fireplace tall enough for a man to stand in. A roaring fire warmed the room. On the dais were massive carved oak chairs, the bigger one with arms and the other without. Both had purple cushions on them.

Men bowed and ladies curtsied. The king and queen strolled the length of the room, looking left and right, nodding to a few, but calling no one toward them. The queen rested her left hand on her swollen belly. Uncertain of her place, Margaret stepped left and stood at the end of the crowd. Several moved away from her and frowned as if she had done something wrong. She spotted them looking at what hung at her side.

The royals reached the dais and climbed the steps. The king seated his queen on her armless throne before taking his. He waved his hand as he commanded, "Let us welcome home Queen Matilda."

Queen Matilda smiled and nodded right and left in recognition of the loud, long, and enthusiastic applause from the invited courtiers. After the din had faded, the king called two persons forward. The couple gave obeisance. Both the king and the queen spoke to them. They dismissed the pair and called another couple forward. While this ceremony continued, Elric stepped to Margaret and whispered. She nodded. They were met at a side door.

"I am Sir Roger, the constable of this castle," announced the tall man who had welcomed the royals.

Margaret spoke Norman because the queen had told her only Norman was used at Court. Unsure of her rank to his, Margaret gave obeisance. "Sir Roger, I am the Lady Margaret."

"The only entrance from this hall to the keep is this way." Sir Roger pointed to a door on the opposite wall. Grateful to have Sir Roger create a path through the crowd, Margaret followed him across the room and outside. Margaret felt the wind blowing through the column of wooden pillars supporting a roof between the hall door and the entry door of the keep.

"Her Royal Highness will live on the top floor. You may deliver the queen's things while Their Highnesses are in the hall. The building supplies His Highness ordered have arrived."

"Thank you, Sir Roger." She turned to the men waiting beside the keep door. "Elborg, Elric, Elstan, Eldene, please see to Her Royal Highness's needs."

Margaret returned to her place in the hall. She watched people jockeying to be noticed. A cough, a gesture, something subtle to gain the royals' attention. Her concern was for the queen. *Can you not see she is tired? I see it from here. Please stop now, please.*

One couple more and the king stood. He took Matilda's hand and guided her to his left. Margaret could not see past the crowd that turned to watch them go. When Henry returned to the dais without Matilda, Margaret wove her way through the people to reach the doorway to the keep.

A knight grabbed her arm and stopped her. "How dare you wear a blade! I shall inform the king."

"Please do so, my lord. As His Royal Highness gave it to me and instructed me to wear it at all times, he will be most pleased with your report." Margaret smiled sweetly at the shocked man. "If you will excuse me, Her Royal Highness has need of me." Margaret pulled away and continued. At the keep door she turned to the two Saxons standing guard.

"No one passes but His Royal Highness. If anyone makes a fuss, make noise—draw attention to yourself until the king or Sir Roger notices."

"With pleasure," answered Elric.

"I always wanted to order a Norman," said Elstan.

"Beware!" Margaret warned. "Insult or touch a Norman and you will be put to death. I advise you only to inform them of the king's orders and then to call for Sir Roger or other Norman of rank who is about."

She stepped between Elric and Elstan and reached for the door handle. She passed through the doorway and closed the door behind her. This ground-floor room had benches against the walls. Margaret thought it was a waiting room of some kind. *Plenty of room for guards. The wood for the new wall and door already here. Did I forget to ask for a lock? I must remember to send for a large, sturdy lock.* Margaret climbed the circular stars against the far wall. *Good. Attackers must gain the whole room to reach the wall stairs guarding the queen. I must ask for a door lock for this inside wall too.*

The room on the second level appeared to be an audience room. Only one chair and a stool stood by a small fireplace on an outside wall. She opt the side door and saw cots and small trunks. *This was probably either a guard's or a servant's room.* The next floor was empty but for a stack of wood beside a larger fireplace. Margaret realized that on each floor the spiral staircase was on a different wall. *Safer. More private. Good planning.* Margaret climbed again and opt the next door. *Found you!*

Before a large fireplace sat Matilda ensconced in an armed chair. Pillows beneath and behind her and a woolen blanket of royal Scottish pattern of blue and black plaid over cream gave her legs warmth and comfort. She had placed her feet upon a padded stool with a wool cover embroidered with dainty spring flowers. Queen Matilda, slim everywhere but her belly, looked at home in the bare room.

"I am ready for my things."

The queen's tone clearly told Margaret she was no longer trusted or a confidant and was again only a servant. Margaret hoped it was only because of the change of homes, not because of any change of the queen's heart. The queen ordered where to build the bed, place her trunks, and all else. Everyone moved with alacrity.

Margaret curtsied deeply. "Your Majesty, may we use the fireplace on the floor lower for cooking?

"Here I am 'Your Royal Highness' at all times. The queen released a long, tired sigh. "I suppose I still must live without the excellent cookery of this castle. But I want better fare!"

"Yes, Your Royal Highness! I am cert we will find edibles to please you. Your Royal Highness, may Caitlin place the kitchen things by the fireplace? May she start the bread?"

"Do not block the arrow slits in case men need them."

"May your guards use the servants' room for sleeping? We women could sleep on the cooking floor."

"I suppose I must surrender my wardrobe room." The queen waved. "I will crowd my wardrobe in here." The queen scowled. "This room and the solar beyond is mine alone." The queen continued her orders. With a wave of her hand, she dismissed Margaret.

In the servants' room, Margaret found the cots had no ticking or pillows, and old blankets. The water in the chamber pot was ice. Margaret's face fell. *Just this? After all I have done for you? You demand better fare? You ate first and best and all that you wanted. What more could I have done with the stores we had? What has happened? Is it this castle? Might it be me? What have I done to displease you so?*

Margaret slipped from the room and asked Elric to ask Father Gregory if he would stay with the Saxons in the servants' room on the first floor below. She explained why. Elric offered to move three cots and trunks to the cooking floor. She added her request for more bedding for the three of them as well as for Father and the Saxons.

"All supplies must be inside before the wooden barrier is complete."

"Are you well, my lady?"

Margaret whispered, "Oh, Elric! I have displeased her and I do not know what I have done. I fear she has turned impossible."

Margaret burst into tears. Elric hugged her and placed her head upon his shoulder. "There. There, now. You are just tired. She is exhausted. We all need a hot meal and a good night's rest. Let me get fresh food upon which to sup." Elric released Margaret and offered his shirt sleeve. "Have you done crying?"

Margaret sniffled. "I suppose so. Does no good."

"The sooner we get her settled and fed, the sooner we are for bed and sleep. My lady, you look much prettier without the tears."

"I do not know what I would do without you. You are so… sensible."

"Sensible, my lady? Handsome or charming or lovable is so much better."

"Oh, Elric! Sometimes you are such a tease!"

Elric showed her a mournful face. "Yes, my lady." He turned and departed.

With furrowed brow, Margaret watched him. *Does he mean it? No. He is just being Elric. Cheering me with a compliment. He does not mean it. He will soon have Aurore.*

Soon Elric returned with a basket containing freshly killed capons, vegetables from the castle garden and more fresh foodstuffs, including a large fresh cod.

Margaret had requested and obtained several unused barrels with covers. She ordered a line of men to pass in buckets of water until the barrels were full. She and Dena placed the half barrel inside their room. Meanwhile, everyone in the hall gossiped and whispered. They realized the queen was being walled away in the keep. They speculated why and guessed terrible reasons.

That evening Sir Roger and his wife, the Lady Gisela, sat at table with the king and queen in what had been the queen's wardrobe room. The long table was set with white linens, gold-lined goblets, and pewter utensils. An evergreen bough had been artfully arranged between gold candlesticks that held fat beeswax candles scenting the whole room with the smell of spring and sweetness. Dried rose petals floated in individual small bowls of warm water for finger washing. The royals wore matching blue and gold garments; their sleeves and the queen's hem were trimmed in rare white ermine. The king and queen sat on the short ends of the table and Sir Roger and Lady Gisela on the longer sides. Elric served the men; Margaret the women. The meal was a rich repast of broth, fish, capons, boiled vegetables, and soft white bread slathered with butter. *How did Caitlin obtain whitened flour? I had best warn her not to do so again. We must crack and grind all our own flour. Flour could easily mask a powdered poison.* Talk was town news and gossip, with the men dominating the conversation. Relieved to have a new dinner companion, Queen Matilda engaged Lady Gisela about the current cost of food and the success of recent markets.

"My stay at Forest Keep was most quiet and restful, Lady Gisela," the queen said. "I fear Court had tired me more than I had realized."

At another of Lady Gisela's probing questions, the queen responded, "Yes, I am quite rested now. I shall stay here and avoid the hustle and throngs of people as before. I will spend Christmastide here and deliver our heir in this castle as well. Thank you for your concern."

Margaret also heard the queen's dismissal of further questions with her change of subject. She had given a plausible reason for retiring to the woodland retreat and had explained why she preferred to stay quiet. *Her remarks will be repeated all over town. Again, I see how clever she is.* The king walked the couple out and returned to sit with his queen for a bit. Margaret placed a warming pan in the queen's bed, checked the fire and disappeared.

When Caitlin arrived to ask if the royals wanted or needed anything, Queen Matilda commented, "That was an excellent meal, Caitlin. You may spit and roast birds that way for us again."

"Thank you, Your Royal Highness, but how I cooked the capons was Lady Margaret's idea, not mine."

As the king left for the night he said, "Well done" to Margaret. Margaret curtsied and kept her eyes down as he passed. She took the plate Caitlin had saved for her and sat on a stool. The queen called down for Dena to help her to bed. Caitlin and Dena cleaned the fireplace area, set the pottage to soak, and started the bread for the next day. They finished the leavings of the meal while standing.

"I am treating this place as a hostile camp. Elric or Elstan will go out to acquire what we need. They will vary the vendors. One of them will stand at the well while the other supervises the Saxons when next they fill the water barrels. The buckets stay with us here when they are not used. Elric said the Saxons will guard the wooden doors in shifts. Inside locks for the main door and for the door on this floor have been sent for." Margaret handed her empty plate to

Dena. She pulled her former nurse close and whispered her order. "Caitlin, never again give me credit like that. I want no attention from the king. Besides, it was your idea."

"I know, but I overheard the queen's favorable comments about the meal. I wanted you to have credit because you need to get back into her good graces. What did you do to anger her so?"

Margaret hugged Caitlin, who hugged her back."I know not. I love you, dear Caitlin. God give you a good night."

"God give a good night to you, my child. Remember as you fall into sleep I am proud of you. If your mother were here, she would tell you so as well."

"I pray for her every night."

"As do I." Caitlin left for her cot.

Margaret moved her cot before the cooking room door and set her sword beside her bed. Seated, she said her evening prayers and then looked around. *So much space. The rooms in this keep are huge. The fireplaces numerous, a whole forest of wood to keep just this one building warm. I never dreamed such luxury. The table and its wares of gold-lined pewter. Who saved the rose petals for use in winter? Who has ever heard of finger bowls for washing and lap cloths for cleaning your hands? The royals have fur-trimmed clothes for daily wear. What more wealth could they wear on royal court occasions? Are other royals like this? Who resides in the large palace that we may not stay there? Do important people from other lands ever visit? What is my part now we are here? Am I only a servant and a person of little rank at Court? Out of her favor I am doomed. I am cert of that much.* Margaret knelt and prayed again. She started by asking God if she had prayed enough for her mother's soul. *Oh God, Father Ambroise heard Mother's confession before she died so I believe she has not been sent to Hell. Has my mother's soul has been purged of any unconfessed sins? Is she in that middle place the priests call Purgatory waiting for prayers to release her from her time of penance? Have my prayers cleansed her soul so she may leave Purgatory and rise to be with You in Heaven for all eternity?*

Margaret listened for an answer, but her heart received none, so she again prayed her mother's penances be fulfilled through her prayers. She reminded God she would pray all her life for her mother to be awarded Heaven. She continued with her usual litany of other persons she prayed for daily and ended with, "Your will, Oh God, in all things." Then she crawled under her blankets. Margaret faced the door, touched the sword hilt on the floor and closed her eyes.

22

Tense Living

Dawn streamed from a window above the sleeper. Margaret half-opt her eyes, closed them, and rolled away from the light. The girl dreamed she slept in a soft bed, in a huge room, surrounded by luxury. She heard soft noises.

"Caitlin says to rise, my lady," instructed Dena. Dena then spoke in full voice. "Her Royal Highness saw where you are and demands you clear the doorway. First Sunday in Advent is High Mass anon."

Startled now, Margaret bolted."I am up! Up!" she promised as she stood, grabbed her bliaut and threw it over her head. She pulled the bed to the outer wall. Taking up her sword, the young woman cleared a path. *I have overslept the time! I never did before! What will she think?*

Father Gregory had set a small altar in the solar beyond the queen's bedroom. The southwest corner of the keep was lit from two directions. The arrow slits gave only dim light, but the double window holes far above them illuminated the whole room with a warm glow, though they also let in the cold that dropped upon them relentlessly. The room filled in order of rank. Margaret stepped to the queen to offer assistance. The queen brushed away the girl's hands and tried to lower herself. Margaret put her hands behind her to hide her offense and stepped back. When Matilda could not lower herself to her wooden kneeler, she looked toward Margaret with an unspoken order. Without meeting Margaret's eyes, the queen accepted her second offer.

Father Gregory turned to the candle-lit altar and began. Margaret knelt well behind everyone. The cold floor numbed her knees, but the ritual comforted her. Thus had begun almost every morning of her life. Margaret lowered her head, stared at the floor and listened. She intoned the proper phrases and tried hard to concentrate on their meaning. As Father said the Mass in Latin, she knew only the parts she had been taught as a child, the parts Father Ambroise had translated for her. Soon the prayers, chants, and responses became rote again. As the priest droned on in Latin, she said her usual prayers and added prayers asking God to take her Mother into Heaven and to show her a way to soften the queen's heart.

Oh, God, Your will in all things. Is that why she is angry? Thinks she I am lacking piety? My Precious Jesus, you know me, know my thoughts have been for her well being, her safety, her needs. Well, not always. Sometimes I do or say things because I must stay in her good will. Now I have lost it, Dear Jesus. Please help me find it again. I confess, I take Communion. Father said I am with the Church. God, is he mistaken? What have I forgotten that she dislikes me so. Oh yes, now I know. I have been thinking of her, of myself, of the babe to come, not You. You sent the king to me. You gave me the ideas for my plan, You let Sir Charles release me. You. I have been forgetting You. No more, My Lord God, Blessed Jesus. Holy Spirit I start my day in prayer. I will pray during the day to know Your will. I will not just attend Mass and think other thoughts. I will pay attention during Mass and Vespers, and be with You as You are with us, with me. Thank you, God. Thank you, Jesus. I will do better, be better, be a true Christian in all I do. I promise. Amen.

After Mass, Father Gregory helped the queen rise. Margaret left first and disappeared to the cooking floor. She carried the queen's breakfast tray into her room. All Margaret saw was the back of her chair. She placed the tray on the small table beside the queen's chair and stepped back. She withdrew when the queen's hand gestured her away.

Margaret had finished her pottage and consulted with Elric, Elborg and Caitlin until she heard a small hand bell from the queen's room.

Please God, let her not be cruel. Oops. Oh God, Your will in all things—including this.

"I want a troubadour at noon today. One with soft, gentle songs to soothe me. Ask Father Gregory to join me. Tell Sir Roger to invite the mayor and three councilmen and their wives to dine with me on the morrow; he and his wife may attend. Make those capons again. I think I can stomach those. Three wines, one for the fish course, one with the capons, and a sweet one to end the meal. That is all."

Margaret did not move. She had no permission to speak, so she did not know how to bring up the subject except by standing still.

"What is it this time?"

"Your safety, Your Royal Highness," was all Margaret dare say. When the queen did not respond, she continued, "Where? This floor is full. Attackers can come to any corner of the hall. Everyone of rank dines there and men wear swords. What if someone wished to approach you? How do we stop him? Each time you step out of the keep, you are in danger." When the queen remained silent,

Margaret dared say more. "One troubadour is easily watched. Eight citizens is another matter. We must treat men of high station well, yet they cannot wander or come close to you. All of them must be unarmed and guarded, even the constable and his wife." Margaret inhaled deeply before asking, "May we clear the cooking floor and use it for dining?"

"Yes."

"May the dinner be smaller?"

"That is a small dinner. We know what we are doing. You must see to our safety."

Royal "we." Invoking your own power or his? Not that it matters.

"Your Royal Highness, your journey was tiring. Would you like to wait several days?"

"This cannot wait. You may ask the men to leave their swords with the Saxons after the door is locked behind them. Then others will not gossip we require my guests remove them. They need their daggers to eat, so they may keep those." Then the queen sentenced Margaret. "As I am confined, so are you. You may not leave the keep. No going to the yard or stable. Stay out of my way. Leave."

As Margaret turned, she heard, "I want Father Gregory." Margaret squeezed her eye lids together to stop tears and swallowed hard. *Not visit Night. No sky except through slits. Why? Why?* Unable to speak without bursting into tears, Margaret gestured to Father Gregory and pointed to the floor above as she fled to the corner of the cooking room and faced the wall.

Dena had thrown blankets over the trunks and piled up the cots. The queen and Father Gregory dined while Margaret stood behind them. The queen ignored the arm that served her. At the end of the meal, the queen motioned Margaret forward and whispered before she excused Father Gregory from her room. The minstrel had been playing beyond the queen's doorway with a Saxon standing behind him.

"You pleased Her Majesty with your voice and instrument. What is your name? From whence came you?"

"I am Will, my lady. Normandy born, but I wander. I have been in England three years."

Since before he was king. Does that make you loyal? I doubt it. "You are to play for Her Royal Highness again on the morrow. She wants you to play before the noon meal to set the mood for her guests. You will play while they eat and sing for the guests afterward."

Will grinned. After playing for the queen, he could brag and set a higher fee.

"Yes, my lady!"

Margaret opt a bag and dropped pennies into his outstretched hand.

"Be cleaner and better dressed on the morrow. They are important guests." After Elborg escorted the man out, Margaret turned to her own meal with Caitlin and Dena.

"Why did you do that?"

"Caitlin, minstrels travel. They both sing and gossip. What better way to impress the morrow's guests in advance they are important to Her Royal Highness than to have the town talking about them before they arrive? Who could better testify to Her Royal Highness's condition to common and high folk alike than one who entertained her? They will love his gossip."

"Be careful!" teased her old nurse as she took her former charge's bowl from her. "You are beginning to think like her."

Margaret walked the room's perimeter, first in one direction and then the other. *My only exercise for… ten? eleven? weeks.*

The next morning Margaret checked and rechecked every detail from the table settings to the sideboard. She approached Caitlin to ask again about the progress of the cooking.

"Stop fluttering like a nervous hen trying to keep her chicks in order. Take slow, measured steps and speak in low tones. Remember your rank. They do not know she is upset with you unless you show it."

"Yes, Caitlin." Margaret stopped and lifted her chin. "I thank you for the reminder. I would not have the mayor or the others speak ill of me."

"The tabards we hemmed will cover the servers' clothing. They will look as if they are in a uniform."

"They expect to be served by Saxons. Think you they will notice a Saxon for every man? She will."

"She charged you with her safety. That is the best you can do."

A half hour later Sir Roger announced the Lord Mayor and his entourage.

Quiet, calm, dignified, pure keeps a lady steadfast and sure. Margaret repeated the phrase her mother had taught her. Ranked as she was, Margaret only nodded to each as she motioned the men forward to a tray of goblets of wine. Margaret ignored the weaponless men staring at her sword.

Sir Roger announced the queen's entrance and opt her door. Matilda glided in dressed in a deep green bliaut over a creamy chemise. She wore her small crown, a golden ring with three triangles above the band. The smaller side ones held a green gem. The taller central triangle held a diamond. At a turn of Matilda's head, the jewels lit up from the sunlight streaming in from the windows above. *An accident? No. I would wager she moved her head to light the jewels to impress them. Does she ever do anything without a purpose. I think not.*

After Sir Roger spoke each man's name, the queen smiled at each man and said his name as if she were ever so glad to see him; the man bowed. Each officer introduced his wife, who curtsied and said, "Your Royal Highness." The queen greeted the mayor's wife warmly, but she only repeated their names to the other women.

Queen Matilda sat at the short end of the table with Father Gregory to her right and the mayor to her left. As a reminder of the king's authority, Dena had set an empty place opposite the queen's place. Talk was of city matters. The queen asked pointed questions and the councilmen responded as if they were presenting formal reports. In general, the city was quiet. Markets were brisk, and the people content. The women spoke not. After the fish course, the mayor's wife broached the subject on everyone's mind.

"If I may say so, Your Royal Highness, you look radiant."

"Thank you. I rest well and feel… " Matilda stopped, gasped, and grabbed the table edge.

"Are you well, Your Royal Highness?" The mayor pushed back his chair and stood as if to catch her.

The queen nodded. "I am fine. Fine." After another deep breath, she added, "He just kicked me again." The queen leaned back in her chair.

"I saw that one even from here," volunteered a woman halfway down the table. "Your babe is strong, vigorous."

The queen laughed at her babe's perfect timing. "Indeed. He gets bigger and stronger every day."

Queen Matilda accepted their congratulations and changed the topic. The next course arrived. After the guests had departed, Margaret coughed before entering the queen's chamber. She saw the queen pacing, smiling to herself, and rubbing her hands together as if she were well pleased with something. When the queen saw Margaret in the doorway, her face turned sour. "I do not want you. Send Dena. Begone unless I send for you."

Crushed, Margaret fled. She prayed for the queen's forgiveness—but for what she did not know.

23

Quiet Deeds

Concerned that the queen had tired herself at the dinner, Margaret sent Caitlin to examine her. Caitlin reported nothing amiss and repeated the lecture she had given the queen about getting enough rest.

"I heard. You always raise your voice when you make a point."

Dena escorted the queen to Mass, attended her, and relayed her instructions. Margaret saw to the household, baked bread, and continued to stay out of the queen's way. On a warmish day after the second Sunday of Advent, Margaret called the Saxons to the main hall door. After accepting linens from the laundry and the food from the market, she issued orders.

"Today may be the last time before spring for you to wash. I want each of you to bathe all over and all at once."

She saw the men glance at Elborg and silently choose him to speak.

"Naked? With soap?"

"Use the strong laundry soap. Wash in parts if you like, but all your parts, hair included, washed during the same cleaning. Is that clear? Use your guard room if you like."

"Yes, my lady," they chimed in unhappy unison.

"Place your usable garments in a pile; take them to the castle laundress for washing and mending. Burn the unusable ones. Her Majesty ordered new clothes for all of you. When you are clean, you may have them."

Margaret spent the morning examining the laundry. She repaired a seam in the queen's sheet, checked the queen's clothes for tears and holes, and resewed part of a hem where Caitlin had stepped on her gunna. After the queen had lain down for her afternoon nap, Margaret escorted Dena to her bed.

"I insist you nap when the queen does. You are just as heavy with child as is she and you need your rest too."

"I confess running and fetching tires me more these days."

"I am sorry for that, but she will not permit me to serve her. Roll over and I will rub your back."

"Oh-h-h! Thank you, my lady. That feels so good." After a few minutes, Dena spoke. "I told her you honeyed the apples yourself, but she silenced me. I do not know what is wrong."

"Neither do I. I have no help for it, Dena. Do not risk her wroth. Now get some rest." Margaret lifted the blanket, patted Dena's shoulder and tiptoed away. Margaret sat on a stool and stared into the fire.

"You look lost, child."

"I was thinking of home. I took Mother's scissors and thimble when I left." Then she spoke of what was really bothering her. "He will never forgive me, will he?"

Caitlin put a hand on Margaret's shoulder. "You can always pray for that. I would not count on him changing. He is a hard man."

"Was he always like that?"

"Oh no. When he bought me as a marriage gift for your mother, he was young, kind, and loving. He adored your mother and was a good man to everyone."

"Tell me the stories again."

Caitlin retold the tales she had repeated over the years of Charles' and Rosamonde's first days together, of Charles' making her mother give up riding after she got with child, of her arrival.

"Grandfather was disappointed I was a girl." Margaret always said that during the stories.

"I confess he was. That you looked like your mother pleased him. You were the only grandchild he ever held." Caitlin always added her traditional sop.

"Does Jorgon still want Dena? If they escape capture, will he wed her?"

"Yes to both questions." Caitlin wondered what caused Margaret's change of topics.

"Will he accept the babe?"

"He has double reason to do so. He loves Dena. As devoted as the man has been to you, I believe he will be as good to your brother or sister. He said as much to me only last week."

"Good. I want my brother or sister treated well. I want the babe to grow up kind like Dena and hard-working like Jorgon. Lord Charles will never claim his child, but we four can look after the babe. My sister or brother will know me to be kind and loving. Mayhap she will love me back. Not that I can tell her—or him—who I am. That will be Jorgan's and Dena's office, if they so choose. I will be a good friend. That needs be enough for me for now."

"What are you sewing at such a hurried pace?"

"Dena needs new clothes. She is bursting from the old ones."

Her shift is sewn; her gunna is half done." Margaret held up the garment. "If I am not interrupted, I will finish it by bedtime. If you will cook, I will find arrow slit under which to work."

With that, Margaret gathered her things and took the stool with her.

Not wanted. He favored Charles and Raymond; Cecily got all his attention. Mother and Caitlin loved me. Mother, you always knew what to say to cheer me when he ignored me or petted Cecily and not me. What would you say to me now? You would tell me to be good and kind. Let the queen's mean ways and hurtful words blow past you like an ill wind. Dear Caitlin. I am lost without you. You remind me how I should be, how I must act. You are always my conscience. I thought powerful friends would lift me to my rank or higher. The king is gone chasing traitors and securing loyalty. She is petulant, angry, mean. I am fourteen, unmarried, with no protector and but one death from a beheading. My state is worse than ever. Margaret remembered her promise to God and sighed. *I know. Your will, Oh God, in all things. You are testing me. I need to accept what You have set before me. I do accept what You have set before me, Oh God. Not my will. Yours. Even the queen's anger is Yours. Your will, Oh God, in all things.* Margaret's biting her lower lip did not stop her tears. She dropped her head and shifted. Anyone looking her way would think she lowered her head to catch the last of the afternoon light.

The next morning Margaret arranged a bath for Dena.

"I need not bathe. I wash my hands and face every day. Washing more is not safe for the babe."

"In two days is Third Advent Sunday. Before your babe comes, you should wash your hair and bathe. I hung a blanket. No one will see you. All you need do is lie on your cot. I will do all the work. I am turning my back. Strip and get under the blanket."

Margaret dipped a rag in the very warm water and handed it off.

"Here, do your face and neck."

"What is that wonderful smell?"

"It is a small square of a gentle soap, something Elstan found in the market. He called it turino soap. The vendor told him it is a pine tree scent. See the tiny specks of green," said Margaret as she displayed the precious item. "He purchased an even more costly one for the queen if she will have it. It smells of a flower called a rose and is from a land called Casteela." After Margaret washed and dried each limb, she covered it well. She held up the blanket for Dena to wash her body and then scrubbed her back for her. Dena shifted so her hair hung past the cot.

"M-m-m. I am warm all over again, my lady, and ready for my hair."

As Margaret brushed her hair, wet and soaped it, Dena chatted. "Do you know I cannot see my feet when I am standing? I used to think myself just a girl, but I am a woman now. Am I not?"

"Yes, you are."

"I am fat. Do you think Jorgon still wants me?"

"You are not fat. You are carrying a child. I am going to rinse your hair twice."

"I am afraid I will not love this babe. Carrying it is not my choosing."

"No, it is not, but it is still your babe. That lord will not claim it. If Jorgon will, what does it matter? You carried it; you will birth it. That makes the babe yours. Jorgon's and yours. "

Dena whispered, "Are you angry with me?"

"Of course not! You did not choose this. The babe may be born a bastard and with Original Sin, but you can have that baptized away. If you two say you are its father and mother, no one will challenge you. Your babe will be as good as you train him to be, or her to be. I would much rather have you both alive and here with me than dead like his first bedmate. I would rather you three be a family than you be gossiped about and shunned. Do you believe me?"

"Yes, you took us away."

"Good. Please know that I am glad I did so." Margaret whisked a clean linen around the girl's head. "Let me dress you. Then you will go to the fireplace to keep yourself warmed. Your hair will dry more quickly there."

"What do you mean Dena is being bathed?" asked the queen as she raised her voice louder with each word.

After hearing muffled words, Margaret and Dena heard the queen again.

"No, I do not want my dinner burned. Send Margaret to me."

"Lady Margaret, Her Royal Highness demands your presence."

Margaret smirked; she knew what Caitlin was about. In a loud voice, she replied, "Please tell Her Royal Highness I am almost finished bathing Dena. I will come anon."

The queen said no more, but the women heard her grumbling.

Margaret reached for her surprise. "These are for you. Clean, new clothes for a clean person."

"Oh, no, my lady. The shift and gunna are yours. I saw you working on them."

"Yours have shrunk. Besides you need a fuller one now. This deep yellow color complements your hair. Please accept my gifts. I have time to sew my Christmas bliaut."

Dena hugged Margaret, who hugged her back. She helped Dena into her new clothes. "I have been neglecting you shamefully. I am sorry."

"You have been busy with… " Dena nodded toward the room where Queen Matilda impatiently waited. "Caitlin has been watching over me. I am fine. Fine. Please go. Caitlin will help me dry my hair."

Before Margaret picked up the queen's dinner tray, she hugged Caitlin hard.

24

Swill

Saturday, 14 December

I have a sour stomach. Food tastes like rot. These rooms have shrunk. The walls close in on me. I am caged and still a servant. She shuns me. What more can I do? Nothing I do is working, not working hard, cooking well or staying away from her. Oh God, why am I treated so? Am suffering Your wroth over a misdeed? Reveal it to me so I may repent. Dark days and nights with bad dreams of my old days at home haunt me. Tell me, Oh Lord, what may I do to change all this? How must I change to regain Your favor? What may I do? Shall I pray more, pray harder? Days of morose thoughts had soured Margaret, including Saturday, December 14. On the morrow, the Third Sunday of Advent, she would be fifteen. In a corner by the wooden barrier, she and Elstan conferred.

"How goes outside?"

"Mostly quiet."

"Mostly?"

"Several have asked to see Her royal Highness. After we refuse them entry, they leave, except for one. A Lady Claire de - something. I forget."

Margaret furrowed her brow.

"She demanded entry. She said she was Her Royal Highness's chief lady-in-waiting and had every right to see to her well-being. She said, 'No sword-wearing country girl will keep me from my queen.' "

"And?"

"I informed her I follow the king's orders, no one else's. Then I said, 'When the king himself escorts you past this door, you may enter.'"

After thanking Elstan, Margaret looked at the arrow slit of light across the room floor and announced she hungered not. She requested the barrier door be opt.

"My lady, are you permitted to leave?"

Margaret lied. In the walkway, Margaret kept a quick pace. Inside the hall she took long strides and set her heels hard upon the stones to warn all to stay away. Margaret kept her hand on her sword hilt as if ready to attack anyone who challenged her. From the corner of her eye, she saw people staring at her, but she looked only straight ahead. At the inner doors to the hall she turned a corner into a stairwell and disappeared. Margaret stepped onto the hall roof and took several steps forward. She lifted her face to the sun. *Sun! Space? Air! Sweet air! Alone once again! Thank you, God.* Margaret flung wide her arms and turned in a circle. Once. Twice. Thrice. Ignoring the cold, she laughed aloud and ran toward a wall.

"My lady!" shouted a sentinel.

Margaret ran on. She stopped herself just as rough hands grabbed her.

"Unhand me, sirrah! "

The guard did not.

"I am a lady of rank and not to be touched!"

"Swear you will not leap to your death."

"What?" Then Margaret understood. "Sirrah, I am only enjoying a short respite from my duties. I want to walk about for a bit. I promise I will use the stairs to return to my post."

The guard held her shoulders still.

"I swear before God above I will not leap off this roof. I swear I will stay alive."

The guard removed his hands but did not move.

Margaret turned and saw a huge chest covered with a fur wrap with wide leather straps binding the pelt to the man. She looked up to see only the guard's chin and nose.

"Sirrah, I have no intention of committing suicide and spending all eternity in Hell. I wish only to see the sun and the town."

The guard stepped back. "My apologies, my lady."

Margaret patted his furry chest. "Follow me around if you like, but do not impede me."

She turned away and looked between the merlons. From below foul odors of stable, rotted food, and worse assaulted her nostrils.

"Wrong side!" She heard a chuckle behind her. Margaret walked to the corner and saw the yard with buildings against the far wall, a well at each end, and many workers going about their duties. Everything in shadow was gray and drab. The setting sun lit the eastern side of the yard with bright shards of light illumining each surface and revealing each space between the outbuildings. Margaret saw mostly the warm browns of the wooden structures, but light and colors made her smile. Moving to another corner and gazing west, she spotted a hill in the distance with bare spots and black circles in front of a blazing sunset of oranges and golds. *So that is where his army stayed the night.*

On the east side of the roof, she looked down to see workers disassembling the old cathedral corner and moving the stones closer to the new cathedral. The church's head faced east and the north and south arms of the building had been built and roofed. Only the window holes need to be filled with glass for that part of the church to be completed. *Just starting the long part. What is it called? The nave! It is just a hole with sides and no roof yet. With no windows in the built part, Mass will be cold and wet and snowy. I wonder where St. Swithin's grave is? Is its location still a mystery?* Margaret saw the men stop work, put tools inside a window hole, and report to a man with papers in his hand. The men rounded a corner and departed. She watched as they walked down this lane or that as they entered town and disappeared. She turned to find herself alone in that corner of the roof. The guards were huddled below the north wall, the windward side. At another corner she spotted the thatch roofs of a different part of town, a bit of river beyond the wall and east gate. *Winchester is a big town and is very busy for it being so close to dusk.*

A couple walked a lane with a girl holding each of their hands and a toddler riding atop his father's shoulders. The man said something and the woman laughed. Together they swung their daughter as she jumped from spot to spot. Margaret leaned well out of the embrasure to follow them. They disappeared. I m*ay never have that.* Margaret turned to the guards. She spotted a stocky, older man clutching a heavy gray mantle to his body. Gray hair straggled out of his woolen cap. His face was well wrinkled and reddened with the cold.

"Please send down for a flagon of wine and a cup."

"From your stocks, my lady?"

"From yours."

"Well watered for cert. It is swill."

"Unwatered."

Margaret turned away.

This guard watched her turn away. He reported to his superior, then disappeared. He returned with a large pitcher and a pottery mug.

"Thank you," said Margaret.

She half-filled the mug and drank. She spewed most of the wine in a fit of coughing. Ignoring the sniggers, Margaret refilled the mug, placed the pitcher against the wall, and walked the perimeter, sipping as she went. The men stood still as she passed. She ignored them. Each time she reached the pitcher she added to her mug. The sun set and the sky darkened.

Margaret heard a man calling out something, but she did not understand his words. She stopped at the north wall to see him walking down High Street, torch in hand. She stopped a guard and pointed.

"What is that man calling out?"

"Covrefeu."

"Why?"

"It is dusk, my lady. Every night, before they go abed, the towns-people must stop their fires and blow out all candles to prevent a fire destroying the town."

"How do they restart them so they can boil their morning pottage, cook their meals, stay warm?"

"They strike two flints over dried straw or bits of wool. Flints are abundant, everywhere. Long ago our ancestors broke apart the stones to make sharp edges and cemented them to the city walls. Anyone who tries to climb our city walls will get cut hands and torn clothes. When they fall, they fall on flint shards and are cut again. Walk the outside of the wall and see for yourself. Winchester is famous for its unclimbable walls."

Each hour she walked with less grace and more wobbling. Outside the keep's guard room door Elstan was talking with a man when they were approached by a castle guard, who whispered in Elstan's ear and left.

"She is in trouble."

"How?"

"She has gotten herself drunk on swill on the hall roof, and she is refusing to move."

"I will help you get her down."

"This is a hellacious way to meet her," Elstan commented as they took the stairs.

"I care not how. I want to see this ferocious girl who brandishes a sword and acts like one of our Saxon women warriors of old."

Elstan led the way. "Lady Margaret. Lady Margaret. Awake!"

"Go way. Am dead." Through slits, she saw two shadows kneeling before her. Behind them she saw stars.

"Not dead," she announced in a cold, flat voice. When she tried to lift the empty mug to her lips, a hand took it from her. "Go way," Margaret enunciated her next words with care. "Want…to…be… dead." Margaret made no sense of the words she heard. Two pairs of hands gently lifted her. She failed to stand. Strong arms supported her.

"I know what to do. You go first."

Margaret laid her head on rough cloth then quickly righted it."Oh-h-h. Hurts."

"Keep your head up."The man moved slowly so as not to jostle his charge.

Trying to get a face into focus, Margaret opt her eyes only a squint. Everything in sight weaved in and out.

"Keep your eyes opt," said the shadowy face.

"Light hurts," she complained.

"Lower the torch. Keep it before you. Be ready to catch us if I stumble."

The bearded man positioned Margaret feet first into the stair-well opening, but he could not see to set his own feet on the narrow spiral stairs. They stood Margaret up; the bearded one sat on the top step and pulled the woman onto his lap.

"What are you doing?" she demanded as she tried to push him away.

"Taking you down the stairs. Relax or we shall both take a bad tumble."

When Margaret looked down the bottomless well of shadows and blackness, she grabbed the man around the neck. By facing behind him and focusing on each step, she could keep her head up and eyes opt. Her stomach contents started roiling; she moaned. The man stopped after lowering them two steps to give Margaret's equilibrium time to adjust.

A voice whispered, "My lady, why are you drunk?"

"Sleep through morrow. Pass without me."

"What is the morrow?"

Margaret started to shake her head in refusal but stopped. She steadied her aching head, swallowed hard, and refocused her eyes on a stair. The voice repeated the question.

"Know what I saw? Wife, husband, two children." She released a long sigh and rested her chin on his shoulder. "Even the meanest Saxon can have what I may never get."

"What is that?"

"Husband. Home. Children." Two steps later she added, "Be fifteen morrow. No hope for any of it."

The voice whispered in her ear, "There are worse things than turning fifteen, my dear."

Margaret whispered back, "Not for a woman. Father disowned me. Queen angry. Not let me see Night!"

Two more steps and a rest.

"You married?"

"I am a third son."

"First born. No help at all." Two steps later, Margaret added, "Servant…I am. Servant remain."

'You will be wed, I promise."

"Hah! Ouch. Hurts."

Margaret felt the silent movement of the man's chest. Angry, she hit his back with the flat of her hand. "Not funny! Oh-h-h, my head."

He stopped. "You are right, Margaret. Your lot is not funny. You have not been properly cared for, protected, loved, wed." Before Margaret could respond, the man pushed her to her feet, stood, and steadied her. She hugged his waist and moaned in her agony. The man holding her instructed the other. "Inform her maid. Bring a blanket to hide her face. We will wait here."

The light disappeared. Margaret felt herself turned from the man's side to his front. Almost senseless, Margaret was unfeeling about being held by a man. Without his body to lean against, she would not have known he was there.

"Margaret, you will forget everything you said," a gentle voice commanded. "Forget who helped you. Forget all but this."

Margaret's mind reeled with feelings of sudden passion, the press of their bodies, the strength of his arms. Margaret let the languorous pleasure pour into her mouth and warm her insides. Then she slipped into darkness.

Those men still in the hall missed the sword tip peeking from the bottom of the blanket. They saw a bearded man carrying a bundle with feet dangling and assumed the hidden woman was meant for the Saxons' physical pleasures. As soon as Elstan and the girl disappeared into the keep, the second man left. Caitlin slipped off the blanket hiding Margaret.

"Child, you have done it this time!" She instructed Elstan, "Set her on her feet and hold her upright." Caitlin roused her charge.

"Caitlin? Stomach."

Caitlin turned Margaret to the chamber pot and held her head as Elstan held her bent over. The stench from the pot was all the catalyst Margaret needed to release her stomach contents. Then she began dry heaving from a stomach too weakened to stop its own churning. She gasped deep breaths and her stomach settled. Caitlin lifted Margaret's head and passed a cool rag over the girl's face.

"Open your mouth. I must clean your mouth or that stuff will rot your teeth." To Elstan, she instructed, "Walk her to her cot and lay her on it." Caitlin ordered, "Margaret. Margaret, stay on your back. Keep one foot on the floor so you know which way is up. A bucket is beside your bed. If you miss it, you will clean up the mess. Do you understand?"

Margaret groaned. "Cold." After Caitlin covered her with two more blankets, she added, "Better." The girl's head rolled right as her eyes closed.

25

Aftermath

"Wake her."

Caitlin called to Margaret and shook her. No response.

"I want to know why she did this."

"She has been abandoned again, Your Royal Highness."

"Explain."

"Her mother is dead. Her father denied her. Now you, her first friend, have forsaken her."

"A queen has no friends."

"I am sorry to hear that, Your Royal Highness."

"She was seen with the king."

"I have been within hearing every time they have met. Their talk has been of you, only you."

The queen harrumphed and left.

Voices seemed distant. Food smells nauseated her. Unwilling to op her eyes, Margaret slowly lifted her foot to her bed. When the untoward did not occur, she risked shifting to her side. That took time. She sighed and slept again. When next she woke, her mouth tasted foul. Someone had tucked her foot under the blankets.

While she was unsticking her tongue from her teeth, someone approached.

"My lady?"

"When?" she whispered.

"Night. Caitlin says no liquids until you are sober."

"Hungry."

"No food either."

Margaret groaned, yawned, and drifted into a deep slumber. Margaret saw a slit of daylight when next she stirred. She lifted herself on an elbow, slowly dropped her legs and sat upright. Margaret offered a wan smile as Caitlin sat on the stool beside her bed.

"Sip only," ordered Caitlin as she handed Margaret a cup.

Margaret rolled the ale around her mouth before she swallowed. After her stomach accepted it, she took another sip.

"I failed."

"How?"

"I wanted to sleep past my birthing date."

"That was yesterday. You missed Third Sunday."

Margaret released a slow, sad sigh.

"The only things for your state are time and temperance. Later today or tomorrow you will feel well. That swill is wicked stuff, bitter and foul, the thick dregs of wine kegs. Fit only for warming the blood, but hard on the stomach. Drink no wine for a ten-day."

"Yes, Caitlin."

"The queen saw you and asked why you were abed." Caitlin lied to the girl. "I said you were ill with stomach troubles, which was a truth, but we did not say with what or why."

"Thank you."

"Finish the ale slowly. I will fetch you the inside of a round."

Bread and ale. Fitting food for a prisoner. By supper, Margaret's head ached only a little and she was ready for broth. Well after bedtime, Margaret crept to Caitlin's cot. Margaret whispered, "Caitlin, I will see the queen on the morrow. I am done being punished for I know not what. Stay clear. Remember, you know nothing."

"About time," replied Margaret's former nurse.

Head high, Margaret stepped into the queen's bedroom. Before Matilda could speak, Margaret did. "I do not know what I did to give offense, Your Royal Highness. What may I do to make amends?"

"Leave this place never to return. Live with ditch women for all I care."

"I cannot leave without a direct order from His Royal Highness."

"You and the king! I know about you two!"

The queen's face went livid. Margaret furrowed her brow. "Know what? There has never been anything between me and His Royal Highness."

"You held hands with my husband!"

"Never!"

"You were seen!"

Margaret glanced about as she tried to recall such a thing. "In the inn? Before we arrived?" she asked.

"More than that? What else!" demanded the woman, mouth hard and eyes fiery.

She is just a woman for all that she is queen. And though she is wrong to suspect me, she is not wrong to suspect her husband.

Margaret looked directly at Matilda. "That was not hand holding. I was being punished." When the queen harrumphed and stated her disbelief, Margaret explained. "You had gone abed. The king asked for me, and we talked about what we have always talked. You.

I reported you were tired, the babe was small, everything you and I said to each other. The king asked me a question and my answered displeased him. He became angry. He grabbed my hands and yanked. He slammed my ribs against the table. When I got back my breath, I apologized. Twice. He warned me never to speak in such a manner again. Then he let go of me. Had you asked me about it afterward, I would have shown you my bruised ribs as proof."

"You expect me to believe this!"

"Call Father Gregory. I will confess aloud before you. Will you believe that? I will fetch him for you." Margaret took a step back to fetch the priest.

"No, No. I do not want him involved." The queen looked hard at Margaret. "At the altar will you swear before God that all you said is true?"

"Yes."

"Follow me."

Hours later Dena reported to both women, "My lady, Her Highness keeps asking about my bath. I think she wants one." Dena smiled broadly. "I told her I could not do it, being with child and all. I said I did not think it proper anyone other than a Norman lady of rank perform such a private service for a queen."

"What did she say?"

"She said she would consider it."

Margaret thanked Dena with a hug. "After her nap bring her the square of Casteela soap," she added.

That evening the queen washed her face and hands with Margaret's gift.

"My skin feels so soft," the queen commented and Dena reported.

Caitlin and Dena made the queen's bed with clean sheets and a washed, repaired coverlet under the furs.

When the queen thanked them for their thoughtfulness, Caitlin retorted, "Thank you, Your Royal Highness, but we are not the ones who thought of it."

When Caitlin and Dena returned from putting the queen to bed, they found Margaret kneeling beside her cot, hands clasped and head lowered in prayer.

26

Reprieve

Between asleep and awake lay dreaminess and languor. Margaret's musings formed and unsettled her. *Held. Carried. Whose lap? Kissed. Kissed?* As Margaret tried to recall more, the place between her legs warmed and ached as did her breasts. Involuntarily, her lips formed a kiss. Margaret's fists clenched as she willed the memory to clear and come alive, but it slipped away. *Who is he? I am cert he has blue eyes. I feel strong arms holding me. William has brown eyes. It was not him. William has no beard. Why was the man bearded? Norman, only Norman men may wear beards. Did I dream him? I remember wanting a husband. Did I just imagine all this? Did I dream of a man kissing me while I slept after drinking swill? Why did I dream he had a beard? Is he real or not?* Margaret stopped wondering and opt her eyes, tried to sort her thoughts and failed. Before Mass she asked Caitlin, "Who brought me home?"

"Elstan."

Throughout Mass, Margaret went through the motions, said the responses, and heard nothing. All she could recall of Elstan was their conversation before she had left.

It is not him. Elstan is clean-shaven. Dare I ask if he had help getting me home? No, do not be a fool twice.

After breakfast, the queen summoned her. "Are you better today?"

"Yes, thank you, Your Royal Highness."

Still in her curtsey, Margaret heard a kitten mewling beside her and watched it trying to crawl up the skirt of her bliaut. She smiled at the gray and white ball of fluff as she gently dislodged it and placed it on the floor.

"You may rise. Thank you for the kittens, Margaret."

"You are most welcome, Your Royal Highness." *Who gave them her? Who gave me credit? Do not question this gift to me.* Margaret counted five of varying shades of cream and gray or brown playing in and around a basket on the floor.

"Have you named them, Your Royal Highness?"

"I had not thought to. Though that one reminds me of my brother Duncan. He keeps trying to climb higher." Matilda smiled and her voice lightened. "I could name them after my brothers."

"Then what will you name the fifth?"

"Matilda, I suppose. Which one?"

"Why the prettiest, of course!"

The queen smiled and chuckled softly. "You pick. The girls are this one and that one."

"Why not call her Tilda. It would not do to call your name whilst you are chasing her."

The queen named Duncan, Edmund, and Alexander.

"The other female I will call 'Edgar.' She is the weakest, and they gang up and attack her. She runs and does not fight back, just as Edgar is running from Magnus."

Margaret brought the queen her namesake. While being petting, Tilda squirmed to escape.

"I do so enjoy watching them. I will miss them. We cannot have one of them sit on our babe's chest and suck the air from his body."

Margaret nodded at the common wisdom. "In the meantime, they will divert you, Your Royal Highness."

"Margaret? Where is the king?" Matilda demanded.

Margaret's eyes widened and she opened her mouth, then shut it. "I do not know, Your Royal Highness. Has he not been sending you messages?"

"What did he tell you? Where he was going? Why?"

"He told me nothing. I trust his abilities. Worry not. He will succeed at whatever he is doing."

Matilda folded her hands and leaned forward.

"Tell me what you know, Margaret. And from whom." The queen was not smiling.

"Your Royal Highness, I should have learned by now I can keep nothing from you, even for your own good. I did not want to worry you, so I have not passed what I overheard the men saying while we were journeying here."

"I want it all."

"They speculated why His Royal Highness would need such a large escort for so popular a queen. They wondered what he wanted with them afterward and guessed he had a campaign planned. They talked of his brother Robert returning or the Earl Robert de Belleme starting trouble again. When the king went north instead of south, I surmised he was chasing de Belleme. Your husband told me nothing. You are the first to ask what I think."

"I fear you are right. He is trying to rid himself of a dangerous thorn."

"His Royal Highness has succeeded in every campaign. Surely he will succeed in this one."

"De Belleme has the advantage," reported the queen. "He is rich with castles, men, and traitors who fund him. Even all our escort may not be enough."

"Worry not, Your Royal Highness. I trust the king to succeed."

The queen leaned over and scooped up a kitten to pet. "You may again call me Your Majesty when we are alone. Is it safe for me to bathe and have my hair washed on the morrow?"

"Yes, Your Majesty." Margaret smiled at being reinstated to her former position. May I assist you?" Margaret asked.

"You may. I want another square of that creamy soap that smells of that flower."

"I will order it fetched immediately." Margaret curtsied and departed.

Thank you, God. She has forgiven me. Mother, you were right. Royals are impossible. Step lightly. She can cost me my head with one complaint, for he will grant anything she asks in order to keep her happy. Again I must hide the real me. No disappointment or disgust at her moods. If she feels it, I am lost. Margaret thought of Caitlin, Jorgon, Dena and the Saxons. *We all will be.*

With three braziers ablaze, the queen was soon fanning herself with her hand. Men hauled buckets of hot water. Margaret piled the linens on a stool. While the queen enjoyed her bath, she talked. "Margaret, what kind of husband would please you?"

"A good man who will give me children and protect us."

"Do you not also want his love?"

"I suppose so. Mother told me it takes time for you to care for each other."

"Nonsense! My lord loved me the moment he saw me and I him. Six years waiting and two years married has only increased our love."

Not wanting to endanger her reinstated position, Margaret decided to choose her words carefully. "I fear you are the exception, Your Majesty. I remember you telling me at Forest Keep you refused other matches. You waited for him despite your brother's wishes. Most women have no choice at all. Her father picks him; her mother tells her it is a good match and packs her off to his estate. His mother trains her. After her courses come, they meet at the church door to be blessed and are put to bed. Where is choice or love in any of that?" Margaret tucked the queen's right leg under the blanket and reached for her left.

"Saxon or Norman?"

"For both I hear."

"I meant do you want him to be Saxon or Norman?"

"Norman. There are no Saxons of rank." When Margaret saw the queen was about to speak, she quickly added, "A lord. Only a full lord. Or His Royal Highness makes him one before we reach the church."

"I agree. A woman marries to raise her rank. He marries for wealth or power. Everyone knows that."

"May I ask why we are talking of marriage?"

"No particular reason," the queen looked away as she dissembled. While Margaret had slept away her birthing day, Elstan and Elric had snuck a man into the keep, past the guards, Dena and even Caitlin, and into the queen's private chamber. The queen heard his request, but sent him away with instructions as to what he must accomplish and acquire before she would give him her answer. Remembering the man's determination to wed Margaret, Matilda smiled. Margaret thought the queen's smile meant she was pleased with her bath.

"Your Majesty, here is the soapy rag for you to wash your front. I shall raise the linen and avert my eyes so you may do this next part yourself."

27

News

Thursday, 19 December

"His Royal Highness has but six days to get home for Midnight Mass before Christmas Day."

Margaret murmured, "Please nap, Your Majesty." She tiptoed out and closed the door.

Elric nodded at Caitlin at the fireplace and addressed Margaret in a hushed tone. "My lady, a messenger from the king is here. He says he will speak only to the queen."

"He will see me first. I want him unarmed, escorted, and between the door and the barrier for secrecy," she ordered as she moved.

The disarmed knight scowled at the armed woman before him and the Saxons on either side of him. Neither did he like the cramped space in which he stood.

"Sirrah, we beg your pardon, but His Royal Highness expressly charged us with Her Royal Highness's safety and health. I would not presume to ask the nature of your business, but I must ask if your message will bring distress to Her Royal Highness. You would not want to be the cause for the untimely arrival of the heir by giving her a shock, would you?"

"No. No. Of course not. I have come with good news and gifts from His Royal Highness, the King. I am cert my messages will cheer her."

"Her Majesty is resting at present. As soon as she wakes, I will tell her of your arrival. May I tell her you have good news?"

"By all means. Assure Her Royal Highness she will be pleased with my messages."

Matilda insisted on receiving the messenger formally in the hall. She requested the presences of Sir Roger, Bishop William Giffard, the mayor and the city council. Those from the main Court in the Great Hall of the unfinished castle near the West Gate of Winchester had been forbidden entrance to the small castle. A few had been sent for and knew of the messenger's arrival; they had walked through town on a cold blustery day and arrived with freezing fingers, red faces and snow on their mantles and boots. Honored to have been selected to enter the small castle, they waited in small clusters near the hall entrance. Margaret had persuaded the queen to sit on her throne with men below. She had asked Sir Roger to provide His Majesty's most trusted men to see the Court saw and heard everything from no closer than the back half of the hall.

"Yes, to the knights at the dais. No to the rest. I want the Court to see I am well and strong and to hear the king's message. I expect them to inspect me and see that I am only seven or eight weeks from delivery. Then they will sup with my guests." Matilda raised her hand to stop Margaret's objections. "This matter is of utmost importance. I will have my way."

"Food and drink, Your Majesty?"

"Serve me something before. I will sup afterward. I will not risk that. While I choose clothing, make preparations."

With strips of sky-blue cloth and strings of pearls to complement the queen's cream shift and dark blue bliaut, Margaret finished the queen's double braids, which hung to the backs of her knees.

Please God, may I soon wear the double braids of a married woman even if mine would be so short. Let him be a lord in his own right or a second or third son from a highly ranked family in great favor with the King. Then I might be called to Court and see Her Majesty a time or two.

The queen ate buttered bread before she set upon her head the crown she wore for formal and state occasions. Twice the height and twice as heavy as her small crown, this one was spiked all around. Round rubies shone from each peak. Rectangular sapphires separated by rectangular diamonds rounded the base. Three inches above that was a second layer of stones with diamonds above the sapphires and sapphires above the diamonds. All the gems glittered brightly in the candlelight. Margaret had marveled at its heaviness as she had lifted it from the chest that had been hidden under the queen's bed. As instructed, Margaret set the crown on Matilda's head and walked around her chair to be cert she had set it evenly. Matilda reached up and pulled the crown down more firmly over her hair.

The keep door, slightly ajar, provided light from the walkway. The sun had not yet set, but was sending deep golden shards streaming between the pillars. Elric, Elstan, and Elborg showed their breaths with every exhale as they stood outside ready to lead the women. As the queen waited, she sipped a hot posset before handing her cup to Dena. The noise in the hall rose and fell like waves against a shore. Trumpets sounded.

"Here! Here! Her Royal Highness, Matilda, Queen of England."

Margaret watched the queen stiffen, become regal, and try to walk smoothly despite her gravid condition. Matilda waddled a bit with her heavy belly pushing her legs father apart than usual. The three Saxons preceded her; Margaret and three more Saxons followed. The queen walked briskly through the pillars and into the hall. She turned right, strode to the dais, raised her mantle and skirts and took the stairs unassisted. Knights already stood before the dais. Margaret prayed they would stop any who tried to reach the queen. The Saxons stood behind the dais. On her throne the Queen of England looked down the hall and smiled. With her left hand upon her sword hilt, Margaret announced she was guarding the left-side steps of the dais. She smiled not. *So many! We could be overrun. No. Enemies will try something subtle, but what? When? They stare. She is right; they need to see her heavy with child.*

The crowd parted. The messenger was tall, thin but with broad shoulders, and better dressed than he had been when he had arrived in traveling clothes. Someone of high rank must have lent him his garments, a fur-lined gray mantle, a clean creamy tunic under a blue-dyed leather jerkin. Because he was so tall, the tunic stopped well above his knees and showed more gray leggings than a more modest man would have done. Proud to show his height with his shoulders back and his head held high, he took long strides from the hall entrance to the dais. A child accompanied him. He stopped before the knights and went to one knee. The child curtsied and knelt on both knees.

"Your Majesty, I am the king's man, Sir Walter de Mare, and his bearer of gifts and good news."

"Welcome, Sir Walter," rang through the hall. "We are eager to hear you."

The messenger stood to display what he carried. He unwrapped a large gold cross. All in the hall gasped. Raised figures and symbols decorated the plain side. The other side was heavily encrusted with large diamonds at each point of the cross and a large ruby at the cross section. In between were gems and stones of varied colors. Many whispered of its beauty and worth. The queen waited for the Court to quiet before she nodded at de Mare.

"This gold cross His Royal Highness gives to you to bestow as you wish along with the cloth of gold in which His Royal Highness wrapped it. His words to you are 'This a sign of God's favor. The cross is from the chapel of Richard of Yorkshire Dales. I have sieged and taken his lands and castle. The traitor is banished.'"

The knight stepped between two knights to place the cloth on the dais floor and the cross on top of that. He stepped back, looked toward the girl beside him and whispered. The girl stood and tried to smile, but she was near to tears with moist, protuberant green eyes staring at the rushes on the floor. The narrow-shouldered, fair-haired girl, with a new, pink scar on her left cheek and skin as pale as milk, quaked with fear. Her hands twisted in front of her. She wore no mantle and her garments were crumpled and dirty at the hem.

"May I present the Lady Adela, orphaned in the siege, an innocent who needs your love and our protection? She is our ward."

"How old are you, Adela?"

"Nine, Your Royal Highness." A tear slid down each cheek.

While the queen could be heard to the end of the hall, her tone was gentle. "Have you any accomplishments, Lady Adela?"

The girl sucked in a deep breath and answered. "Needlework and sewing, Your Royal Highness. I also play the lute and sing."

245

"Welcome to our Court, Adela." Matilda looked about and called, "Lady Claire de Clerkx."

A tall woman with angular features and thin, pursed lips stepped forward and gave obeisance. She was almost as richly dressed as the queen in her mink-lined and trimmed blue mantle, matching bliaut and leather slippers. Her smile did not reach her eyes.

"Take the Lady Adela into your excellent care. See to her needs. Instruct her in the manners of our Court. Keep her with you."

Lady Claire nodded, took the girl by the hand and taught her to walk back three steps before turning. They disappeared into the crowd.

"Bishop Giffard, please come forward."

"Accept this gift from His Royal Highness, King Henry. Please bless this cross to its new purpose. Display it on the High Altar so all may know His Royal Highness's support of our Holy Mother Church and St. Swithin's Cathedral."

The bishop re-consecrated the cross to God and to king's lawful rule over England. He thanked the queen for her generosity and continued support. He held the cross high as he left the hall. All crossed themselves as he passed.

"Your Royal Highness," called out the messenger. "The king has asked me to convey three messages."

Margaret watched the queen slip her hands from her lap to beside her thighs and clench them into tight fists.

"First, he sends his felicitations for your continued good health. Second, he wishes you to be the first to know he has routed all who went against him in July. Only those who have sworn allegiance to the him and to his rightful rule have been permitted to keep their lands. The others have forfeited all they possess and are banished. Finally, Your Royal Highness, the king has asked me to tell you he is but five or six days behind me. He said, 'I will be home for Christmastide and we will celebrate Midnight Mass together.'"

Matilda un-pursed her lips as she slowly loosened her fingers. The queen motioned Sir Roger forward. From her left hand she removed a silver ring with a green stone and held it out for him to take. She had worn it should she need to give a reward. She leaned forward and reached out while Sire Roger stepped between two knights at the dais' edge and watched her drop the ring onto his open hand.

"Sir Walter de Mare, accept this ring as a token of my gratitude for your good news."

Sir Roger handed over the ring, which Sir Walter placed on the smallest finger of his left hand. All saw Queen Matilda hold her stomach with both hands; Sir Roger smiled and nodded as she watched her bliaut move in a ripple as the babe shifted in its home. Matilda patted her belly then rubbed it gently as if to quiet the one within.

"We are pleased to have you sup with us, Sir Walter. Please take a place at our first table," said the queen as she motioned to the table where the bishop, Sir Roger and the others of importance would dine.

With her hands above and below her bulbous stomach, Matilda oversaw the Court as they supped. A few stepped toward the dais. Each time a knight shook his head or took a step forward, giving the warning the queen was not to be approached. When the queen stood to leave, all talk stopped, all in the Court stood and all remained silent until she disappeared through the doorway to the keep.

After serving the queen her meal and helping her to bed, Margaret rubbed her back. "Is there anything I may do for you Your Majesty?"

"No. Leave me."

Margaret slipped away. Later she put her ear to the bedroom door.

Margaret whispered to Caitlin, "The queen is crying. What shall I do?"

Caitlin lifted her head from her pillow. "She is most likely crying with relief he is safe and coming home. Never tell her you heard her. Go to bed. "

Margaret knelt at her cot and was a long time praying, for her mother, Caitlin, the queen and her babe, Dena and her babe, Jorgon, the Bishop, Adela, and many more. She returned to the queen's door and noted silence. She offered another prayer for the queen's good rest and tiptoed to her own cot. Once abed she prayed for herself with hands clasped under her heavy coverings.

Oh God, I thank you I am not the queen. I never want a life like hers. Lonely. Dangerous. If it be Your will, protect her child and bring it safely into this world. Protect Dena's child too. Even if it is a bastard, it is still my brother or sister. Holy Spirit, please enter their bodies and give them their souls that they might live. Jesus, the Christ, if it be it your will, please send me a good husband who will care for me and protect me. I vow to be as good a wife as I know how to be. Let the king be generous and grant my boons. Grant me the wisdom to ask for the right things. Mary, Mother of God, watch over Her Majesty in her hour of birth. She needs you. Please let Caitlin, Dena, Jorgon and Night continue to be safely under your care. Oh God, what happens to me is Yours to decide, but do not let them die because of me. Your will, Oh God, in all things. Margaret sighed and remembered to thank God for the rest as well. *Thank you, God, for the king returning triumphant, for helping me choose the right side in the struggle for the crown, and for getting me back into the queen's good graces. Thank You, God, for everything.* Margaret rolled over, touched her sheathed sword on the floor, and smiled to herself. She immediately fell into a peaceful, deep, and dreamless sleep.

28

Christmastide 1101 A.D.

December twenty-third began with Elric requesting to speak with the queen. When he left her chamber, he winked at Margaret.

"Attend her. She will be in a tizzy. We will clean and cook," ordered Caitlin.

Margaret had no chance to respond, for the queen had barked her name. She cleaned the solar and the bedchamber. Then she re-folded the queen's clothing and made room for the king's while Father Gregory and the queen prayed in the solar. Matilda returned from prayers in a calm and serene mood, which she slowly abandoned before dinner. She dropped stitches and mumbled. Suddenly needlework bored her, so she stood and paced. At noon Matilda declined to dine and stared through an arrow slit. Margaret insisted the queen eat all her dinner and rest, even if she did not nap. Matilda tried to lie down after dinner, but she soon popped up and returned to pacing with hands together in prayer. The queen ate only half her supper and spent the evening kneeling before her altar in prayer. Finally tired, the queen took to her bed. Exhausted by the queen's emotional swings from calm to worried to distressed and back again, Margaret slept hard.

In relay, the news passed from pages to Saxons to Lady Margaret to the queen. King Henry entered the west gate; he approached the castle; he met Sir Roger at the portcullis. Huzzahs and applause announced His Royal Highness's arrival in the hall. The noon meal simmered. With backs against the wall, the women gave obeisance as the king passed and did not move until he climbed the stairs to the queen's floor. When summoned, Margaret reported with tray in hand and promptly left.

"Put her to her nap," the king said as he departed.

Elric reported the king dined a second time with the Court.

"For the queen's benefit, Midnight Mass will be in the hall as well as in the cathedral," said Elric. "Too icy for her to walk. They will sup afterward with the Court."

Margaret gasped.

"My lady, she will sup from our stores. The king has already informed several people his queen is eating special foods to keep her in good health. No one dare speak any suspicions. I will serve her."

"Thank you, Elric."

A holy day, Christmas was a solemn occasion begun with Midnight Mass and an early breakfast to break the Advent fast. The royals and couriers ate a full meal that began with a meat and vegetable soup in bone broth, bread and butter, ale and wine. The second course was roasted small game, such as birds and rabbit, followed by more bread served with a variety of cheeses. Simple folk ate vegetable soup with meat—if they had it—bread and butter and ale. Those not working took to their beds with full, happy stomachs to sleep well past dawn. At noon those of the Court dined on a sumptuous feast with a soup course followed by two fish courses, three meat courses, and many trays of accompaniments. Wine and ale flowed through toasts and talk. Sweets finished the meal, which had lasted hours. Between courses, musicians, jugglers and others entertained those in the hall. Tables set against one wall held leftovers.

From time to time, Margaret peeked from the doorway. The queen looked to be enjoying herself immensely. Late in the afternoon, Margaret noted her slightly drooping shoulders and a rounding of her back; Matilda was tiring but Margaret could say nothing, do nothing.

Caitlin and Dena had outdone themselves for those in the keep and served a meal much like that of the court, but with only one fish and one meat course followed by honeyed stewed fruits. The men drank ale in moderation as they had to take turns at guard duty.

At dark, the queen returned and Margaret bathed her face, hands, and feet in warm water and Casteela soap to help her relax before bed. The king and the Court celebrated until late into the night.

The next days were spent in the same routine. In the solar, Father Gregory celebrated Mass with the king and queen and those not on duty. The royals broke their fasts in a private meal, and the king departed for the hall to hold Christmas court to hear and rule on the pleas from any Norman or Saxon, who came with needs or grievances, as his father had done during his reign. Each morning a Saxon escorted one person into the queen's presence for a brief visit. The first to appear were the Lady Claire de Clerkx and Lady Adela. Lady Claire, still thin-lipped and stiff-backed, scowled at Margaret and lifted her nose as she passed. Lady Adela tried to curtsey, but Lady Claire pulled her up and dragged her away. Margaret smiled at the girl. As she departed, Lady Claire frowned with disdain at all she saw, the women, their surroundings, and the smells from the cooking pots. Lady Adela meekly followed. While the queen napped, the king hunted or gambled with his courtiers. New Year's Eve was for men to drink and game after they had supped. They yelled in the new year to frighten away evil and to usher in the goodness and holiness they had prayed for that morning.

As January 1 was the feast day of Saint Almachius the Martyr and Saint Basil the Bishop of Aix, a High Mass was held in the hall so the queen could attend. On this day each baron and earl in the realm renewed his allegiance to the king and repeated his oath to serve and defend the realm at the king's command. Winchester overflowed with the arrivals of nobles. A few had brought their wives. As with all Court events, the nobles had reserved every room or house available. Many families, both Norman and Saxon, crowded together to share the rent from their vacant homes. The profits would see them through their winter needs should their stored food, drink or medicines fall short.

Dressed in finery that included fur-lined and edged mantles, richly dyed, and their larger, matching bejeweled court crowns, the king escorted the queen to their thrones. Once again, six Saxons stood behind the dais. Margaret stood inside the hall door nearest to the keep and watched the proceedings from the shadows. Sir Roger announced a lord, who stepped forward and knelt. He placed his sword upon the dais, swore his allegiance and made his oaths. The king accepted the man and told him to take back his sword. Of most men the king asked about their lands or local conditions. Some he congratulated; he talked quietly to each man.

Margaret waited to see Sir William. Her heart jumped when Sir Roger called his name. She flushed when she saw him stride forward in high polished boots and resplendent in blue and brown. Hoping he might look her way, Margaret took a step forward. He did not, and her heart seemed to fall into her stomach. His part over, he took three steps backward, turned left, and disappeared into the crowd. Margaret's mood dropped further as she waited through a dozen more men.

Surely he knows I am here. Why did he not move where we might at least look at each other if we cannot speak? Has he forgotten me? Has he forgotten his promise to champion my reputation? Was he attentive because I was the only Norman lady of rank with him? Please, God, let him remember me as I do him.

Despairing of seeing William, Margaret was about to leave, when she spotted him. Now only a few feet away, William was slowly turning so the man speaking to him was forced to turn as well. When William was finally facing Margaret's direction, he looked up. And he smiled. His eyes looked down at the man speaking and darted up to catch her gaze. Margaret held her breath as her heart raced. *Do that again and I will know you purpose me to smile back.* Margaret did so. She looked away to hide her purpose as well. When next she glanced at William, to his smile he added a tiny tilt of his head and a minuscule shrug.

If we speak, they will talk. She will learn of it and we will have trouble. William gave a tiny nod as if he had heard her thoughts. *Drat! My face shows all.* Margaret repeated his nod and added a tiny shrug. She watched William place a hand on the man's shoulder. She felt the weight of his hand upon her shoulder too and lowered her eyes. When Margaret looked up, she saw William raise his brows as if to ask, "Dare we?" Margaret gave him the tiniest shake of her head. Then, in front of her waist, she clasped her hands together with fingers entwined. *I shall pray for you, for us.* William sucked in his lips to stop a grin, gave a final small nod and turned to walk beside the man. The crowd swallowed them. Margaret dropped her head so no one would see her flushed face and notice her breast rising and falling so fast. She turned and disappeared into the walkway to the keep.

We spoke not, yet I heard his voice in my head. We touched not, but I feel him. His lips when he kissed my forehead. I am warmed in places I should not be. Oh William, I do want you. To be your wife would be heavenly. I want your arms around me again, always. I want whatever married couples do in bed. Margaret shook her head to stop that thought and climbed the stairs, grabbed a stool and placed it in a corner. She leaned back against the walls and hugged herself. The fireplace *is too warm. Dear William! You do care! Thank you, God, for giving me hope. Now I am sure of my boons. I want a dowry great enough to suit him. No, I must not be so specific, or the king will know my thinking. A dowry great enough to … to… attract a family of good rank. No, a family of suitable rank, my rank is high enough. I will specify he must loyal to the king; the king will like I add that condition. Ask for that before I ask for a lord. No. I must hide my thoughts. I will ask for a man who is already a lord or a man the king will make a lord before we meet at the church door. Please, God, tell the king to let me have William. I want William.* The memory of being kissed, the languor, the warmth in her breast and loins jostled her mind. *That was not William I dreamed. I know it. Forget the kiss. It was just a drunken desire and not a true memory.*

In the hall the proceedings took two more hours. The Court would dine well but the custom was to save the greatest feast for Epiphany, final day of Christmas Court. Caitlin saw Margaret hugging herself in a corner and ignored her because she was unwilling to suffer whatever mood the girl was in. Not until Dena came to the fireplace to request the queen's dinner did Margaret stand and join the pair at the fireplace.

The next morning the exodus began. Soon the Court and the town were almost back to normal size and in their regular winter routines. King Henry invited only the most privileged barons and earls to stay for the Epiphany feast, the finale of Christmas Court. Two days before Epiphany, the queen was ready for her nap.

"As I rest, fetch your mantle and scarf. Go with Elric and Elstan."

"I am to go outside?"

Margaret was so surprised she forgot to say, "Your Majesty."

"An early Epiphany gift. They will escort you."

The men met her at the barrier.

"My lady, the courtiers gossip about you because they have seen you only from a distance. May I suggest how you conduct yourself now will be talked about for days."

"I understand, Elric, but I am not parting with my sword."

"No. No. Some courtiers want to see you with it. Mayhap anger you into using it? We can be of no help to you."

"Stand behind me. I will show them I am more than an 'ignorant country girl' as the Lady Claire calls me."

In the hall Margaret first looked toward the king, but he was in conversation. She found a path to the door. She walked halfway when someone stepped right and turned her back. Margaret stopped behind the woman.

She leaned forward and whispered, "I am on the queen's business. Please move."

Frowning, the woman turned and looked down her nose at Margaret as if she had just seen her for the first time.

"Mine men and I need space."

Hands out, Margaret flicked her wrists to indicate the party should separate. No one moved.

"I shall call the king's attention to your lack of cooperation," Margaret threatened.

People stepped back. Grasping her hilt, Margaret swung her scabbard out. Beside her people jumped back so as to not have their knees knocked. She continued out the door at a brisk pace and with eyes forward.

Will I be allowed out of the grounds?

At the bottom of the stairs, Elric said, "Left, please."

Night! Stern of face, Margaret marched as she turned the corner and strode down the side yard.

"Well done, my lady. They learned not to trifle with you."

Margaret grinned as she picked up her pace. "Thank you, Elstan. Visit or ride?"

"Visit. Sorry. Mayhap you may walk the yard with him. Do you want him brought out?"

"I shall meet him at his stall. See his conditions."

Jorgon stood at Night's stall. When Margaret entered the stables, she waved as she walked toward him. Jargon pulled on his forelock as he lowered his head and stepped back.

Night's nicker became a full whinny. Other horses answered. Margaret enjoyed their noise and even barn smells of hay and manure. Night kicked his door.

I have missed you so! She unlatched the top half-door. Night pushed it open and nickered at her before he lipped her shoulder. Margaret leaned against the door as she hugged his face hard. "Night. My Night! I have not abandoned you." She kissed his cheek and kept talking and stroking him. "She keeps us apart, my friend." Night nickered. "I like it not any more than you do." Margaret stroked the Percheron's neck and talked to him for several minutes as they both calmed themselves. Elric touched her elbow. Looking down, she saw a halved apple. Margaret began her ritual with her beloved fifteen-hand pet. Night crunched and ate. He looked over her shoulder and, as usual, found the second half behind her back. Night enjoyed his treat, but Margaret was frowning. She stroked his forehead and face; she examined his muzzle.

Gray starting on your muzzle. Are you getting old? You are well groomed and have been brushed. How well do you move?

"Jorgon." The hostler stepped forward. "Thank you for taking such good care of him. He looks… older. Has he stiffened?"

"Yes, but only a bit, my lady. As a Saxon may not ride; I only trot him around the yard. He has been anxious of late because he has not been ridden."

"And his tricks?"

"He will not do them for me. He is waiting for you and is getting testy too. He nips at the other horses if they come near him. I exercise him very early or very late. We have no rank, he and I."

Everyone stopped and stood aside as Margaret ran her horse to the center of the yard. A few men called to others to watch the girl and her gelding. Margaret's hair was mussed by the wind and her mantle flapped. She handed Night's halter rope to Jorgon. As she walked away, her mantle billowed open, and cold again rushed up the skirt of her bliaut and chilled her legs. Margaret's scarf had fallen back. She tucked her hair behind her ears to keep it out of her face. Night perked his ears.

Margaret turned back and curtsied. With one forefoot bent, Night bowed. Margaret clapped her hands and called out praise. She pumped her hands. Night pranced his front legs. Margaret stopped sooner than usual and he stopped too. Margaret spun left, Night right. Someone in the yard laughed at Jorgon running to keep the gelding from tangling his halter rope. Margaret did not hear the laughter. Her hair danced in the wind, but she knew it not. Only Night existed. She watched him side step with excitement.

"Wait for it!" she commanded.

Margaret stood still until Night did. She raised her arms and shook her hands. Night neighed as he stood on his hind legs and pawed the air. Instead of staying in the air, he dropped his forefeet to the ground. *You are getting old, poor baby. No more jumping fences for us.* Margaret ended with a curtsey. Night bowed. She ran to her horse. This time Night waited for her. Just then a knight walked a stallion out of the stable. Margaret grabbed Night's halter and pulled his head downward.

"No!" Margaret commanded when Night tried to turn his head toward the stallion,

"Obey!"

That she controlled a man's horse surprised the dozen or so Normans and Saxons standing about in the yard. They could see how strong she was, how the gelding obeyed her. With her free hand Margaret accepted the coiled rope from Jorgon. She kept Night's head down until a knight mounted and rode away.

"Good boy," said Margaret as she loosed his head but kept her hand close to the halter.

"Jorgon, have you circled him?"

"This morning, my lady. A short walk might do him good. He needs cooling."

Margaret turned a circle as she loosed the rope. Each time Night walked a round, she gave him more rope. Jorgon stood aside and watched. Elstan and Elric visited. When Night slowed his pace, Margaret stopped and led him back to his stall. Jargon threw Night's blanket over his back and tied its leather thongs under his belly.

Margaret asked about Night's food and water regimen and approved of what Jorgon had been doing. With many strokes on her horse's neck and back, Margaret talked to Night. She gave him oats in his food bag and shut the bottom door.

"Jorgon, have you seen Dena lately?"

"Not since we arrived."

"I will ask the queen for you to visit. I will remind her you two are betrothed. I cannot predict what she will say."

"Thank you, my lady."

Margaret finger-combed her hair. At the stable door, Elric and Elstan joined her. They returned to the keep without incident. Hair properly combed but still flushed from the cold, Margaret knelt before the queen and kissed her hand.

"Thank you, Your Majesty. You have given me the best Epiphany gift ever."

The queen sat in her chair with her needlework in her lap. "He is well?"

"Yes. He still loves apples and remembers our tricks." Margaret related her visit with Night. Still on her knees, she spoke for Jorgon. "Your Majesty, I am sure you remember Dena and my hostler Jorgon are betrothed. They have not seen each other since we arrived. May they have a similar Epiphany gift? May Jorgon visit her here?"

"Yes. He may enter the keep this evening after we sup. They must be supervised, of course. They are only betrothed and not yet married."

"Yes, Your Majesty. Thank you, Your Majesty."

Matilda resumed her needlework. Glad at having been allowed outside, Margaret stood with her just-brushed hair shining in the sunlight streaming into the solar. Margaret waited until she was dismissed. Her voice and step were light as she left the room with a cheery, "Thank you, Your Majesty."

In memory of the Magi and of their gifts to the baby Jesus, on Epiphany friends and families gave each other gifts and ate the best dinner they could afford. The queen gave her gifts before her appearance at Court. Dena received clothes for her babe. Caitlin received a new mantle and matching scarf of gray wool. Margaret 's mantle and scarf were blue wool and edged in rabbit fur. Each Saxon received a new shirt and a leather belt.

The Feast of the Epiphany celebration was second only to the Easter celebration. Course after course with matching wines arrived, each course more lavish than the one before. The broth was thick with chunks of meat and vegetables. In each second course of three different fishes, the fish swam in a sauce of buttered white wine. Each pair of persons on the dais could reach a tray of bread and a tub of butter. Bread and butter dotted the tables for the rest of the Court invited to the feast. Warmed red wines had been dribbled over large platters of the meats to moisten and flavor them. One set of pages lumbered into the hall with full trays in hand as another set of pages whisked away the empty platters. The boys sweated with the hard work of carrying the heavy loads and holding them between pairs of diners. Each person used his or her dagger to spear meat and lift it to their plates. The pages waited between courses to refill goblets, cups, and mugs. Ale, wine, and cider flowed. Troubadours sang between the performances of the dancers. Margaret dined not. She stood beside the fireplace behind the royals and watched the queen for signs of tiredness. By now the Court expected the royals would stay on their thrones and dine privately.

After the long feast, their own meals, and with the queen abed, Margaret, Caitlin, Dena and the Saxons exchanged gifts. From the women, the men received a joint gift of either a shirt or knitted leggings. Margaret received two squares of turino soap. She gushed her gratitude at so fine a gift and promised to wash her face and hands with one that very night. The men gave Caitlin a shawl. Dena received two blankets in which to swaddle her babe. Caitlin had sewn the nursing shift with a scooped front, and Margaret presented Dena with the nursing gunna, which had a panel over the holes for breasts, so Dena could lift one side or the other to nurse. Both Margaret and Caitlin gave Dena two dozen bottoms for her babe. Dena gave each woman a strip of linen to tie up their hair when they bathed. Earlier she had passed Jorgon's gift to Elborg to deliver as had Caitlin and Margaret.

All remained calm for two weeks.

29

Dilemma

Dena closed the queen's door behind her. Pale and shaking, Dena reached the bottom of the stairs and collapsed against the wall and groaned. Caitlin and Margaret rushed to her.

"Are you well? Is the babe coming?"

When Margaret saw the girl's tears, she repeated her questions to no avail.

"To her cot," advised Caitlin. "Talk later."

Margaret stood beside her and held her hand. Caitlin insisted on examining Dena and pushed her hands away when the girl objected.

"You are not wet. Not bleeding. Not in labor. What has upset you?" asked Caitlin.

Dena had covered her face with her arm. Before Caitlin received an answer, a man called her away. Once Margaret and Dena were alone, Margaret continued to worry about the girl.

"How has the queen upset you? What may I do to make it better?"

"Nothing," came Dena's muffled response. After a time, she added, "I am lost. We are lost. All has been for naught."

Still holding Dena's hand, Margaret knelt beside her. "Dena, Caitlin and I brought you. I am responsible for you. We are your friends. Surely one of us can help you."

Dena wiped her nose with her sleeve and whispered. "She forbade me to tell." Then Dena told part. "The queen knows we ran away. She has threatened to send Jorgon and me back. Unless…unless."

"Unless you do something she wants," guessed Margaret.

Dena placed her arms around her belly. As Margaret watched as Dena caressed her unborn child with fear in her eyes. Margaret gave voice to her suspicion.

She whispered, "She has kept you hidden. If you have a boy and she has a girl, she wants your son."

Dena nodded as more tears freshened her cheeks. She turned into her pillow to hide the noises of her sobbing.

"Sh-h. Sh-h." Margaret hugged Dena's back. "She cannot do it without Caitlin and me knowing. We are to deliver her babe."

Raising her head a bit, Dena answered, "If she sends us back, he will kill us. Me for carrying his bastard. My babe for being his, and Jorgon for taking me away."

"Dena, she will not return you. She made an idle threat. She needs you and your babe."

"Not if I have a girl. If I give her my son, I place him in great danger. Someone poisoned her first son; they could poison mine too." Dena sat up and put her hands to her face to muffle her words, "I am going to lose. If I birth a girl, she, Jorgon and I will die. If I birth a boy and she a girl, she will take him, and I will never see him again. Either way I lose my child. We are lost, lost!"

Margaret looked across the room toward the light from an arrow slit. "Mayhap not. Dena, stop crying. Let me think." The silence unnerved Dena further; tears coursed down her cheeks. Margaret whispered, "We cannot stop her. She is the queen and can order anything she desires. She can force you to do as she wishes and then eliminate you, all of us." Margaret paused. "If she does take your son, he will be a prince, heir to the kingdom. You will be giving him a good life; you can watch from afar and be proud of him." Dena stopped sniveling, so Margaret continued. "A girl is another matter. Margaret sighed and thought aloud. "As long as the queen thinks you might have a son, you have what she wants. This is your advantage over her. A small one. How do we use it?" Margaret pondered again. "I know, I know! Before you deliver, you must wrest your freedom and other promises from her."

Dena raised her head from her hands. "What promises?"

Trying to convey hope, Margaret smiled at Dena. "Tell her she may have your son for a price. She will take him anyway. Say you want royal decrees declaring you and Jorgon are free Saxons. You want an immediate marriage. You want coin to start a new life. Royals know they must pay for what they want. She will believe you mean it if you ask for money. Then promise you will leave and never return. Tell her she is buying your silence. But you must mean it. Disappearing is your only way to be safe from her plotting."

Dena pulled away from Margaret. "You ask her for me. You tell her what I want."

"I cannot. She forbade you to tell anyone, remember? What I can do is to help you form your requests."

"I cannot. I cannot," demurred the girl as she started to weep.

Margaret shook Dena's shoulders as she ordered, "You must do it yourself. You must do it today."

Margaret talked, advised, and cajoled, until Dena stopped crying, sat up straight and began to ask questions. Dena practiced what she wanted to say, but she broke down halfway through her recitation. With Margaret's encouragement Dena began again and repeated it several times. With each telling Dena began to take more charge of her situation. Her courage grew. She practiced on Margaret, who pretended to be the queen. Margaret knew she was not being nearly as stern or as hard as she knew the queen could be.

"You must withstand her threats, her attacks. Stand still and straight and just listen to her rant. Remain calm no matter what she says. You have something she needs. You may not get all you want, but you can stay out of Sir Charles's clutches if you remain firm. Insist upon at least that. She has the power to grant both your freedoms. Demand it. Threaten to return to Sir Charles yourselves. Stand and stare at her in silence. She hates that. She will not send you away as long as you might be carrying a son."

"If she does, we go to our deaths, Jorgon, the babe, me."

"Trust me, she will not do it. Remember, if your freedom is not written and stamped with the queen's seal, then she can go back on her word. You must get your papers."

"I will. I promise."

"Good." Then Margaret thought of something else. "Wait until tonight and after we sup. Take a nap now and sup well yourself. Asking her before her bedtime will give her all night to worry over what she might lose if she refuses you."

From the other room, the pair heard Caitlin calling.

"The queen is asking for you, my lady."

After hugging Dena and making her lie back, Margaret forced herself to smile and put on a pleasant countenance before she went to the queen.

Smile. Be cheerful. Play ignorant. Stay uninformed.

30

Contracts and Confinements

Two days later the queen's babe shifted head down and Dena went into her first false labor. The next day Caitlin noted Sir Roger's comings and goings, but Margaret pleaded ignorance when Caitlin asked about what the queen was doing. Margaret sat under an arrow slit and kept sewing christening gifts for the coming babes.

Dena pulled both women toward the fireplace and whispered her news. "Her Royal Highness has paid Sir Charles the wergild for his losing Jorgon and me. Our banns are being announced in a church in town. In two days, Father will bless our wedding outside the solar before Mass." Dena accepted hugs and congratulations. "Will you be my witnesses?"

"Of course we will," blubbered Caitlin as she wiped her eyes.

Because Dena had been confined to the Queen's rooms, Jorgon shopped for their new clothes, a bed, bedding and a screen and had paid for all from the bag of coins the queen had given them. Dena stayed away from everyone and only smiled when Caitlin asked questions. Margaret asked nothing to the girl as she worried about her part in the plot. *Oh God, I pray Dena deliver a girl, but I fear she will not. Her skin is clear, not muddy as it would be if she were carrying a girl. Her hair is longer, thicker, and shiny. All signs she is carrying a boy. The queen's face and hair tell me she is not. Why, God? Why?* Margaret sighed. *I know. Your will, Oh God, in all things. Praying I am wrong has done no good.*

First Margaret fretted over her part in the queen's trickery; then she worried she had condemned her soul to eternal Hell. She dared not confess to Father Gregory, for that would make him part of the plot. *It matters not priests are sworn to secrecy and cannot reveal what is confessed. His very actions could reveal my words and condemn us both to death. I cannot undo what I have done. God, will you ever forgive me? I pray that You will. I remember. Your will, Oh God, in all things.* She prayed several times a day.

Dena finally took Margaret aside and confided, "I did what you said. These are the documents from the king's scribe with the king's seal. Our marriage certificate reads 'Dena, Saxon Free Woman' and 'Jorgon, Saxon Free Man.' Jorgon says I am to keep these papers with me and never leave them where they can be taken or destroyed. We are so grateful, my lady. With your help, we are free!" Dena hugged Margaret hard.

The risks! "Are you sure?" was all Margaret dare ask.

"I prayed." Dena rubbed her belly. "I gave my babe to God. He will decide its fate, and I will bear whatever comes." But Dena sighed as if she were unsure of her decision.

"And Jorgon?"

"Knows none of this. Only we are free, to be wed, and paid by the queen for our service. She told me we are free to leave after the prince is weaned. Until then we get a bed and screen here. Jorgon may sleep with me." Dena saw Margaret frown. "I know. I know.

I should not lie to him about any of this, but she has ordered me never to tell him."

On the fourth day after Queen Matilda and Dena had bargained, Queen Matilda waited inside the solar for Mass to begin. Jorgon, Dena, Caitlin and Margaret stood outside the solar door. Father Gregory read aloud the marriage contract and asked the usual questions.

"Do you, Dena, Saxon Free Woman, enter this marriage contract of your own free will?"

"Yes, Father."

The priest asked the same of Jorgon.

"This marriage is valid in the eyes of God and is as everlasting as is His Church. Let all witnesses say, "Aye." After they did so, Father Gregory gave the ritual blessing.

After Mass, the couple enjoyed a small celebration, breaking their fasts with Margaret, Caitlin, Elric, and several of the other Saxon guards.

"Now we put you to bed, Dena, and Jorgon goes to you," Caitlin announced.

"That is silly." Dena giggled. "I will deliver in days. What good is inspecting sheets now?

After you have put us to bed, you will not find the blood of my lost virginity on the sheets."

Caitlin disagreed. "It is not silly. You will follow custom and not mock it. Someday you can tell your children you two were put to bed for the first time in a royal castle in Winchester under the Queen of England's supervision. How many can say that?"

"How many would believe it?" countered Dena. "Oh, well. I want a nap. Jorgon can rub my back."

After the putting of the couple to bed and the guests' departures, Margaret went to the queen. "I am sorry, Your Majesty. He is out of the channel and sideways again."

"I felt him moving."

"Even if this son does not turn down again, Caitlin has a way of rubbing your belly so he will."

"If my counting is correct, His Highness has less than a dozen days to get home for his heir's birth."

Margaret said nothing. Two days later, Dena suffered another set of false labor pains. "When will this be real? It is years since I saw my feet. I want this over!"

Caitlin laughed. "When the real pains start, you will know. Know you why it takes nine months to deliver? To make you willing to suffer even as did Eve and to give a man time to realize he is a father."

For two more days Dena paced. Sat. Became uncomfortable. Walked. Napped. Tried to sew. Paced and started all over again. Her best distraction was Jorgon, who joined them for meals and gave them news from the yard. He and Caitlin were as busy with Dena as Margaret and Father Gregory were with the queen.

Another day, another supper, another evening of her sitting fireside. She is petulant and distressed and hopeful and then worried. She asked for the king's whereabouts again. I want all this to be over as much as she does.

On a sunny but cold afternoon, Dena emitted half a scream, half a groan as she leaned back and almost fell from her stool. Caitlin and Margaret came running. As they helped Dena rise, she doubled over. A gush of fluid wet their shoes.

Jorgon became frantic.

"What do I do? What do I do?" he asked as he rang his hands.

"Clean that up," ordered Caitlin. "Build a high fire and boil plenty of water. We will see to her."

The women disappeared behind the bed screen.

Soon Jorgon called out, "The fire is high and the water is heating. What do I do now, Caitlin?"

"Leave the wing and do not return until we call you. This could be all night and all the morrow."

Margaret added, "This is her first, Jorgon. Nothing for you to do. Visit Night. Sleep. We will send for you."

Dena's howl of pain drove Jorgon off the floor and out of the building.

"Stop that," ordered Caitlin. "You have hours to go. I will not have you scaring the queen!"

"But it hurts!" said Dena. "The other ones were tiny compared to this."

"And they will get worse," predicted Caitlin. "The babe is head down. The more you walk the faster you will deliver."

Margaret and Caitlin each put a hand under Dena's armpit as she walked back and forth. At each set of rolling pains, they supported her. Hours later, Caitlin announced the babe had pushed the ring open; she could feel the top of its head. Dena used the bedpost to steady herself as the pains came faster and faster.

"He will be down the channel and out soon. Then we will send for Father to baptize him."

"Caitlin, Dena is going to birth a girl."

"We will know soon enough."

"You do not comprehend, Caitlin. Dena is going to have a girl no matter which it is."

"I knew something was wrong about them suddenly being free and paid. This is her doings! You cannot do this! God will punish you both for defying His will, His plan for who will rule England." Caitlin scowled. "She ordered this. Bought the babe with their freedom. When the king finds out what you and she have done, he will know the lie and we will die for it." Caitlin objected. She raged and refused to cooperate. After much persuasion, she relented. "I will not speak a lie. You say 'girl,' not I. I pray you three know what you are doing. Either way, a babe's life is in danger. Why it must be a poor Saxon's rather than a rich Norman's is beyond my ken."

At Dena's next real howl, the women positioned her on the birthing stool. Margaret ran for hot water. Caitlin rinsed her hands again and checked the babe's progress. Caitlin massaged Dena's stomach as she suffered wave after wave of contractions. Dena was too busy to scream about the pain.

"I see its head. Keep pushing, Dena. Once its shoulders are past your bones, it will just slip out."

In a final burst of strength, Dena heaved herself upon on her hands and bore down with all her might. Then she fell back against Margaret. The babe let out a lusty yell.

Between sobs, Dena called out, "My babe! My babe!" as she reached out.

Still attached to his mother through the pulsing umbilical cord, the babe wailed. Caitlin tied threads around the cord three inches apart and waited until the cord stopped pulsing and flattened. She cut the cord, wrapped the babe in clean cloth, handed up the child, and placed the babe on Dena's chest. Margaret covered him with a cloth to keep him warm against his mother's skin. Dena hugged the babe close and cooed to it until it quieted.

From Caitlin's nod, Margaret knew Dena had delivered the birth bag and was not bleeding unduly.

"Dena, it is a girl."

Margaret undid the cloth and showed Dena the genitals that made her remark a lie. Tired as she was, Dena smiled as she stroked her son's back. Margaret took the boy and wiped him with clean rags, wrapped his bottom and tightly swaddled him. She returned the babe to his mother's chest. Dena grabbed her son and began softly crying.

"Jorgon. I want Jorgon."

"Not yet," advised Caitlin. "First, we clean you up and put you in a new shift. Once you are abed, we will call him. As soon as the babe starts nuzzling you, you must nurse. His work will bring on your milk."

"Her work," Margaret corrected her.

Caitlin glared.

Tired from no sleep and sixteen hours' work, Margaret arched her back. Only then did she notice daylight streaming through the slits. *Has she slept through any of this?*

Margaret knocked on the queen's door and entered.

Shaking her head in the negative, Margaret reported, "Dena has borne a healthy girl. Please do not undress her in the presence of others."

Matilda covered her face with her hands. Then with one hand, she waved Margaret away.

Margaret departed and softly closed the door behind herself. She returned to mother and child and hugged Caitlin. "Are they not beautiful?"

Caitlin sniffed. "Someday, God willing, a powerful lord will pace outside your room." Caitlin pulled them around the screen and whispered, "Does Jorgon know of this?"

"No. And he is not to be told. Only you, me, Dena and the royals." Margaret reached for a stool and set her former nurse upon it. "You rest. I will send for Jorgon."

The new father rounded the screen and froze. Then he tiptoed to the bed. All Margaret's attention was for Caitlin as she walked her to her cot and put her to bed.

"Sleep the remainder of the day. I will cook."

Caitlin only grunted as she rolled to the wall. Margaret covered her former nurse and patted her shoulder before she tiptoed away. Before they supped, the queen visited Dena and the child for a few moments. Caitlin woke in time to eat. Jorgon wolfed down his food, so he could hold his child while Dena ate. As he helped Caitlin at the fire, Margaret visited Dena.

"'She' has a lusty appetite. 'She' sucks hard." Dena smiled. "Jorgon chose his mother's name for 'her.'"

"Do not say 'she' and 'her' like that," admonished Margaret. "Someone might suspect.

Treat her like a girl; call her a girl. Use the name her father gave her."

Dena blurted a whisper. "I hate fooling Jorgon this way!"

Margaret rasped her whisper in return. "You must. You agreed. He must believe and talk as if you have a daughter. It is safer that way."

"Safer for who?" challenged Dena. "Certainly not for my child! If it is true, what they say. That their firstborn was poisoned in her womb. Might they not poison my son to keep them from having an heir? Even if she makes him a prince, he's mine. Mine. His life will be in danger every minute." Dena hugged her son so hard he stirred in his sleep and she had to loosen her grip on him. "And what if she has a boy? Then what? I did not think of that when I agreed to her plan. What do we do then? What do we tell Jorgon?"

Margaret spoke in low, measured words. "We will keep your babe as safe as possible. You will stay with it; we will stay with you. If she also has a son, we will… " Margaret looked away. "We will think of what we need do then."

"I hate the bargain we made. I wish we had never done it. We are not really free. We are in more danger than ever."

"If you break your bargain with the queen, what will she do? I shudder to think of it."

Dena kissed her sleeping child's head and hugged her babe close. "Please, God, give her a son, so I may keep mine," prayed Dena.

Margaret chose silence and slipped around the bed screen as Dena repeated her prayer. Afraid Caitlin was awake and glaring at her, she looked at the floor as she passed Caitlin abed. Kneeling beside her cot, Margaret was a long time praying. *Please, God, give the royals their own son, so Dena may keep hers. Even though he is unbaptized and not yet a Christian, he is an innocent in all this. My idea, my sin of plotting. I turned Dena's mind; she only did what I helped her to do. My little brother, a prince then the king, always in danger.* Margaret shook her head in refusal. *Rather a poor Saxon's son and safe. I know. I know. Your will in all things. But did I do Your will? Did you plant this idea in my head? If that, so be it. Your will in all things. What if the Devil planted the idea? Then what happens next is all my fault for having fallen into the Devil's clutches. I will have sinned against You, Oh God. I will have taken those I love into Hell with me. My sin, my sin. I am too rash. I do before I think of the consequences, of what is the worst that can happen. Too late. I cannot stop it now. All I can do is pray for Dena, her son, Jorgon, all of us. Your will, Oh God, in all things. Your will, Your will, not mine, never mine, no matter how good my intentions.* Margaret's tears came as she continued to pray. Finally she crept under her bedding but slept not.

Two days later the queen grabbed her armrests and half lifted herself from her chair.

"Too soon!" she gasped. Her body tensed in rejection of birth. "This babe cannot come now! He is not here!"

Margaret called Caitlin. They watched the queen twist and grimace through the next contraction. Margaret asked permission of the queen for Caitlin and her to touch her.

"Send for the mayor. Tell him to bring three councilmen of his choosing. Send for Bishop Giffard. Tell Sir Roger I need three lords from the Great Council if he can muster them now. They must see I am in labor." Another spasm overtook the queen. That over, she waved Margaret away. "Prepare."

Margaret stood firm and begged, "Your Majesty, we must check the babe's head. You need to walk and stand to keep him in the birthing position. We need to touch you Please, Your Majesty."

Matilda released the lungful of air she had been holding and nodded. She let the women assist her to rise and step to the bed. Once Matilda clutched the bed post, Margaret supported her with their backs together as Caitlin knelt.

"Head down. Dropped into the channel. Pushing hard to arrive." Caitlin stood and locked eyes with the queen. "We dare not stop him. You are in childbirth, Your Majesty."

"He is early!"

"All we can do is send a messenger. If you fight this, you will harm the babe." Caitlin stopped the queen's objection with, "If you fight the birth, you could tear and bleed to death. Is that what you want?"

"No. No."

"Then do as we say."

"Men. Witnesses … " was all Matilda could gasp before the next wave struck her.

Margaret dashed away so as to return in time for the next pains. Word spread quickly through the castle and town. Saxons stacked firewood in a corner of the queen's bedroom and fill the braziers before disappearing from the queen's chamber.

"I am sweating and you are using warm cloths on my face and hands," complained the queen.

"To avoid chill and ague." Caitlin added, "Cool water is for drinking."

Behind the door, Sir Roger reported, "All except the bishop are here as you requested."

"After my next contraction, help me lie on the bed. Cover my body except my belly."

After an interval, the queen called out, "You may enter."

Queen Matilda commanded of her visitors, "Examine the room, see my women, witness my contractions."

The three council members looked about nervously. The others, having already witnessed Queen Matilda's miscarriage, remembered seeing ropes tied to the bedposts. They watched the queen idly twisting them. Suddenly she pulled them taut and gasped. The mayor took a step toward the bed. Margaret moved so she stood between the queen's head and the men.

The queen dug her heels into the bedding. The witnesses watch in fascination as the ripples of her stomach muscles rolled rhythmically top to bottom, top to bottom. Several veins seemed ready to pop out of her skin.

"You are indeed in labor, Your Royal Highness," said the mayor. You have our prayers," said Father Gregory

We will wait outside for your summons," said a lord.

The men departed.

"Thank you, Margaret, for standing so they did not see my face."

Impetuously, Margaret bent and pecked the queen's cheek. "Up with you now, Your Majesty. You need to be walking again."

Having birthed once before, the queen's labor was not as long as Dena's. Every hour one witness or another walked to the queen's door and called her name. "I am fine," was her only response.

After several hours, Sir Roger called out, "We have not heard your voice."

Matilda pulled a rag from her mouth, "I am still here, sirrah. Just busy."

Sir Roger apologized and walked away from the door between them.

"Mayhap you should scream once," teased Margaret.

"Queens do not cry out." Matilda glared at the girl.

Chastened, Margaret apologized. "I am sorry. Please forgive me, Your Majesty. I was only trying to lighten your mood."

Well past the middle of the night, the queen yelled. With a cloth in her mouth, the queen's muffled cries sounded distant, hollow, not serious. Caitlin fetched the basket of birthing cloths. Dena accompanied her. A sleeping babe lay hidden under a domed cover of cloths; Dena uncovered his face to keep him from smothering. All three women worked hard to assist the queen give birth. The babe in the basket slept on.

Margaret caught Matilda's babe and held it aloft. The queen strained upward, saw her child and fell back. No one spoke. The newborn's cry was soft, restrained.

"No. No," murmured Matilda as she feebly pushed away the

child whom Margaret was trying to lay on her belly.

"You must use the babe's weight to push out the birthing bag," Margaret said.

Caitlin grasped the queen's wrist and held it. Matilda turned her face to the wall.

"Transfer the mess," Margaret instructed.

Dena worked quickly. Her son soon bore all the signs of birth, a blood-soaked belly wrap, streaks of blood and a waxy substance everywhere. She rubbed some behind his ears and between his fingers and toes. He was rewrapped in fine linen.

"Nurse her. Put her to sleep," Instructed Margaret.

Caitlin, who had positioned herself so she did not see the switch, cared for the queen. Caitlin washed her face with warm water; she helped the queen into a clean chemise. Matilda tolerated Caitlin combing her loose tendrils back toward her single braid before she laid back against a bank of pillows.

The noise levels beyond the door increased. "May I announce you will be ready to receive them in a few moments, Your Royal Highness?"

"Where is the king?"

"I do not know."

"Reveal nothing. Send them in."

"Remove the mess. It is not fitting that it should be here when Her Royal Highness is receiving guests," Margaret said loudly enough to be heard beyond the door.

Dena placed the sleeping princess in the basket, formed a hood of cloths so she could breathe and covered her with dirty cloths. She placed the afterbirth bag above the babe's feet so it peeked from under the top cloth.

Caitlin and Dena took up the handles and left. A lord stepped forward and grimaced at the mess on top. The women disappeared behind Dena's screen as Margaret stood at the chamber door and distracted the men with, "Her Royal Highness, Queen Matilda, is ready to receive you."

The men filed in. They saw a quiet, subdued queen with a newborn, still a bit messy, nestled in her arm.

"This is the child." The queen said no more.

"Born on the seventh day of February, in the year of Our Lord 1102," intoned Bishop Giffard. He blessed the queen and the babe before he asked, "Is it the prince?"

"When the king arrives. Not before."

The day wore on. Neither Jorgon nor any of the Saxons were allowed on the queen's floor. Dena nursed the babe and put it to sleep in the cradle with the royal crest on the headboard. She stroked her son's cheek as he fell asleep with a full belly. The queen rolled away and appeared to be sleeping. Margaret and Caitlin took turns sitting in the queen's chamber between times to eat. Dena nursed her new daughter behind her bed screen. While Dena lay beside the sleeping child, she shed tears for her son now gone from her arms, but she dared not cry aloud. No one rested. Darkness fell.

31

Bells Chime

Speculation flowed from hall to town. Some guessed disappointment. Others claimed the queen only wanted the king to know her good news first. Everyone whispered and waited while the day finally waned.

Just before sunset a wave of noise flowed from the castle gate into yard, Margaret left her stool, walked into the queen's chamber and announced, "Your Royal Highness, noise in the yard."

Matilda refused to look Margaret's way. All she said was, "Leave us."

The king saw no one as he dashed up stairs, passed individuals with their backs to the walls, and raced through the rooms. He reappeared with the babe in his arms and stepped carefully down the spiral staircases.

"We have a son!" roared Henry as he entered the hall. He held the babe aloft. "See our heir, the Prince William!" he shouted.

The uproar in the hall spilled into the yard, out the gate, and to the town. One set of church bells set off another until the whole town was awake for the news. The bells would peal all night.

"See the proof!" commanded the king as he stripped off cloths. Henry held high the boy, who was naked from the waist.

"Ah-h-h! I am pissed on by mine own son!" as King Henry saw liquid dribble down his shirt and jerkin.

The courtiers howled with laughter. The king joined them.

"Long live King Henry! Long live Prince William!" resounded from the hall to the yard and beyond.

"'Tis a warning," joked the king, "to treat him in a more royal fashion."

Henry stuffed the cloths into the boy's crotch and returned to his wife.

From the open door, those nearby heard him say, "Well done, my love. He is strong, healthy. Oh, Aedygyth, we have an heir!"

Henry kissed his wife and strutted to the celebration in the hall.

Behind the bed screen, Dena murmured, "Poor thing. Which is worse? To be wanted but a bastard or royal but unwanted? She did not even look at you." Dena kissed the princess. "Soft and perfect."

At the fireplace Margaret looked at Caitlin and opt her mouth. "Not a word! You agreed to this. I will hear neither your complaints nor your fears!" Margaret sucked in her lips and nodded. She left for the queen's chamber.

The Church's law was babes must be three days or older to be baptized, so the priests scheduled the christening for Tuesday. In the meantime, the king fawned on the queen and his heir, ordered special meals, and granted her desire for company. Court members were permitted to visit the queen in pairs. All had been instructed to touch neither Her Royal Highness nor her son. Twice a day Matilda lay abed against a bank of pillows wearing a bright blue short blouse over her chemise. With her hair bound in two braids as would any proper wife in public, she gave the impression she was properly dressed from head to toe under the coverlet over her bedding. Her eyes were bright and her expression a happy one; she spoke in a calm and serene voice. They only looked at the prince sweetly sleeping in the cradle his father had once occupied; no one touched him. Margaret stood so she could study the faces of those who cooed over the royal heir. She offered no food or drink; Caitlin disposed of any gifts of food or drink. Queen Matilda's visitors believed her charade, and their report of all being well with the royal family passed through the town and over the land.

As soon as her guests departed, Matilda turned to the side of the bed opposite where the cradle had been set on the floor. The queen had stopped calling Margaret by name; she only gestured in her direction when she spoke her commands. She demanded Margaret remove her blouse and leave. Matilda ate her meals sitting up on side of the bed with her back to the babe in the cradle. She ate and drank little, ordered the tray removed and crawled back into bed. Because the king conducted business in the hall, he was away from the queen much of the day. He left her to sleep away what he thought was her tiredness.

While Margaret served the queen, she knew to look not toward the cradle. Even in only glances at the queen, Margaret easily read her moods. Margaret saw sadness in the droop of her shoulders, worry in the furrow of her brow, and regret in the way Matilda looked only down, never meeting Margaret's eyes, never acknowledging her presence. She decided to ignore the queen's constant sighs even as she worried the queen was not breathing easily and might also be ill. After each meal, Margaret set the tray aside to lift the queen's bedding as she crawled back into her bed and hid beneath her coverings.

Getting the babe fed was even harder than trying to feed the queen. Dena crept into the chamber without looking toward the bed. She nursed her son in silence, burped him without cooing at him or making any noise at all. She did insist on rocking him back to sleep before she crept out of the room. Each time she returned from the queen's chamber, Dena hid behind her bed screen; Caitlin scowled at Margaret when they both heard her softly crying into her pillow.

On the second day, after serving the queen dinner, Margaret had placed a tray at a side table when a woman appeared at the chamber door.

"Your Royal Highness, it is I, the Lady Claire de Clerkx. I have come as you requested."

Matilda straightened her back and plastered a smile on her face before turning to the woman. Margaret heard, "Enter. I have been awaiting you." The queen waved Margaret toward the door. Without a word, Margaret took up the tray, curtsied, and rose to leave. Dressed in rich fabrics with fur cuffs on her sleeves and a small train on her gown, Lady Claire looked down her nose at Margaret before she gave obeisance to their queen. "I am pleased to see you again, Your Royal Highness. I have missed you."

"The Lady Claire will serve me now. I dismiss you," the queen said in Margaret's direction. When she saw Margaret look toward the cradle, she commanded, "Go!" Margaret curtsied and left the room without looking at either woman. Lady Claire closed the door.

Margaret sat on a stool by the fireplace as she watched women arrive, stay long in the queen's chamber, and depart only to have another two or three women arrive to spend time with the queen. *How can he remain safe with all those women about? Is she deliberately putting him in harm's way?* Margaret heard Dena's soft crooning. *Dena is falling in love with the princess. That is not good. Nothing is. The queen may send Dena away and get a new wet-nurse. She will not feel safe as long as those of us who know are near. We are in great danger. Banished at any time. Death if we tell. Death even if we do not tell and the queen fears us.*

A strange lady approached Margaret and told her to fetch the prince's wet-nurse.

"Dena, go nurse the prince. I will take your daughter."

Dena moved with alacrity. Margaret sat on her bed and rocked the sleeping princess.

Margaret was sent away to dine in the hall, but she was sad at her diminished status. The sycophants followed the queen's example and ignored her. They looked her way only to snigger at her clothes and point to her sword. She sat in a middle seat, farthest from the royal ends, and the place for those of the lowest rank. Old men sat on either side of her. Her plate was wooden and her spoon had a bent handle. The only one who spoke to her was a Lord Cai. He had greeted her with kindness and tried to engage her in talk of the food and the weather. The meal over, Sir Cai asked her to stay.

"I have a tale about your grandparents I want you to know. I was on the same ship as your grandfather when we crossed the Narrow Sea in Anno Domini 1066. As we were leaving the harbor, the fog lifted a bit, and we spotted a woman standing on a hill with her unbound hair waving in the wind. A man asked who she might be. Your grandfather answered, 'My beacon. The woman I will marry as soon as we win land.' He refused to tell us her name and warned us away. 'Beware. She has red hair and the temper to match.' We watched her until the fog shifted and hid her. Your grandmother reminded us all of what we sought, land so we could marry."

"I am named after her. I am the Lady Margaret, my lord."

"The sword-wearing one. I dare say you are more like her than you know."

"Did you ever meet my grandmother?"

"No. I served King William. He gave me land far from here, near the fens."

Margaret curtsied. "Thank you for your story, Sir Cai. Mayhap we will talk again."

"I hope so."

Margaret departed with a bounce in her step. *Grandmother had red hair! I wager she had the temper to match. My hair has reddish and gold glints in it at the end of each summer. I bear her name, why not some of her hair coloring too?*

Each morning, each afternoon, Margaret went to the queen's chamber door and asked after the queen's health. The ladies rebuffed her offered services; the noblewomen looked upon her with disdain. Margaret kept Dena company behind her screen. Father Gregory prayed with them each morning and evening.

On Tuesday the eleventh day of February, the third full day after his birth, the prince was baptized. As only baptized members may enter a church, Anselm, Archbishop of Canterbury, Gerard, Archbishop of York, and William Giffard, Bishop of Winchester, baptized the boy outside the south door of St. Swithin's Cathedral. As a new member of the Christian Church, the prince would attend High Mass in King Henry's arms. Lady Claire and several other women attended the queen rather than the baptism. Having birthed a son, the queen was unclean for twenty days and could attend neither the baptism nor the High Mass that followed, nor any Mass or church service for that matter. After a cleansing and a blessing, she could then enter a church. Had she birthed a girl, the wait would have been forty days.

Should I go to the cathedral? No. With so many attending, she may need me. Even as Margaret wished it, she knew it would not be so. *Better to guard the princess. Stay nearby in case of attack.*

With Caitlin about and Dena and babe behind the screen, Margaret unlocked the barrier door. She wrapped her mantle tightly around herself to keep out the cold winds as she strode down the roofed walkway. She peeked at the hall. Banners decorated the walls. Down the center of the tables ribs of colored cloth wove between candlesticks and evergreens. *I would rather sit fireside with Caitlin than attend the feast at the lowest place in the hall.* After Margaret re-sealed the door, she stole to her cot. Margaret grabbed a pillow and cried into it as she prayed.

Dear God, please forgive me my plotting. In thinking of how to help Dena, I ignored what might happen as a result. How could I have been so stupid? How can she maintain this charade? If the boy passes as the king's heir, what will she do to the girl? Will she hate her, refuse to feed her, let her sicken and die? What if the boy grows up to look like Sir Charles, his father, instead of looking like the king? She needs us gone to be sure she can keep her secret. Soon we will be dead. Sent away and killed on the road. She will cry false tears even as she claims it was likely robbers. Our deaths will be on my head. Only then is she safe. Dear God, please protect the princess… protect them all. I dare not confess. If I do, the priest may talk and I will die. If I do not and am killed, I will spend eternity in Hell for my sins. I will never meet Mother in Heaven. Dear God, please fix this for the others. I am already lost and bound for Hell, I know it. Margaret continued to cry for herself, for the others, and for the unwanted girl babe with the wrong parents.

After Mass the feast began with many toasts. Fireside in the keep, Margaret's food turned to dirt in her mouth. She gave up eating. She listened to distant happy noises with only half an ear. *No one needs me. No one wants me. He has forgotten my boons. Not that she will let me have them. Oh, God, if it be Your will, I will die. But I would rather live, if it pleases You.*

A woman rushed from the queen's chamber and ordered the barrier door opt. Margaret followed as far as the door and stared out. She watched the woman dashed into the hall. Inside the hall the lady sought and approached Sir Roger at a table close to the dais. She whispered in his ear. His face fell and paled as he stood and stepped over the bench upon which he had been sitting. He took the dais stairs, stood behind the king, and spoke to him quietly. Sir Roger stepped back. The king looked stricken. He turned to the queen and spoke. She gasped. The royals rose and the company followed. Henry took Matilda's hand.

"SIT!" he roared. "Lock the doors! No one leaves!"

32

❦

Treachery

All immediately sat. They watched the royals descend the stairs and rush to the side door. Margaret dashed inside the keep and ordered everyone to the walls.

In the hall, the messenger covered her face with her hands and sobbed out, "The prince is convulsing."

From the dais Sir Roger announced, "The prince … is … not … well."

Stunned silence. Archbishop Anselm rose. "Let us pray." The party became a congregation both deeply afraid and very eager to pray for the prince and his parents.

Margaret stepped round Dena's screen and saw her wide-eyed and clutching bedding. She had stuffed a corner of a blanket into her mouth. Tears streamed down her cheeks.

I am the cause. I brought her. I advised her. Please God, let her keep her son. My poor baby brother! How could this have happened?

Not daring to catch Dena's eye, Margaret stood beside Caitlin, who was seated next to the cradle beside Dena's bed. Margaret leaned over the crib. *Are you alive, little one? Thank you, God. Dena's milk is safe.* Margaret touched the sleeping babe's cheek. *So tiny. So precious. Still safe. Who did this? How did they accomplish this with all of us guarding my brother? Would they have done this to you, little princess? No. They would have waited for a son.*

Margaret faced away from Dena, knelt beside the cradle and clasped her hands together. *Please, God. Let him fight and win and live. Please, God, save my brother. Bastard or prince, let him live. The worst has happened. How did they reach him? We guarded him well. No one but Dena touched him, fed him. I watched to be sure.* Crying and rocking in the bed, Dena distracted Margaret, who glanced her way but could not bear to look directly at her. *Please, God, for Dena's sake, save her son. She loves him so. He is a sweet babe and does not deserve to be punished. Punish me instead. Her idea to switch them. I am the guilty one for not fighting the queen's plan. I promise to tell the truth. I will lose my head. I deserve it, not the babe. Let not Dena suffer, let not her son die. Please. Please.* Margaret shed tears for her brother, for Dena, even for the queen, so desperate for a son she was willing to lie to her husband, to the country.

The hall was grim in its silence. The royal chamber was silent. The afternoon waned. At hearing a long, low moan, Margaret's head snapped up and she stopped praying. A woman's voice cried out. Margaret shook her down-turned head at the failure of her prayers to keep her brother alive and she wept. Caitlin lifted the princess out of her cradle and handed the babe to Margaret. Dena turned in her bed and wailed into her pillow. Caitlin sat on the bed and held her. If physicians and attendants leaving the royal chamber wondered why those behind the screen were crying as hard as those within the chamber, they did not ask.

A wave of sorrow swept into the hall, through the other buildings, out the yard, beyond the locked gate, over the moat, and through the town. All the day's joys became bleakness. Into her pillow, Matilda wept bitter tears while Henry paced and swore. Each grieved apart. Henry was afraid to touch his wife, who had waved him away when he tried to approach. As he paced, Henry thought of those who had visited his son. He searched his mind to ferret out who might have murdered his second boy too; he sought whom to blame. Matilda sobbed out her grief at her failure to present her husband with a son. She wept because she was cert Henry would now set her aside, force her into a convent or have the pope annul their marriage. If he learned what she had done, he could accuse her of treason and have her executed. Then he could have a new wife. She feared she might already be too old to bear more healthy children. Most women bore healthy babes into their thirties and some into their forties, but Matilda was too irrational to remember that. Matilda knew she had failed her beloved husband. The terror that Henry might seek a new, younger wife, one who could bear him sons, tore at her soul. At the thought of losing Henry, Matilda sobbed anew.

Archbishop Anselm arrived in the keep, knocked at the royal bedchamber door and announced himself. Hearing muffled words, the Archbishop motioned Bishop Gifford to remain outside before he entered the chamber and closed the door behind himself. Giffard heard faint crying beyond the door; then he heard silence. He noticed crying was also coming from behind a screen at the other end of the room, but it too was muffled. After a time, the chamber door opt, and the archbishop stepped through holding the king's heir wrapped in silk cloth. Bishop Giffard accepted the body of the dead prince. He hugged him close to his chest as the archbishop gave instructions.

Giffard nodded his understanding, turned, walked across the room and waited at the top of the stairway. The archbishop returned to the chamber. Closing the door behind himself, Henry followed the archbishop out of the queen's bedchamber and to the stairs. The men left the keep and castle. Two priests at the gate joined them as they processed to the cathedral to lay the prince in state. A third priest led all in the hall to the church. Citizens doused fires; darkness covered the town and crept into the hearts of its residents.

In the keep, Margaret surmised the king and the priests had left to take her brother to the cathedral for a Mass of Burial and then to the cemetery. *Please, God, accept his soul into heaven. Let him rejoice with your angels and saints. If Mother is in heaven too, let her welcome him and tell him he is loved in heaven and on earth. I will pray for him all my days. I am so sorry. I am so sorry.* Margaret opt her eyes and looked down at the babe in her arms. Margaret continued praying until she heard the king returning to the queen and closing the door behind him. Determined to save the princess, she stood and approached the bed.

"Caitlin." Margaret shook the woman's shoulder. "Caitlin." Margaret pulled her to the end of the screen. "We dare wait no longer. We must protect her."

"Who?"

"This babe is still not baptized," Margaret whispered in a rush. "The king will be furious when he learns of her. If he dashes her brains against the wall before she is baptized, she will not see heaven. I could not bear to have her not see heaven. She must be baptized. A Christian may not kill another Christian without cause, and she is innocent. The princess did not plot; I did. Mayhap, if she is made a Christian, he will not kill her. At least not before he kills me. We dare tell no one who she really is until she is Christian. Father Gregory could baptize her. I trust him."

Caitlin's shoulders sagged. "When will this deception end?"

"It will end as soon as we baptize her," promised Margaret. "Get the water yourself. From the stable well. I trust nothing from this building. No one will think to poison that."

"What are you thinking?" demanded Caitlin.

"Of her. The queen must have her child. He must see his true babe. Now. She must go to them a Christian. Then they dare not harm her."

Margaret watched Caitlin leave. Then she turned and saw Dena staring at her.

"My son is dead and it is all your fault. Take her with you. I never want to see her again. Or you either. Go away!" Dena turned to her pillow, dropped her face into it and cried anew.

"Dena, I beg you to… "

Still with her head in her pillow, Dena cut her off with a gesture. Margaret heard footsteps on the stone stairs below. She took the princess with her as she rounded the screen and walked toward the priest just stepping into the room.

"Father, I have much to confess. In doing so, I have much to tell. Please step behind the screen with me. I want Dena to hear me."

Shocked that another might hear her confession, Father Gregory objected. Margaret stopped him by beginning the opening prayer for confession as she walked backward to Dena's bedside. Father Gregory followed her.

"Go away! Go away!"

"Not until you and Father Gregory hear my confession. You do no have to look at me, but you will hear me." By the time Caitlin returned, Father knew almost everything.

"He would not let me take the bucket. Insisted on escorting me and wants it back when we are finished," Caitlin said.

"I must take it back," explained the tall, gangly stable boy. "I am responsible for it, no matter who uses it." He shuffled from one foot to the other as he pushed his blond, stringy hair from his face.

Father Gregory sat the boy on a stool. "We are about to baptize this babe and you are another witness."

Caitlin placed the bucket at the priest's feet. Margaret handed him the child. Everyone watched Father Gregory speak Latin words over the water. When he bent to scoop up a handful, the boy interrupted.

"You did not pour in the blessing like he did for the prince."

Everyone froze. "What blessing?" Father murmured.

"The blessing in the little bottle the priest poured into the water on the altar in the cathedral," came the innocent reply.

"What priest, my son?"

"The one in St. Swithin's."

The water dribbled through the priest's fingers. He looked kindly at the boy. He spoke softly. "What did you see, my son?"

"I snuck away," the boy admitted as his cheeks flushed. He looked at the floor.

"That is good. We are glad you snuck away. I need to know what you saw."

The boy looked up to see Father's friendly smile. He began haltingly. When he admitted to leaving the grounds ahead of the royal train and no one scolded him, he told more.

"I wanted to be inside the church to see them baptize the prince. It was dark and empty. I thought I was in time. I snuck behind the pillars all the way to the front."

"And then…" Father added when the boy stopped.

"And then a priest came in with water in a gold bowl. I watched him be careful not to spill it. He set it on the altar and left."

"And then … "

"And then I waited for everyone to come in. A little bit later a different priest came in. I stayed hiding because I did not want him to send me away. He took out a tiny bottle. He poured it into the gold bowl and left." The boy thought a moment and added. "He left fast, like he was in a hurry."

"And then … "

The boy took his cue. "And then I waited and waited, but no one came. Outside, people made noises. A line of priests came out a door by the altar. One picked up the bowl, and they all marched from the front and out the side door."

The boy turned crestfallen and his mouth drooped.

"I missed it. They did it outside, I guess. Because the next thing I saw was the bowl, the priests, the king holding the prince, and everybody else coming into the church. We had Mass, High Mass. Tall people surrounded me and did not see that part, just heard it."

"You are a good boy for telling us this story. We are happy you saw what you did. Would you recognize that priest if you saw him again?"

The boy nodded.

"Are you certain?" Father added, "It is important you would know him."

"I saw his face." The boy paused, "and he had funny feet."

"Funny feet?"

"You know how priests have sandals and their feet get sun darkened?"

"M-m-m-m."

"He was wearing sandals, but his feet were all white. And I think he was wearing a sword under his robe. I saw the tip. I also saw his face; I would know him."

"Excellent. Now we must baptize this very special babe. We want you to be a witness. Would you like that?"

"Yes, Father. Is she a lady's babe?"

"A very important lady's babe."

The boy's blue eyes brightened at the prospect. "Good. I get to see somebody baptized."

Soon you will know who. See a royal baptized after all.

"I have already blessed the water with holy words," explained Father Gregory. "We need nothing else."

The priest looked at Margaret.

"Matilda." Margaret glanced in the direction of the royal chamber. "Name her Matilda."

"Like the queen!" chimed the boy.

"I baptize thee Matilda, in the name of God the Father … " He made a tiny cross on the babe's forehead…"and of Jesus the Son…" He made a second cross on the infant's lips…"and of the Holy Spirit… " He made a cross on over the babe's heart. "May God guide you. May Jesus defend you. May the Holy Spirt fill our soul with the love of God's holy church. Amen."

Margaret gasped. She realized a priest had unwittingly placed poisoned water on her brother's lips. He had licked it. Suckled it into his body when he nursed—and died. She asked the boy to stay with the bucket while she talked with Father and Caitlin. She led them around the screen. She whispered how she thought the babe had taken in the poison.

"I thank God Dena has not nursed little Matilda since the baptism. Caitlin, wash Dena's breasts. Use lye soap. She dare not nurse this child, or it too may die."

"Father, will you go with me to tell them?"

"I will stay with the boy. You must face them alone. You took part in this charade, these lies. You must set aright what you have done wrong with no help from me nor from anyone else."

"Yes, Father."

Poor princess. He will not want you. She may never accept you. Margaret kissed the sleeping babe and held her close. *Oh God, do not let her die too. I beg you. Please let her live.* Margaret walked toward the queen's chamber. *If I die because of what I have done, so be it.* Margaret's eyes clouded over with fear. Suddenly, Margaret's senses heightened. She stopped after only two steps. In her arms she felt the soft rise and fall of the babe's breathing and the blanket wrap her hands touched as she clutched the child. She smelled the ashes of a dying fire, heard night sounds leaking into the room through arrow slits and the soft hiss of candles burning. The cold in the floor seeped through the soles of her slippers and chilled her toes. Her back ached, her stomach churned, and her breathing became rough and irregular. Determined to do what was right, Margaret shook off her dread and stepped forward.

The guards stopped her well before the door.

Margaret stiffened her resolve and spoke with authority. "Please tell His Royal Highness I know how the babe was murdered. Please tell them I have a witness."

I should *have pissed first. Stand still. Stop shaking. Will do no good.*

The royals saw how reluctant she was to enter. The king stopped pacing and stood with his arms across his chest. The queen, who had been sitting on the edge of her bed, lay back and refused to meet Margaret's eyes.

She did *not tell him the boy was not his. Does she ever intend to? If not, what was she going to have me do with the princess? Dare I interfere*

297

and tell him myself? If she planned to have us all killed to keep her secret, I had best save us all right now. I will tell him myself and take the blame so the others might live. God, give me strength; please help me. I must be strong.

"Out with it. Who killed my son?"

The king ignored the bundle in her arms.

Margaret looked to the empty cradle. *Put her in it? No. Needs my protection against his rage.* "Your child is not dead. Your child lives." *I am holding her for my own protection. He may wish to kill us both but not at the same moment.*

"Your Majesty, your child is safe, but she is in need of a wet nurse."

Margaret faced the queen. "Your Royal Highness, do you not want your daughter back now?" She turned to the stunned king. "Her Royal Highness handed you Dena's boy, born days before the princess. Dena nursed them both." Margaret looked at the queen as if to include her. "Her Highness thought having a son might reveal the poisoners. It did, but from a quarter we did not expect."

After a long silence, the king turned and looked at the queen. Margaret could see neither of their faces. The air was electric.

Have I done the right thing? Will he let me live? Will she ever forgive me? Margaret looked down. *You are a princess. Your birthright is to be royal.* Margaret took in a deep breath.

"The weeping you hear is from Dena over her dead son. Your daughter is here. We baptized her Matilda after her mother. She is safe and well."

Henry stared at the babe. After a time, he pointed at the cradle.

Margaret placed the sleeping infant in the cradle and covered her. *God's blessings upon you all your life. You will need them. It is not easy to be a girl, even for a princess.*

Margaret spun on her heel.

"Your Highnesses, I found a witness to the poisoning. He says he can identify the man. An innocent boy who does not understand what he saw. He thinks he did something wrong and he is terrified. He spoke to Father Gregory in front of me."

Not once during her retelling did Margaret look in the queen's direction.

"Send in the boy and the priest."

Margaret curtsied low. "Yes, Your Royal Highness." Only half rising she turned in the queen's direction and curtsied again. "Your Royal Highness."

Margaret backed out of the room, turned and fled. She walked toward the screen and rounded the corner. While her smile was forced, her voice was even as she addressed the stable boy.

"Have you ever seen the king?" she asked kindly.

"Many times," replied the boy. "Once, Father let me hand him his reins. He touched my shoulder and smiled at me."

"The king would like to see you again. He wants to learn your story."

"The whole thing?" The boy shook so hard his hair fell back onto his face.

"The whole thing."

The boy pushed back his hair and looked to the priest. "What should I tell him?"

"Only what is true and honest," replied Father Gregory.

"The king is thrilled to talk with you. He wants to know everything." Then Margaret added, "If the king becomes angry, it will not be at you. I think he will become angry with the man with the little bottle. Will you remember that?"

"Yes, my lady."

"Father Gregory is to go with you. Remember, the king likes stories, but only the true and honest ones."

Once the boy and priest left, Margaret approached Caitlin. "Let his wroth fall only upon me," she whispered. "If you would save your lives, get Dena, Jorgon, and yourself gone from this place. I command it of you." Before Caitlin could answer, Margaret said, "Now! You have only moments to spare." Margaret pulled a coin bag from her sleeve.

"Take this. Hide. Take your papers with you. Tell no one your names. Get off this floor. Wait in the stables until the main gate is opt and find an errand to do. Do not return. Pray he forgets you were ever here. Take these coins with you; they are all I have."

Father Gregory returned alone to see Dena's and Caitlin's backs at the stair well.

"If they can stay out of his sight. If the gate is opt before he remembers them, they may escape. If not, their souls too will be upon your head." The priest's voice was hard, unforgiving.

"Think not, Father, I was alone in this," Margaret warned, "but I am the one who will bear the blame."

Margaret headed to the privy. Afterward she took to the shadows. She saw a guard leave, several knights in full armor arrive. Two escorted the king, who had his arm around the boy and talked to him as they walked. She turned to the wall to disappear. Margaret fought the urge to soil herself. *Cease this thinking! What if they drag you out of the privy? The gossip!* She decided to hide behind the screen. When she reached it, she found two armed guards awaiting her.

"Lady Margaret, you are not to leave. We are here to guard you."

"May I rest?"

"You may, but you will have no privacy. We must keep you in sight at all times."

"I understand."

One stepped forward. "Your sword and scabbard. Now your dagger. And any other weapon you have hidden upon your person."

"I would not harm you, nor anyone else. I am removing my boots and taking to this bed now."

She tucked her skirt around her ankles before lifting her legs. Once under the blankets she rolled away from one guard's stare to find herself looking at the other.

"Tell me truth," she whispered. "Were you told to murder me in my bed?"

"No, my lady. To stand guard. No one may speak to you."

"Then God's grace upon you. May He give you a good night."

She pulled the covers over her head and prayed. When she was still alive at the end, Margaret peeked. The guards still faced her. With a sigh, she settled into the bed even though she did not believe sleep would come. It did. When she awoke, two different men guarded her. A soft dawn had arrived.

"Have I the freedom of this floor?"

"No. You must stay behind this screen. We escort you to the privy. A servant will bring you food."

The privy? How embarrassing! No help for it. Must go. A bucket of cold water and a rag arrived. Margret washed her face and hands. She asked for and received her things. She brushed her hair. Pottage for breakfast. Back into the bed. A long day of waiting. She ate not and only sipped a bit of ale before offering the guards her meals. A long night of worrying. With closed eyes she could ignore her guards but not her thoughts.

I must start with You, Oh Lord. Oh God, I am a bag of sins. Where shall I begin? Yes, at the beginning. I am willful. When Father refused to teach me to ride when I was of six years, I leaped up on Night to show him I could ride. I am defiant. He did not want me to learn to read, but I begged Mother and she taught me letters and my name. I am sneaky. I worked around him when he was drunk and ran the estate the way I wanted it run. I hid Night from his wroth for two years and snuck him away when I left. I am vengeful. When I found out he poisoned Mother, I poisoned his favorite hunting dog. I am unkind. I was glad Mother paid more attention to me than to Cecily. I am froward. I created a plan to escape my lot at home by convincing the king he needed me. I am mean. I claim Caitlin is no longer a servant and then I order her around as if she still is one. I am proud. I liked surprising the king and Lord William when I revealed my rank. I am thoughtless. I tricked Dena into asking for her freedom, marriage and coin. Then I blamed the queen for giving those things to her. I do not remember the seven deadly sins the Church teaches God hates, but I am sure I have committed them all. I am going to die. I must face it. I am going to die. If not for my recent deeds, then because God has been counting up my sins, and I have exceeded His limit. I will be a long time confessing before I am hanged. Or will the king behead me? Margaret shuddered. Her eyes filled with tears. *Will the king let me confess before he executes me? I hope so. I pray so. Who will pray for me after I am dead? No one. Well, mayhap Caitlin.* Then Margaret reconsidered her recent treatment of her former nurse. *No one. I have offended You, Oh God. I beg Your forgiveness.* Margaret paused in her ruminations. *The truth, Oh God, is that I do not deserve Your forgiveness. Nor the king's either. I am going to die unforgiven. I am going to die and be condemned to Hell for all eternity.* Margaret wept anew for her innocent baby brother even though she was cert God had taken him into Heaven. She began her litany of offenses against others by asking her baby brother to forgive her for putting him in mortal danger. She started the rest of her long list with Caitlin's name. Rather than sleep, Margaret spent the night praying for all whom she believed she had harmed and might have offended.

Thursday morning the new guards exchanged news with the old ones. "Two nights ago king charged out in the middle of the night with a stable boy in tow, raided the cathedral and the abbey, and sent knights to chase down a man. Found on the road to Dover, someone had been dragged back to Winchester and thrown into this castle's donjon. Other guards are protecting the queen, the princess, and a wet nurse. Last night the king was alone with the man in the donjon, probably torturing him for information. The abbot and bishop were demanding entry to retrieve the priest, but had been refused because the castle had been sealed by the king's command."

"Who hid the royal babe and saved her from the poisoner?" asked Margaret's current guard.

"Why, the Lady Margaret, the woman you are guarding," replied the man's replacement.

They switched places.

They think well of me? When they know, they will be glad to see me beheaded. At least I will go to the block well rested. Margaret turned away and ordered herself to sleep. She slept through her dinner, so her guards ate it. By the time she awakened, she had new guards.

"May I know what has transpired since this morning?"

"Of course, my lady," replied the man to her left.

"The princess and a wet nurse are in the chamber, guarded of course. The queen has walked about with a lady at each arm. She dines in the chamber. The king returned from the donjon after noon and held counsel with his lords. He heard the abbot's and the bishop's demands for the return of the monk, priest, knight—not sure who he was." The guard smiled across the bed at his mate. "The king turned over the body. It looked more like a knight's than a priest's." He paused for her reaction and got none. "At this moment the king is in the chamber with his family."

Who sent him to kill a babe and destroy King Henry's reign? Rebellious barons and earls, his brother, the Church the king has been defying? All three factions? Is Princess Matilda still in danger? No, she cannot rule. Is the king still in danger? Yes.

"Did His Royal Highness gain a confession?"

"If he did, he told no one. You will sup in an hour. Nothing in the hall tonight."

"Please wake me when my meal arrives."

"Yes, my lady."

Likely, it is my last meal. Margaret swallowed hard. *I want it not. The longer he waits, the greater my self-torture. Fool the king. I will spend these last hours repenting and praying. Mother, will I join you in Purgatory? Will you wait for me in heaven if you have already reached it? Forget about dying. I am already dead. All I can do now is save my soul. Oh God, I am afraid, I pray You send me not to Hell but Purgatory. I will spend centuries in Purgatory if it be Thy will. For my soul to leave Purgatory, someone on earth must pray for me, pray for me for years and years. She must pray all the penance I owe God, so I can leave Purgatory and ascend to heaven someday. Someday. Who will pray for me? Does anyone care? What is it like to be dead? Mother, I fear. I am not brave at all. Your will, Oh God, in all things.* Again Margaret pulled covers over her head and prayed, mostly for forgiveness.

33

Truths

Margaret stopped just inside the tall, heavy entry doors of the hall. The guards closed them behind her. She listened for them to be locked but heard nothing. On the floor in front of her, she noticed a trap door with a heavy iron ring on it. *The donjon. Will he send me there to rot and die?* Margaret shuddered. She stepped forward, shifted her path a bit to the right to avoid stepping on the door, and stopped halfway to the dais. She glanced up. King Henry sat upon his throne; the queen's was empty. Behind him firelight flickered, but he sat in a darkness that hid his chest and face. To his left stood two fat beeswax candles on tall pedestals. *Very expensive candles.* She did not spot the two guards standing behind the thrones. Margaret looked at her feet and willed them to move. She took in a deep breath and took a step and then another. Without looking up from the floor, Margaret walked to the dais. *They should be beyond the city wall. Be far away. Stay out of his reach, Please, God, keep Caitlin, Jorgon, and Dena safe. Your will, Oh God, in all things. Even this.*

At the dais, Margaret curtsied, went to her knees and stayed, chin to her breast.

"What is in this box, Margaret?"

Margaret looked up. Stunned, she gasped at seeing the box of poison she had stolen from her father. *Who dug it up from the forest floor when we left to go with the king? Not William. He was standing beside the king. Too far away to see. The knight who guarded us from the road? He must have turned around and seen me burying it. What was his name?* Margaret glanced at the king and saw feral eyes. *He has had it all this time! He* already *knows what it is. No point in lying.*

"Poison, Your Royal Highness." *I just gave him what he needs. He summoned me at night so I can disappear. No one to know why. Or care.*

"Who has used it?"

Dear God, please forgive me. Even if he was cruel to me, I do not want my father to die. "Sir Charles of Royal Oaks," she admitted.

"Tell us."

Royal "us." Now there is no hope for either of us. Oh, Father, our sinful deeds have come due.

"The latest was a Saxon wench Sir Charles had gotten with child. She wanted him to marry her and make her a lady."

"Your proof?"

Do not implicate Caitlin. Let him forget her.

"I saw him hide the box. After the girl died, I put a bit of it inside meat for a dog." *Poor Yolo.* "Within hours the dog died the same way she did."

"Who else has died?"

"My mother, I think." Margaret was careful not to accuse. "On her deathbed she claimed Father had poisoned her. I did not believe her."

"But you do now." Margaret chose not to respond. "Why did you not tell us this the first we talked or at least when we arrived at Forest Keep?"

306

"Would you have you left your queen to be guarded by the daughter of a known poisoner?" Margaret could no longer bear the suspense. "Is it the same, Your Royal Highness. The same used on … " Margaret could not finish the question.

"I had it tested. My physicians tell me it is of a different kind."

On whom did they test it? Who else has died? God, please forgive me his or her death. I did not do it. Margaret burst into tears. She covered her face with her hands but could not contain her tears, so great was her relief. They spilled through her fingers, down her hands and into her sleeves.

Henry waited. From experience, he knew they always told more when he did.

Margaret shook. "Afraid … I thought … I tried to show you my loyalty."

Margaret pressed her fingertips into her eyes to stop the flow. She wiped her face with the backs of her hands and dropped them to her sides.

"And the boons?" Her evasiveness regarding those wishes still piqued his curiosity.

"I told you one thing, but I was thinking something else. If I needed to save them. I have two brothers and a sis … "

"Think you if your father was party to the poisoning of my heir, I would let you save his sons? My firstborn was poisoned in the womb, remember. Now the false prince. Had Sir Charles been party to any of this, none of his seed would live! Three promised boons would not even save your life!"

Margaret's face was still, head bowed, but she was tired of being mouse to his cat, tired of being oh-so-careful, always deferential. *If you will pounce, do so! I am done with this! I already know my fate.*

"I have spoken with Her Royal Highness and I want an answer!" he commanded as he leaned forward. "Whose idea was it to switch the babes and claim we had a son?"

Blame the queen and I am dead! If she said it was me, I am dead already. Did she tell him the truth, that is was her idea, her plan? Will the right answer save me? Margaret decided. *Mayhap an equivocation will save my life.* Before speaking she said a quick prayer, feeling as if she were stepping off a cliff. *So be it.* Margaret looked straight into the king's eyes ."Your Royal Highness, it was the idea of whomever the Her Royal Highness, the queen, named."

The king sat back and asked, "If she said it was your idea?"

"Why then, Your Royal Highness, it was."

"It was your idea. You talked Her Majesty into the lie against her better judgment. You promised you would save our daughter and the Saxon boy at the same time."

So that is what he will tell everyone. "Yes, Your Royal Highness."

"That you succeeded in helping us catch the poisoner is cause for our appreciation. That you failed to save the boy is cause for our sorrow."

Already worded for Court.

The king shifted on his throne. "You will confess your failure to save the boy. You alone will bear the penance given."

Has my using his formal title softened him? I think not. Wait! He did not say confess to thinking the plan, only failure to succeed in it. He knows! Mayhap I am not dead. Mayhap she has spoken for me, defended me. Mayhap I am not dead.

"Yes, Your Royal Highness."

Not really a lie. I can re-confess to Father Gregory. This time I can confess to my failure to save my brother. Did I already do that? I remember not. Oh, well. Better to confess twice than not at all. Will it matter that I confess to my failure, to save my poor brother but not the idea? I will ask Father. I will do the penance for my brother, for her, and for myself.

"Rise. Despite your part in the trickery you have plotted, I have decided to grant you the three boons I promised you. I do so only as a reward for your helping us to catch the poisoner. Before we discuss boons, you will settle another matter. On the morrow and in open Court, you will accuse Sir Charles of the deaths of your mother and the Saxon girl. You will testify before the Royal Court of Law, and you will use this box as proof."

The king tapped the lid to punctuate his last four words.

Swiftly, Margaret looked about and was relieved the Hall was still empty. No one else appeared to have heard him. She shifted from one foot to the other as she tried to find the right words. "Your Royal Highness, I cannot do that."

"Cannot? You will."

"Had you asked this of me six months ago, I would have done it. Now I cannot because I now know it will do no good, only harm."

The king harrumphed; he was not accustomed to being denied. "Explain."

Margaret nervously clenched and unclenched her fingers. Trying to marshal her thoughts into order, she sighed. "Accusing him will not bring back my mother. It would only destroy those whom she held most precious, her children. Young Charles will inherit. Who would wed his daughter, his family, to a poisoner's son? No one. Raymond needs a place; no one would give him one. Cecily would not be asked for and no convent would take her. And I? Sir Charles could claim the box is mine. That my accusation is revenge for his disinheriting me. He could swear I had poisoned the girl so she could not take my mother's place. I would be ruined too, my reputation destroyed. Among Normans his reputation is spotless. All would believe him, not me.

If you sentence him, others will say it is in payment for my services to you. A mess. Ruin. Everyone would suffer, even your and Her Royal Highness's reputations. My silence protects my siblings, our family name. My mother would want my silence."

Margaret pleaded with her eyes as she begged. "Please let her children have a future, Your Royal Highness. Please, forget what cannot be undone. Please go no further."

Henry rubbed his chin. "What am I do with this?" He gestured to the box and rag he had set at his feet.

"Send it away to be burned on some barren spot," Margaret offered. With a small smile she added, "If you do not like the servant, you could order him to stand downwind."

He smiled at her. "Margaret! Again you reveal you are wiser than your years. You seek for the greater good rather than for personal revenge. Your answer was almost statesmanlike in its reasoning." In a husky voice, dripping with desire, the king added, "What am I to do with you, my dear?"

"I hope you will grant my boons, marry me to a lord, and send me off to a good future."

Margaret looked at the floor. *Please, God, keep him away. I must stay pure. I will run away; I will fight him. Please, God, save me from him, save my reputation.*

While Margaret prayed, the king called for a servant to remove the rag and box and to send for his scribe. She heard footsteps, the scraping of wood on wood. Fearful of what was coming and holding her hands against her legs so as not to shake, she willed herself to look. Through her eyelashes, she saw a man beside the king. He stood at a tall wooden desk that had been set between the throne and the pillared candles. The top of an ink pot and a quill poked above the desktop. She watched the king place his hand before his mouth and turn. She heard first the king murmur as he dictated and then the priest scratching a quill across vellum.

"Lady Margaret, I like not surprises. We will discuss the matter of boons now. State them."

Margaret raised her head and addressed the king with a directness she hoped he would accept.

"Your Royal Highness, once I told you I might want clothing and jewelry befitting my station. I have changed my mind for coin instead. Your Royal Highness, my first boon is to request a box of coins sufficient to my purchase of all the dowry items I want and all the household goods I need to establish a home and to attract a good family of rank."

This king whispered to the scribe. While the man whispered back what he had written, the king looked her way.

"Done. Your second boon?"

"Your Royal Highness, I request that you deed me lands, properties, goods, and chattel commensurate to my rank for my dowry to a marriage to a lord or to a good man you make a lord before we meet at the church door. My formal boon ends here; but, if it please Your Royal Highness, I make a personal request. Because you will provide the dowry, I ask your assistance in finding me a husband of rank. He must be whole, younger than twenty-six, strong, a good fighter. Have I omitted some good aspect of dowry or manly quality?"

"No." Then the king added, "Are you cert you want to limit yourself to that age? What of a man older than twenty-six? Might he not do?"

"I think not, Your Royal Highness. I want him to live to see his heir reach the age of ten. If I have a daughter first, he would be thirty-eight and nearing old age."

The king stared at her, his reluctance to yield on that point evident.

Margaret accepted his stare, but did not flinch. "Surely, Your Royal Highness, your realm has enough good men between sixteen and twenty-five who would be to your liking."

The king did not look pleased. "As long as this is not written but only agreed between us, I will accept your request."

That part not a boon and changeable. We shall see.

"Your final boon?"

Margaret looked at her feet. "Your Royal Highness, I have heard marriage contracts among the ranked must carry three signatures. Is this true?" At the king's nod, Margaret continued in as brave a voice as she could muster. "Your Royal Highness, as the king, your signature and seal will be on the marriage contact, will it not?"

"I approve all marriages of rank."

"Will my husband's seal be on it as well?"

"He will sign his own contract if he is eighteen. If not, his father will sign."

Henry furrowed his brows. He wondered where this was leading.

"Then my final boon, Your Royal Highness, is the last signature on the marriage contact be mine own."

"ABSOLUTELY NOT!" roared the king as he half rose from his seat. "Unheard of! No woman signs her own contract. Only her father. I forbid it! I grant not this his boon. Choose another," he ordered. He leaned back and waved a hand in her direction.

Margaret did not stir, did not cower. She looked as high as the king's chin and appeared unmovable through the angry storm of words washing over her. Margaret waited until she was sure the king would not speak.

"Your Royal Highness, I must give my consent aloud to the priest before the church door for the marriage to be valid. My signing the contract is your assurance you will have it." Despite the king's rage-filled face, Margaret was resolute. "Your Royal Highness, you may not remember my father took back my dowry and falsely soiled my good name. I trusted him with my future once. He betrayed me. I will not trust him again."

The king challenged her. "You trust me, do you not? Let me sign for you."

Margaret curtsied before she answered. "Your Royal Highness, I trust you to provide the dowry sufficient to your gratitude. I trust you to find me a good husband. I trust you to make him a lord if he is not one already. I trust you will serve my best interests and will act accordingly." Margaret took a deep breath and finished with, "But a valid contract requires three set of signs and seals. I want who signs for me to be myself. I have learned more of men in these last months than in my old life before. I know men can be good or bad, trustworthy or not. I know you to be both good and trustworthy." *I will have to confess that lie.* "I also know you to be wise and fair. You will not sign unless you find me a good man, I know that. But other than yourself, I trust no other, man or priest, not really. Thus, I ask to sign for myself because I cannot be tricked or cheated against myself. Please, Your Royal Highness, help me do this." Her heart was beating wildly yet she was, almost, not afraid.

"No decent family will have you if I grant this boon. They will see you as a willful, froward girl and refuse to be aligned with you."

Margaret thought before she answered, "Then I will live a maid." Margaret swallowed hard at the loss of her dream. "If I die unwed, then all you had given me, coin, lands, goods, property, chattel, plus all I have husbanded will return to the Crown. If no good family will have me, the royal coffers lose nothing—only gain. I will have stewarded your property and been your very loyal subject unto my death." *Cry not. Cry and he has you. Do…not…cry.*

"If you die without lawful issue, the same fate?"

"Yes, Your Royal Highness. "*No tears. Please, God, let me have healthy children. Let me die before they do.*

"Signing your own contract is not right. Unprecedented. Unheard of."

"Your Majesty, I told you I would ask only boons within your power to grant. This is within your power. I ask it as my final boon."

The king sat back and stared hard. "You will not yield?"

Margaret shook her head. *Mother, if you could see me! I am not weak.*

"I grant the first two boons. I grant not the final one. It remains unwrit. On the morrow you will hear these same objections."

"I understand." Margaret bobbed a respectful curtsey. *Needs to object in public. Wants to set no precedent.*

Henry bargained. "If you change your mind, I will be most generous. Find someone else, priest, knight, lord. In open court I will accept your signature with his counter." The king paused, waiting for assent. When he was met with silence and a stare, he finished with, "I cannot grant such a boon; I will not. Expect a fight."

I have already seen it. Margaret's eyes smiled, which she tried to hide when she again gave obeisance.

Henry had seen it and scowled. Roughly dismissed, Margaret stepped back several paces before she turned and left the hall. As the girl departed, only the scribe saw the King of England's lust-filled stare.

34

Court

Even before Mass, many had heard the gossip. The Lady Margaret would be challenging king and custom. Word passed down the tables as the invited courtiers broke their fasts. No one left after the meal. They milled about and waited as servants pulled the table trestles and boards to the far wall.

King Henry and Queen Matilda left the head table and proceeded to the dais to sit upon their thrones. The king's scribe, guards, and retainers took their places. After the king first conducted official business, he called for petitioners to step forward, two did so. The king signed two copies of a marriage contract. His chancellor applied the royal seal. The second matter was about the sale of cattle that had sickened and died. Sorting the details and issuing a decision took a while. During the first part of the proceedings Margaret hid beside a window behind an archway.

I have already re-confessed to Father and begun saying my penances. This morn I will either be free or on my way to the block. I want my freedom. Be bold. I must be bold and surprise them. I care not for the courtiers' favors. Oh, William, I would you were here to speak well of me. Are you king's man or mine? The king's, I fear. If I name you to sign for me, will you still want me to wife? If you want me, you cannot sign twice, and all will know my feelings toward you. I dare not risk that. Father Gregory? A good man, but he will do as the Church demands. No help there. In truth, I trust no man. Oh God, again I ask for your guidance. Reveal to me another path and I will take it. To be free is everything to me. You know all I desire. Your will, Oh God, in all things. Now mean it. Your will, Oh God in all things. If You will my death so be it. You know I will ask for my freedom. Do as you will, Oh God, and I will obey. I promise.

Next the king's seneschal called, "The Lady Margaret of Royal Oaks, present your petition."

The crowd stirred and looked around. Margaret appeared from behind the arch closest to the entry door. The courtiers made a center aisle for her.

Margaret wore her best gunna of deep blue wool and matching leather slippers. From her girdle, embroidered as her mother's had been, hung the signs of a lady: a pair of scissors, a small pouch of fragrant herbs. Margaret had included her dinner dagger, but had left off her sword. She had fastened her side hair back so it would not fall when she lowered her head but the rest of her hair was free, announcing to all she was still a maid. Margaret was a picture of loveliness and grace.

Quiet, calm, dignified, pure keeps a lady steadfast and sure. Margaret repeated her mother's dictum in a rhythm for every eight steps she walked. At a dignified distance Margaret gave obeisance.

"Thank you, Your Royal Highnesses, for hearing my petition."

Margaret bowed toward King Henry and began in a manner unexpected.

"Your Royal Highness, I would remind you of the bargain we stuck last June. With your permission I should like to make public the agreement." At the king's solemn nod, she continued. "I promised to help Her Royal Highness, our queen, deliver a healthy child. Further, I promised that, should I fail, I would of mine own free will appear at Court and offer you my head for the block."

Courtiers behind her murmured.

"Your Royal Highness, have I helped your queen to deliver a healthy child? Does that child live?"

"You have, Lady Margaret. She does," answered King Henry.

"May I keep my head upon my shoulders, Your Royal Highness?"

Your chance to be rid of me. Any cause. Switching the babes? Not wanting to grant my boons? Margaret's tone indicated she was unsure of his answer.

"You may keep your head upon your shoulders, Lady Margaret."

Margaret's relief was visible in her breathing and stance. She curtsied. "I most gratefully thank you, Your Royal Highness."

King Henry waved her to be silent and looked past her. He announced to the Court, "You located the witness who saw the babe's murderer pour the poison into the baptismal water. Because of your quick work, we found the poisoner and learned who had sent him. You hid and protected our daughter. You kept our beloved queen safe through all the treachery. Know, Lady Margaret, our appreciation of your efforts. Praise God, our child is safe and well." Henry paused and placed his hand over Matilda's as he gazed into her eyes. "God grant our next child will be our heir."

In unison the Court repeated his words. Henry returned his hand to his chair arm and his eyes to Lady Margaret. "I grant three boons to you, Lady Margaret of Royal Oaks, as our thanks for your service to us."

At the king's nod she made her first request exactly as she had asked the previous night. The king waved two men forward. They placed a nail-studded chest at Margaret's feet and handed her a key.

"Lady Margaret, accept this chest holding one hundred eleven pounds coin in token of our gratitude."

Many in the room gasped and then repeated the amount to those farther back in the Hall. "That is a small fortune!" exclaimed one. "A large fortune!" retorted another.

Margaret grinned and curtsied low. "Your Royal Highnesses! Your reputed generosity is well founded. I am overwhelmed!"

"You have helped us rid our realm of poisoners. As we punish traitors, so do we reward loyal subjects." The king had spoken the words for more than her. Margaret waited. "Your second boon, my lady?"

Margaret made it. This time the king's scribe stepped forward and unrolled a scroll with the royal seal stamped in wax on the bottom. The man translated the written Latin to Norman.

"Heretofore may it be known to all the land, on this fifteenth day of February in the year of Our Lord, eleven hundred and two, that Henry, King of England, does grant to the Lady Margaret of Royal Oaks... "

The scribe droned on as Margaret and the Court listened. The gift lay in Worcestershire, about twenty-five miles north and a bit west of Winchester. Five hides translated to about a square mile, diverse in assets in an area known for rich, black soil and deep oak forests. The king had just handed Margaret a rich pearl.

Margaret tried to concentrate on the list of what was included. *All that Sir Charles holds and half again. Can support five knights on retainer. I am rich!*

Again, the courtiers gasped and gossiped. The Court also heard the conditions and judged them reasonable given the uncertainties of living. The scribe stopped, re-rolled and secured the deed. The scribe handed down the document to one of his men below the dais; he placed it in Margaret's empty hand.

"Lady Margaret, you look stunned."

Speechless, Margaret nodded again and then again as she stared at the key in her right hand and the scroll in her left. Pleased with himself, King Henry chuckled. He announced, "This land once belonged to the traitor, William de Warenne, now banished. I turn it over to you, dear lady, until I can arrange a suitable marriage for you. Be it known, only my most loyal subjects will be considered for this land and this lady. They are both great prizes." The king waved men toward Lady Margaret. "I send to you these knights: Sir Roussel, Sir Cachier, Sir Gailard. Until Lady Margaret is married, guard her well and see her safe. The Lady Margaret is under my special protection."

"As you will it, Your Royal Highness," said each man in turn. They took up positions right, left, and behind her.

"Do you wish to save your third boon?" asked the king in a helpful tone.

Margaret bit her bottom lip in consternation. *How can I be so ungrateful? Should I wait? Will it matter? I am in more danger than ever from those who want the land and coin and not me.* She frowned. *Have I explained why? Would it matter to him? Should I try?*

In the hall those who had heard the rumors leaned forward in anticipation. Would she? Dare she? Many hoped she would, so they could watch her defeat, or worse.

In the quiet, Margaret's thoughts rushed at her. *Wait and he may still deny it. Ask now? A boon denied is a boon not granted, so saved. What else do I want? Nothing. I want myself.*

"Here it is!" thought many in the room. As Margaret began, those in the back pressed forward to hear better.

Uncertain how to start, Margaret asked in a soft voice, "May I explain before I ask, Your Royal Highness?"

Matilda watched her husband casually shrug and nod before he leaned into his throne's back. She frowned at this exchange, which appeared formal but was more personal than she liked. She wondered what was between them that lay unspoken. She watched Margaret carefully to discern what she might be missing.

"Your Royal Highness, almost three years ago, I was betrothed to the first-born son from a fine family. Sir Charles of Royal Oaks, my father, decided he did not like the terms of the contract he had signed. To break the contract, he lied to the other family, saying I had lain with a man and was no longer was a virgin." Margaret paused when she heard whispering behind her and then continued. "It was a lie; my nurse swore it was a lie. Everyone on the estate knew it was a lie. Still, the contract was broken. When you visited the estate, you heard my father disown me. I dare not trust him ever again to take good care of me. I will not trust him to sign anything on my behalf ever again. When you charged me with Her Royal Highness's care, I learned I could trust you. I do trust you. You may not know this, but I have no one else upon whom I dare rely. Since leaving my father's estate, I have learned men can be good or bad or both at the same time, trustworthy or not. I fear I truly trust no one but you and Her Royal Highness." Margaret sucked in a deep breath and slowly exhaled. "Your Royal Highness, should I wait to ask for my third boon?"

King Henry sighed as if he were tired. "Well, if you will not change your mind, best everyone hear it."

"Your Royal Highness, my final boon," Margaret tried to steady her voice, but its wavering betrayed her, "is my request that, in addition to your signature and seal and my husband's or his father's sign on the marriage contract, I be permitted to sign for myself. That way you are assured of my consent at the church door." Margaret ignored the gasps from the courtiers.

Still facing straight ahead, Queen Matilda gave her husband a quick side glance and raised but one eyebrow at the look she saw. Matilda thought, *I can still read your mind, Henry. I am not blind. You want to bed her. You are angry still. Your revenge for my plan to trick you with a false son. Or is she your next queen? Act now or lose the moment.*

"Margaret, Margaret," chided Queen Matilda. "How could you be so bold? Do you not see His Royal Highness has your best interest? Has he not proved more generous than any other father you know? He has given you almost as much as he would his own daughter." How she stressed that last word cause Henry to glance her way for just a moment. He clenched his jaw ever so lightly as his wife continued. "Yet, there you stand defying His Royal Highness, your liege lord. You are also defying custom." The queen shook her head. "You know His Royal Highness will do what is right. He knows what is best for you. Leave this to his good head, his good heart. If you trust the king so well, then trust him to choose a guardian to protect you to be married well and properly. As for this last boon… " Matilda paused. When Margaret did not respond, the queen demanded, "Lady Margaret, rescind this boon. Ask for a guardian or save it."

Trust a man I do not know, may have never met? That is a worse danger than even Sir Charles.

Silence.

"Do not step beyond the bounds of polite society."

Margaret hung her head. The queen's threat was real. Without their approval, she would be a pariah. No one would ask for her hand. No one would visit. Once the royals dismissed her from Court, they would not see her. Perhaps ever.

Margaret returned a soft answer, gently spoken. "Your Royal Highness, you told me yourself several men asked for you and you spurned them. Your father and your brother, both kings, out of love and respect for you, let you refuse each offer. His Royal Highness, our king, asked for you and you accepted. Your sign was not on the contract, but your brother would not have signed it without your consent. My father loves me not. He falsely took a dowry and a marriage from me and slandered my name. He betrayed me and I cannot trust him. I have had to protect myself, seek my own way in this world. I am all the family I have. My consent cannot be unseen as was yours. As my father was swayed by coin, so may any other man, even a good one. With this boon granted, no one can bribe me against myself."

Margaret turned to the king. "I trust you, Your Royal Highness, but you have the realm's interests and needs to serve first. You want a loyal, powerful lord to oversee the land. So do I. You want a man from a good family. So do I. I want a family to accept me and to know what my father did. I believe you do too. I want a good man who will give me children. I believe you want the same. We are not so far apart, Your Royal Highness, you and me. We agreed you should be the one to find him. Your Royal Highness, please remember you may select my lord, but I am the one who has to live with him."

King Henry glared into the crowd searching for the unseen woman who had barked a short, loud laugh.

"Your Royal Highnesses, without my assent, there is no marriage. All my sign does is guarantee you will have it at the church door. I have prayed hard over this. I wish to set no precedent; I only ask what is right for me. As I have no father who loves me nor family who will protect me, please permit me to have this small say in my future." Margaret looked at the floor as she waited for one or the other royal to rail against her. Neither spoke. In the silence, all Margaret heard was her wildly beating heart.

"You will regret this, Lady Margaret. I am cert. Against my best advice, you still demand this boon. Against Her Royal Highness's wise counsel, you have not relented. So be it." King Henry waved his hand in dismissal. "Leave for your new home. If any man asks for you, I will send him to you. God grant you the wisdom to choose wisely, as if any woman could be that wise."

Margaret gave obeisance, stepped backward several times, and retreated. Sir Roussel signaled the other two knights to take up the chest. They followed the lady as she walked through a silent Court of men and women who turned their backs on her as she passed them.

Author's Note

King Henry, Queen Matilda, and Lady Margaret, are living at a time where nothing is certain, and each faces dangers.

Henry's first challenge is from his older brother Robert Curthose, Duke of Normandy, who demanded the throne. After a failed attack by his brother, Henry paid him to renounce his claim. Henry is sure he has only bought himself time before Robert goes back on their agreement and attacks again.

Lord de Belleme is a baron with great power and wealth, who also desires to be king. Henry knew Lord de Belleme was part of his brother's attack, but De Belleme and his forces slipped away and are now somewhere in the countryside. Henry is unsure of the size of de Belleme's army and what the traitor plans to do.

King Henry still denies Archbishop Anselm's claim that only he can choose the Church's bishops in England. The king knows he must have Anselm's approval before he may annul his marriage to Matilda. Henry may need to give in to gain his support.

Queen Matilda failed in her second attempt to provide her husband with an heir. She worries Henry will ask her to step aside so he can try for an heir with a younger wife. Matilda needs to become pregnant at once and deliver a son.

Lady Margaret believes she owns a rich estate as a dowry. She expects her suitors will be lords or barons or their heirs and that she will have a choice in the matter. Margaret is riding toward uncertainty and distressing surprises. She will need the best of her wits to survive.

The futures of more than three people hang on the birth of a babe who has yet to be conceived.

Preview

Lady Margaret's Challenge
Henry's Spare Queen Book Two

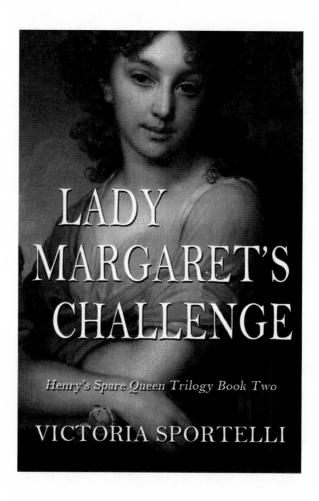

An excerpt

1

—— ✤ ——

Demoted

15 February 1101 A.D.

Margaret backed four steps before turning away from Queen Matilda and King Henry, who, in an angry voice, had dismissed her, no ordered her, to leave immediately. She passed the curtained sleeping bays between the hall pillars as she walked an aisle the couriers left for her. As she passed, they showed first their frowns and then their backs.

No privileged screened area for me. Stop shuffling. Pick up your feet. Look up. Up! Smile as if all is well. Shoulders back. March.

She continued toward the main doors and gray daylight. From the entrance steps, Sir Roussel directed her around the right corner of the building. A bitter wind slapped her in the face and tore at her clothes. The thin-soled slippers the queen had provided were no protection from the pebbles covering the courtyard dirt. Within two yards, Margaret started limping toward the distant stone outer wall and a wooden structure. Winter continued its attack, whipping her skirt tightly around her legs as she fought to take steps. Her hair flew over her face, blocking her sight. Margaret shook her head to free her locks, crossed her hands over her chest and shivered. *May I have my mantle, my things?* Margaret stumbled on a hole in the stones. *Purchase sturdy boots.* Beyond the hall wall, another wintery blast rounded the corner, pushed her hair left and tried to freeze her right cheek and ear. She blinked and squinted to protect her eyes. *Two doors, no windows. Servants' quarters?*

Sir Roussel opt the right door. He was the eldest of the three and the tallest. All three men wore the uniform of King Henry's special group, gray clothing, brown jerkin and boots, and gray mantles. Each man had shaved clean the back of his head to make room for the padding at the back of his helmet. His remaining hair was pulled forward and cut in an arch from the top of one ear to the top of the other, leaving little bang. Their swords were sheathed in wood and covered with the same gray cloth as their uniforms. Such a uniform enabled a man to slip between trees, hide in the dark, and move about almost unseen in bad weather.

Women's side. Cots and clothing on pegs. Where goes that back door? Margaret strode through the double line of cots and opt the door at the end of the room. She smelled midden from a slim window slit. She grimaced and forced herself not to pinch her nostrils closed. The tiny room had lately held firewood for the braziers in the dormitory. A cot, a chamber pot, a stool, and one lit, fat candle on a small table filled the tiny space. *A message. I can bear it. I must. Oh, Mother, what have I done? I can hear you saying, 'Too bold, too bold. Be a lady.'* Margaret sighed. *Too late.*

At the outer door, Sir Roussel turned to see they had not been followed before the wind slammed the door shut. Gailard and Cachier carried the money chest through the second doorway and lifted the trunk over the table and cot to deposit it in the far corner. Margaret smelled onions. *Their breaths or outside? Do not ask.*

"We did not choose this place, my lady."

"Of course not, Sir Cachier. You may depart."

"We stand guard at all times. That chest will draw thieves and murderers."

"Sir Roussel, Sir Gailard, Sir Cachier, make a show, but promise me one thing."

"My lady?" they replied in unison.

"If you are attacked, die not. You are more valuable than either the chest or me."

Margaret's gesture halted their objections. "Promise."

"I promise," they replied in half-hearted tones.

Probably mean it not. The king's charge is more important. I tried.

All four turned at hearing the outer door open and close. Sir Roger, the king's constable, approached. He stopped halfway into the dormitory, wrinkled his nose, and coughed twice. "You will attend Mass elsewhere but not in the cathedral. You will dine and sup in your room. Do not enter the hall, the keep nor any other part of the castle. Stay in this room unless you are leaving the grounds. The king orders you to depart before Ash Wednesday."

"Please inform His Royal Highness I obey. Today I must hire men and wagons and purchase what I need. As the morrow is Sunday, I shall confine myself to this room as soon as I return from Mass. I plan to leave Winchester Tuesday morn."

Sir Roger nodded as he turned to flee the odors wafting toward him. The group watched him wrap his cloak around his body and slip through the doorway. Again the wind slammed the door shut. Sir Roger opt the door for a moment to free a corner of his mantle.

Next to march to Margaret's door was the Lady Claire de Clerkx, resplendent in a mink fur-lined and edged mantle and matching scarf. She glowered at each of them. The knights stepped aside, but she refused to enter the room.

"A fitting place for you," sneered the woman. "A cubby for a badger."

Pretend this is the best room in the palace. Thwart her.

Margaret's smile seemed genuine. She curtsied. "God give you a good day, my lady." Margaret's cheerful tone hid her dismay at her loss of station.

The woman gestured servants forward. The first deposited her bedding on the cot, the second her personal belongs and her clothing. Margaret eyes widened when the final servant held out her sword in its scabbard. As Lady Claire talked, Margaret took it from the man.

"Her Highness says you are to keep that thing until His Highness calls for it." She made a rude noise. "Why she would trust you with it is beyond me. She has no need of you or it."

"Did you protect Her Royal Highness during her first child bearing?"

"I have served the queen since her coronation."

"You failed to protect her first babe and the heir died. I served her and her second babe lived." Margaret lifted her scabbard so the sword's upright handle and the guard was but inches from Lady Claire's nose. The weapon was now a cross, the kind men at arms use to make oaths. Her back straightened. Sir Cachier shivered at the fire in Margaret's gaze. In a low, resonant voice, Margaret threatened, "I swear by this cross before you. Fail her again and you will answer to me." Margaret's eyes dared the woman to speak; she blinked not, moved not. The woman turned on her heel and marched away.

"Are you going to wear that?" asked Sir Roussel.

"No need." Margaret smiled at him. "I have you."

She turned and placed the weapon on the table.

"Two to guard, one to escort me? Or the opposite?"

"Two to guard. Where are you bound?"

"I need wagons and oxen. I will order them today, fill them Monday to be ready Tuesday dawn."

"All you rent or buy will cost you dear, my lady. Everyone knows of your wealth."

Margaret leaned toward Sir Roussel as if sharing a secret. "But they know not how well I bargain." *Not cert about that among city folk. Distract them.* "Sirs, please tell me about yourselves."

Sir Roussel answered for the other two as well. "We are of His Royal Highness's corps d' elite. An inner circle among his knights."

"Have you lands? Are you married?"

"Not yet. I have served His Royal Highness two years now. Sir Gailard one. Sir Cachier since January. If we do well, after five years the king will award us our own mail, sword, horse, lance and land. Then we may marry."

"I am honored to have your protection."

At that moment a knock on the outer door put the men on alert. All three drew swords as Margaret backed into a corner and looked toward her sword.

"Who goes there?" demanded Sir Roussel as he strode to the door.

"Cormac mac Cennedig. Unarmed. Alone. Me lady, may I speak wi' ya?"

"Of course! Of course," Margaret called out.

Beside the entry door Sir Gailard put his back to the wall as Sir Roussel, sword in his right hand, opened the door. Cormac stayed outside until Roussel motioned him forward. Half expecting to be cut down from behind, the Scot glanced over each shoulder as he walked toward Margaret. He wrinkled his nose while he pulled his forelock.

"We can talk at my door. Open, of course, to protect my reputation. Have you come from Her Royal Highness?"

"Nay, me lady. I have not. I have come for meself."

"Oh." Margaret's voice drooped. "What want you?"

"Well. 'Tis like this, me lady. I like the warmer weather here. I have no real reason to return to Scotland and reason to stay. I am older than some, but I am an experience seneschal. I am hoping ye are in need of one. Hopefully me."

Margaret looked to Roussel.

"He went with the traitor."

Eager to be accepted, Cormac listed his abilities. "I speak Norman, Saxon, Scots and a little Latin. I read and write and figure so I can keep track of things for you. I gain the confidence of people quickly. They like to talk to me and often tell me more than they realize. I can turn away those ye want not to see without 'em gettin' angry. In Scotland I ran a smooth household for more than one king."

"What reason to stay? Why my household?" *Do you also spy for the royals? Better one I know than one I do not.*

Cormac blurted, "Where ye are Caitlin is sure to be, soon or late. Me lady, she has been missin' four days. Where is she?"

"Cormac! After all the teasing you have done? After she purposely ladled hot soup onto your lap? I knew you two are now friendly and smile at each other. Are you saying there is more between you?" Cormac's expression betrayed him. Margaret teased, "Cormac, why did you not tell me!"

"She stopped whackin' me with her cooking spoon. She even smiled at me once or twice. I took that as a hopeful sign. I have walked with her a time or two. If I am at ye new home, she may come round more." Cormac added, "She will return to ye, will she not?"

"I hope so." Margaret was pleased to see relief spread over his face. "But if you stay, or how long is Caitlin's choice. I will not have her upset. If she makes a fit at seeing you, you must leave."

"Agreed." Cormac rubbed his hands together in pleasure. "Now I am in ye employ, what may I do for ye?"

"Tell me what you have heard." Margaret waved toward the outer door. "Has anyone asked for me?"

Cormac saw her men look away. "Not that I have heard, me lady. Talk is that His Royal Highness is still piqued at ye. Talk is that any interested family will wait until ye are gone and he is calmer."

"Piqued? Calmer? You are a diplomat, Cormac." Margaret changed the subject. "I need wagons and oxen to haul goods and gear. Will you accompany me to the market? I want to purchase or rent them today to order them ready for departure Tuesday."

"Gladly, me lady. May I suggest that you bargain with all of the stablemen first. Tell them ye will hire the one who costs ye the least. Make them work for ye business."

"Good thinking, Cormac. Please wait while I ready myself."

After Margaret closed the door to her room, she relieved herself and brushed her hair. She removed the key from her sleeve pocket and knelt. The key turned hard in the new lock. Margaret's eyes widened at the silver coins. She ran her fingers through her wealth. *So many. Thousands of them. More than I will ever need.* Margaret smiled as she dipped both hands into the chest, brought them together beneath the coins, lifted her hands, and created a waterfall of tinkling silver that piled up in the center of her treasure. She smoothed the coins evenly and patted them. "Now get me a husband," she ordered her wealth.

Lord William? I like him. Margaret sighed. *Two boons granted, coins and land. King Henry hates the third. Will he ever grant it me? I told him I want no precedent. He does have the power to grant me the right to sign mine own marriage contract. Do I still want that? Wait, as Cormac suggested, until he is calmer and sees the right of honoring my boon.*

Margaret hid a few coins in each sleeve pocket before she dragged her purse through the coins until it filled. Margaret pulled the strings tight. She closed the lid and locked the box. *Shall I hang it from my girdle? No, too easy to snatch. Where?* She looked around and decided she must wear the key too. She untied the leather thong from around the sword's scabbard to make a necklace. She tied the key in one place and the pouch in another before knotting the leather strip at her nape. She dropped the items between her bliaut and chemise so her girdle would catch it should her makeshift necklace fail. She picked up her mantle and hugged it as images of the queen flashed in her mind. Margaret sighed. *Shoulders back. Head up. Do not let them think I am defeated. I must go about my business as if all is well even if it is not. Ah, Mother, I do remember. Quiet, calm, dignified, pure keeps a lady steadfast and sure.* Margaret gritted her teeth and squinted away her coming tears. She tied her scarf under her chin, swirled her mantle round her shoulders and fastened it with her old brooch. Margaret stiffened her back, ordered herself to smile, and opt the door. "I am ready," she announced. Margaret spotted a fifth man talking to the others. "Elstan?"

"My lady," he replied in Saxon. "May I serve you? I have no other place to go," he added in a rush.

Saxon tongues are swifter than Norman hooves. The dictum Sir Charles's reeve taught me. I wager he can learn about my estate by asking other Saxons. I need him. She motioned him forward and whispered, "Someone told me 'Saxon tongues are faster than Norman hooves.' I go to market Monday. Can you know by then what I need to add to my estate?"

Elstan whispered back, "I promise I shall."

Margaret spoke aloud so the other four would hear, "Then you may serve, Elstan. Cormac and I go to bargain for oxen and wagons. Join us."

Sir Cachier led Margaret; the Scot and Saxon followed. They were ignored all the way across the bailey and out the barbican.

Coming Late November 2020

Lady Margaret's Challenge
Henry's Spare Queen Book Two

Margaret arrives at her new estate
to find it has been stripped bare,
her villeins are starving, and her crops are not planted.
While she tries to set things aright,
she worries King Henry has forgotten her.

Acknowledgements

Without T. M. Evenson's encouragement and support, I would not be an author. This trilogy would never have been more than ideas rolling around in my head and stories I would tell her. She is an accomplished author and computer expert, who introduced me to the program National Novel Writing Month (NaNoWriMo. org). She read the first draft of *Lady Margaret's Escape*, Book One of the Henry's Spare Queen Trilogy. After she helped me edit it, she taught me how to be published. Dear Sister, I am forever grateful for all you have taught me and your help, all the while you launched *Emergence: The Journey Begins*, the prequel to *The Destiny Saga* and began your first book in the series, *Providence: A New Beginning*.

By phone Kathy Carlson listened to me read from Chapter 1 of *Lady Margaret's Escape*. Kathy has taken every late-night call. When I ask, "Is this clear?" or "Does this make sense?" she makes suggestions. Kathy encourages me every step of the way. Kathy, you are a true friend and a sister-of-the-heart to me. Dick Carlson is part of my inspiration for all my heroes. Thank you, Dick, for your patience while Kathy and I worked together.

My beta readers examined an early draft of my writings; their comments and ideas helped me greatly. Thank you N. Boyt, Ann Burrish, Gail Klein, Christy Lennon, Carol Oakland, Ginger Westberg.

Any "horse sense" in this story comes from my friend Joyce sharing her equine knowledge and from my meeting her American saddle-bred horse Gizmo.

Thank you, T. Wiering, for helping me locate Creazzo Publishing.

Producing a good-looking book is an endeavor that can best be done by finding the right people; thankfully I have. Thank you, Jenny Q. of Historical Fiction Book Covers, for book cover designs I am proud to call mine as well as for your patience with me when I needed several versions. Margaret Diehl, my book editor, "gets" me. She not only edits copy, she also writes me pages of single-spaced notes, explaining what I need to do to add depth to my ideas. If my writing has improved, it is because of Margaret's able assistance. Wordzworth is an interior book design company that understood what I meant when I said, "I want my interiors to meet the industry standards for historical fiction novels." They are so good at it that I plan to continue to use their services. Jenny, Margaret and Wordzworth are exactly what I need.

Glossary

Advent. A time of prayer and fasting from the fourth Sunday before Christmas to midnight Mass on Christmas Eve.

ague. Any illness involving fever and shivering.

All Saints Day. November 1.

All Souls Day. October 31.

A.D./Anno Domini. Latin for "In the year of Our Lord." We now use C. E. (Common Era).

anon. Immediately.

bailey. A large area, usually protected by a dry or wet moat, surrounded by a tall wooden or stone wall called a palisade, which encircles the hall, keep, kitchen, garrison, chapel, and other buildings where a lord, his family and his retainers reside. Part of an early Norman castle.

barbican. A fortified entrance to a castle or to a town of towers on either side of a passageway to enable guards to shoot arrows, or to drop rocks or boiling water over invaders. They may also drop a portcullis to stop an invasion.

bedmate. Polite term for any woman a man takes to his bed and uses for his pleasure, whether for a night or longer. Usually a Saxon who had no choice in the matter.

betrothed. A formal arrangement of a marriage with the first step a contract between families. The second step is a blessing of the couple by a priest; the third step is the couple bedding together and the woman proving she was a virgin.

birthing stool. A wooden chair with a back and arms that has a hole in the seat and is open in front for a midwife to reach for and catch a babe as it is born.

bliaut. *(pronounced blout)* A Norman-French word for a woman's outer garment to the wrists and ankles, fitted to the elbows for fashion, then flared to the wrist and fitted to her hips, then flared below for easy walking, usually wool in winter and linen in summer.

boon. A gift or favor granted by one person to another.

breech. A kind of birth where the babe comes feet or buttocks first down the birthing channel.

C. E. Common Era is the modern term used to describe years. It replaced "A.D." (Anno Domini): Latin for "In the year of Our Lord."

capon. A rooster that has been castrated as a chick and then fattened.

Casteela. A region on the Iberian peninsula where scented, gentle soaps were first created in the eighth century. The modern spelling of this region of Spain is Castile.

Catholic. A person who follows the teachings of Jesus the Christ but does so through the **Church,** whom he/she considers as the path to Jesus. A Catholic believes in the special authority of the pope.

cert. The medieval word for certain. The opposite is uncert.

chatelaine. Usually the landholder's wife; she is responsible for everything on the estate except its safety and men's hunting practices.

chattel. A person who considered property even though he or she is not a slave.

chausses. A male's loose-fitting pants covering the legs and feet which require belting and cross gartering and which are a part of a Norman's or knight's clothing.

chemise. A soft undergarment of linen or wool slightly smaller than a bliaut worn by a Norman woman to protect her skin from chaffing. Called a **shift** by Saxons.

Christmastide. The days from Midnight Mass on December 24 through the Epiphany on January 6.

Christening. Giving a baby a Christian name in a ceremony that includes blessed water, religious prayers and blessings as a sign of admission to the Christian **Church**.

Church. The one, catholic, true religion taught by Jesus the Christ and practiced throughout Western Europe with the pope in Rome as its head; it is also called the Christian Church. After the Protestant Reformation it was renamed the Catholic Church.

close. A piece of land held as private property, usually walled and gated. European cathedrals and churches are often surrounded by a close that may also encircle other buildings, such as a convent, abbey or other religious place. Because a close may be locked, it protects the religious from attack.

Confession. A requirement to state one's sins to a priest, to receive absolution, and to do penance before being permitted to receive Holy Communion during **Mass**.

convent. Enclosed buildings and its surrounding property which houses women who have chosen to become servants of God and are called nuns.

coronet. A relatively small metal crown consisting of a band with only one peak, which may be plain or decorated, especially with a gem or jewel.

courses. a euphemism for a woman's menstrual cycle during which her uterus sheds it bloody lining because she is not with child.

covrefeu. Old Norman-French for "cover fire." With most buildings of wood, a single spark could burn a town. During this time in England, all fires in homes in a town had to be doused every night at dusk. From this word and custom we get the word "curfew."

crenels. The spaces between stone merlins on the battlements at the top of a **keep** or castle.

curtsey. A woman's or girl's formal greeting and/or sign of respect made by bending the knees with one foot in front of the other to one who is of superior rank.

dais. In a hall, a platform two to four steps high upon which sit a table and benches, stools or chairs and from which the lord of the estate and his family dine and rule.

daub. The mud used to fill in the spaces between willow branches that form the walls of Saxon huts. See **wattle and daub.**

ditch woman. A girl/woman whose father/husband has thrown her out of her family for unacceptable behavior, such as disobedience, having had sexual relations outside marriage, running away, etc. She lives in fear of her life because anyone can do anything to her. See also **pariah.**

donjon. The below-ground level of a keep or medieval castle which originally was a storage room for food, weapons, and other supplies. Later it became a prison. The modern spelling is "dungeon."

dowry. The money, goods, and other items a woman's family agrees to give so she can bring it to her husband and her husband's family at her marriage. The amount of wealth she brings often determines her value as a wife. The verb form is "to dower."

Epiphany. January 6. The twelfth day after Christmas, believed to be the day the Magi visited the Christ Child and gave him gifts; a time of gift giving and feasting.

excommunicate. A severe penalty for a gross offense to the **Church** that results in a person's inability to receive the sacraments or to be buried in holy ground. One must still attend **Mass**. The penalty is reversible if one repents, goes to **Confession**, completes a **penance** and changes one's ways. One is then readmitted to the group of Christ's followers and to His **Church**.

farthing. A coin equal to one/fourth of a penny. The obverse side was scored with a cross so a penny could be broken in half, a ha-penny, and then again into a farthing (a fourth thing.)

feudalism. All of England was owned by the king. He portioned out some of it to be held by those beneath him, who worked and protected it on his behalf. A baron held vast tracts of land and answered directly to the king. With royal permission, a baron could separate his lands into earldoms and raise a lord or knight to that station. In turn, either the earl or lord could then assign land within the property he held to a knight who could then marry because he was a landholder. Each rank owed military service and taxes to the station directly above his.

forelock. The front portion of hair, which a Saxon male grabs and pulls down over his forehead when he lowers his head as a sign of respect toward a Norman or to one who is of superior rank.

froward. The medieval form of forward. The act of behaving in an outrageous, unbecoming manner.

gelding. A castrated male horse.

girdle. A belt of leather or stiff fabric, decorated or not, that women wear around their waists. They hang their personal dagger, a scissors, household keys etc. from it. We now call it a belt.

girl. Any unmarried female no matter her age.

Grand Crusade. In 1095, Pope Urban II called all of Christendom to a crusade to free Eastern Christians from Turkish rule and to take possession of the Holy City of Jerusalem. When Jerusalem fell to the Turks in 1147, a second Crusade was called and the custom of numbering the Crusades began; this one was then renamed the First Crusade.

gunna. *(pronounced goona)* An Old Saxon word for a long-sleeved woolen dress worn to the ankles and fastened to the body with a girdle (belt). Most Saxon women owned only one, which they wore until they were annually given cloth by their lord to make another one in preparation for Easter. Similar to a **bliaut**, but straight from shoulder to hem and shoulder to cuff.

half penny/half pence. A silver penny with a cross on the obverse side that can be used to cut it in half or quarters. See also **penny/pence**. The Old Saxon word was "pfenning."

hall. The building where the Norman members of an estate dine and conduct business.

hand. One hand equals 4 inches. A measurement of a horse from the ground to the top of its shoulder.

High Mass. A regular religious service lead by a priest or higher member of the Christian Church for a special occasion to which has been added additional elements such as a procession, special prayers and the use of incense.

hide. A unit of land comprising about 120 acres.

Holy Communion. A piece of bread and a sip of wine transformed into the body and blood of Jesus the Christ by a priest during Mass and served to the faithful.. The ceremony unites all of Christendom, and only those in good standing with the **Church** may partake in it.

hostler. A person who trains, works, and takes care of horses.

jerkin. A sleeveless jacket, often leather, that evolved into what we call a vest.

keep. A square building usually of stone, sometimes of wood, where the Norman lord and his family may flee for safety if his estate is attacked and his bailey is breached; generally the family lives and sleeps there. It is built on a motte, a hill, either natural or man-made.

kneeler. A bench for kneeling on with an upper part upon which one may place her/his hands.

knight errant. Designates a fighter in arms who serves or is hired by one of rank without his being given land; he is called "Sir" out of politeness but bears no rank.

knight landed or just **knight.** A knight errant who has been given land and who may now marry; he serves a man of a noble rank above him; his is the lowest noble title during these times. See **titles**.

linsey-woolsy. A textile made with a flax warp and a wool (worsted) weft.

litter. A curtained and canopied conveyance for a lady of rank. She sits or lies among cushions, blankets and furs on a wooden plank while the device is attached to horses front and back. No real lady rides unless she must.

mayhap. The medieval word meaning "maybe."

mantle. A hoodless, sleeveless warm outer covering worn by women. We call it a cape. In this time, the same garment worn by a man was called a cloak.

mark. A measure of money equivalent to 160 pennies. In 1096, 10,000 Marks was 1.6 million pennies when two pennies bought an adult boar pig, one penny bought a sow, and piglets were two for a penny.

marriage chest. A wooden chest, carved or plain, into which a girl placed the linens she has hemmed and all manner of clothing, fabrics, household goods and items she has made or acquired and will take with her to her new home as part of her dowry. During the 20th century, it was called a "hope chest."

Mass. A religious service led by a priest or higher member of the Church to which Christians attend and those in good standing with the **Church** receive **Holy Communion** as a way of uniting all Christendom and of keeping its members faithful.

May Day. May 1.

merlin. The solid part of the top of a wall that is separated by spaces called crenels, part of the top of the battlement of a castle.

Michaelmas. September 29.

Midsummer. The summer solstice, usually June 21 or 22, depending on the moon cycles in that year.

minstrel. A servant who was the entertainer of an estate or was the court musician for a king. Men who traveled as minstrels were for hire. The word 'minstrel' means "little servant."

morrow. The next day, The medieval word for tomorrow.

motte. A mound topped with a tower called a **keep**, which is within a **bailey**, the whole of which comprised an early Norman castle. Motte and bailey are the modern terms for this kind of castle arrangement.

mortal sin. A misdeed that will cause your soul to be sent to Hell if it is not forgiven and which is more serious than a venial sin, which is a misdeed and a minor offense against God and/or the **Church**.

Norman. Both the name of the group and the language the Normans of England and Normandy spoke during the twelfth century. We now call the language Old Norman-French.

nonce. For now or for the time being.

op/opt. (sounds like oap/oapt) The medieval words for open and opened.

Orignal Sin. The sin held to be inherited from Adam in consequence of his and Eve's expulsion from the Garden of Eden. The **Church** held that only the ceremony of Baptism removed the sin from a person so that individual could then become a member of the **Church**.

palfrey. A gentle horse, usually female, women and priests ride.

palisade. The wall of wooden timbers or of stone which surrounds the bailey and all within; usually has either a dry or wet moat around it for further protection and only one gate for entrance.

pariah. A person who is despised, avoided and treated badly. During this time in England, anyone declared a pariah could be hurt, maimed or killed without any penalty. It was not a crime to kill a pariah.

parchment. See also **vellum**. Sheep skin that has been pounded thin, stretched and upon which records are written.

penance. Prayers and good deeds that must be completed before one's sins are expunged and before one can receive **Holy Communion** during **Mass**.

penny/pence. A coin/coins of the realm. Pence was also another word for a penny; the word is sometimes used for a single coin or a number of coins, as in six pence. In Old Saxon the word was "pfenning."

people/s. A group of persons related by common elements such as descent, heredity, history, language, cultural traits, social norms or geography. In the early medieval period, the chief determiners of a separate peoples were language and geography, so the groups were: Saxon, Norman, Scot, Irish, etc. One of the most shocking of King Henry I's policies was his mixing of Saxons and Normans through marriage to create a new peoples he called English.

Percheron. A horse, usually black but sometimes gray, from Perche, a region in northwestern France.

portcullis. A strong, heavy metal grating that can be lowered down grooves on each side of a gateway or a barbican to block entry.

pottage. Soaked grains such as cracked wheat, cracked rye, smashed oats, or a combination of grains into which can be thrown leftover vegetables and meats; it is cooked and turned into a soup/stew served in the morning. This word was later changed to porridge.

pound. A unit of money in silver pennies/pence. In this era 240 **pence** equaled 1 pound.

psaltery. An ancient musical instrument. In the medieval period, the sound box was often shaped as a triangle with a long neck. The number of strings, which were plucked, often varied from three to six. Round the edges and it looks like a precursor of a guitar.

Purgatory. A middling place between Hell and Heaven to which souls went for a time. For a soul to reach Heaven, those on earth had to pray or do the good works the dead person needed to complete before her/his death. During the early 21st century, the Catholic Church removed Purgatory from its religious practices.

rank. See **titles**. Within each title, men are ranked according to how much land they held, their level of wealth, and how the royals favoredt hem. Wives, sons, and daughters held the same rank as the head of their household.

reeve. On an estate, a man who has been elected each January by his fellow Saxons to oversee all the assigning of land, planting, growing, and harvesting of crops. Rather than speak his name, all often just said his title. Traditionally, he may elected only three times before another man must be chosen.

rib. Any narrow strip of cloth. See **wedding rib**.

riding platform. An early medieval woman's saddle, upon which she sat sideways with her legs to the left side of a horse with a sandbag counterweight behind her on the other side of the horse. No self respecting or honorable woman spread her legs around a horse's back.

roundsey. Icelandic/Norwegian horse who was the size of a large modern pony. Not only could it carry heavy weights, its five-gaited walk was much desired. In addition to walk, trot, canter and gallop, a roundsey ambled, a gait the pony could maintain for hours. This created easy riding for humans because it was so smooth. Roundseys still exist and are now called Icelandic ponies.

rushes. The general term for any hollow stalks, which after the harvest were strewn on the floors of halls, keeps, and other buildings to keep down dirt/dust and to catch food and other fallen debris. In addition, they were also strewn on barn floors for animals to stand upon. After rushes dried, they became a fire hazard.

Saracen. A term that was brought back to Europe after the Grand Crusade. It referred to any Arab or Muslim.

Saxon. Both the people of England who were invaded in 1066 by King William I (the Conqueror) and the language they spoke. We now call their language Old Saxon.

scabbard. A sheath for a sword, usually of leather or cloth-covered wood.

serf. See also **villein**. Term for a person tied to the land owned by the king, earls, barons, and lords, as part of the **feudalism** system common on the European continent. Usually serfs are not free, but they neither are serfs bought or sold as if they were slaves. This term was used on the European continent, not England. In England, the term used was villein.

shift. A soft undergarment of linen or wool slightly smaller than a gunna worn by Saxon women to protect their skin from chafing. A Norman woman called it a **chemise**.

simples. Ointments, creams, powders, and other simple remedies for a variety of illnesses and ailments; most used pig fat as a base.

slattern. A woman with a bad reputation because she has had sexual relations outside of marriage or with many men.

solar. The English form of the Latin word "solarium," a room in which the sun shines during a major part of the day.

squire. The second step toward a Norman boy becoming a knight after having served as a page. Usually a squire began this position at the age of 14. A Saxon might become a page or a squire, but he was never permitted to rise to knighthood.

stone. A unit of weight equal to 14 pounds.

surcoat. A man's loose robe worn over armor, a sleeveless garment worn as part of the insignia of an order of knighthood, or an outer coat of rich material worn by a man of rank.

swill. Usually contains the wine and lees from the bottom of a barrel of wine. It tastes terrible.

tabbard. A strip of cloth with a hole in the middle for the wearer's head to be worn over armor or one's clothing for protection and warmth. Often it was also belted. By the late 12th century, a man's tabard was often emblazoned with a coat of arms. In winter, Norman women wore plain woolen ones to keep warm. Now it is spelled "tabard."

ticking. Cloth case for a mattress or pillow into which is stuffed hair, feathers, straw or the like.

titles. Royal: King/Queen
Prince/Princess

Noble — Baron/Baroness (called Lady)
Earl/Countess (called Lady)
Lord (sometimes addressed as Sir/Sirrah)/Lady
Sir(Sirrah)/Lady (a knight who owns land)
During these years titles of address were fluid. All the nobles except for knights landed could be—and often were—addressed as "Lord"—even the barons and earls. Many times the barons/earls and lords were informally addressed as "Sir" by their equals. "Sirrah" was its most informal form.

tonsure. A part of a monk's or priest's head left bare on top by shaving off the crown of his hair.

trestle table. A wooden table composed of a top of boards set upon a triangular A-frame (think sawhorse).

troubadour. A Norman-French word for a composer and performer of lyric poetry who usually accompanied his works with a musical instrument such as a lyre or psaltery. The Old Saxon word is scop.

turino. During the medieval period, a region in what is now north-western Italy. During the ninth century, a man stole the process for making soft, body soap from what is now Castile, Spain, and took the knowledge to this area. Because the climate did not support roses well, he used pine to scent his soaps. The principal city in the area is now known as Turin in English.

uncert. The medieval form of uncertain. The opposite is "cert."

vassal. Under the feudal system, any person who holds land and owes taxes, homage, fealty and/or military service to an individual of higher rank; in England all are vassals except the king.

vellum. Sheep skin that has been pounded thin, stretched and upon which records are written. The word was used interchangeably with **parchment**.

villein. Term used in England for those tied to the land, who are not free, but they neither are they bought or sold as if they were slaves. See also **serf**.

walkway. Structure attached to and behind the **palisade** upon which guards may stand and defend the **bailey**.

warrior priest. A priest who has been trained as a swordsman and fighter and who guards the Church's property. After King William II prevented Archbishop Anselm from appointing bishops and took their lands for the income, several of England's remaining bishops created these men to protect themselves and their bishoprics.

wattle and daub. A form of construction using softened willow sticks woven together (wattle) and a mud of dirt, straw and other debris (daub) to form walls of a hut that is then roofed with thatch. A common type of home for Saxons during this era. Wattles were also used as fencing.

wedding rib. A strip of woven, lightweight cloth 3 to 6 inches wide that is used as decorative trim on clothing or is wrapped around a married woman's long hair when she wears it in two braids. Thinner ribs are often woven into braids for decoration. We now call them ribbons.

wench. A female servant, whether girl or woman.

wergeld. Means "man payment" in Old Saxon. It is the amount of compensation paid by a person committing an offense to the injured party by paying a debt, paying for a person's freedom, or, in case of death, a debt to his family determined by the dead person's worth.

wimple. A woman's head-cloth drawn in folds about the head and around the neck; it usually covered the forehead as well. Originally worn out of doors, it later became popular for covering one's hair indoors. Nuns started wearing it to cover their hair from being seen by men.

withies. Thin willow branches, soaked and woven together to build exterior walls called wattles. They are then covered with mud and straw mixed together to form house walls and white washed to inhibit rain damage. See also **wattle and daub**.

wroth. The Old Saxon form of the word wrath.

About the Author

Ms. Sportelli is a life-long Anglophile, who loves British history, culture, manners, folklore, customs, and humor. How women worked and struggled, what they wore and ate, and how their families survived are the focus of her novels.

She has been to the places she writes about. One of her exciting finds is in the hall to the Queen's Wing of the Great Hall, which is all that remains of the large castle in Winchester. Hanging there is a photograph of a royal treasury chest King Henry I used.

During 25 years of reading and research, Ms. Sportelli concluded that Henry I of England was an under-rated king. She found compelling King Henry's struggles, and the dangers he faced amid the conflicts between the Normans and the Saxons.

In college, she majored in English with a special interest in the Anglo-Saxon and the early Medieval periods. She learned to read, write and speak basic Anglo-Saxon.

Now Ms. Sportelli off to Italy to research her next historical fiction novel, which is set in Venice.

Find Victoria online and on social media:
Author Website: victoriasportelli.com
Facebook: victoriasportelli and HenrysSpareQueen
Pinterest: VictoriaSportelli

A Note for You:
The author will be grateful if you leave an honest review online.
Thank you!

Made in United States
North Haven, CT
23 May 2022

19454679R00224